ROADHOUSE JUSTICE

HATTIE LEE BARNES
AND THE KILLING

LOUISIANA STATE UNIVERSITY PRESS BATON ROUGE

OF A WHITE MAN

IN 1950s MISSISSIPPI

ROADHOUSE JUSTICE

TRENT BROWN

Published by Louisiana State University Press
lsupress.org

Manufactured in the United States of America
First printing

DESIGNER: Michelle A. Neustrom
TYPEFACE: Adobe Minion Pro
PRINTER AND BINDER: Versa Press

Jacket image: iStock.com/greenleaf123

LIBRARY OF CONGRESS CATALOGING-IN-PUBLICATION DATA

Names: Brown, Trent, author.
Title: Roadhouse justice : Hattie Lee Barnes and the killing of a white man in 1950s Mississippi / Trent Brown.
Description: Baton Rouge : Louisiana State University Press, [2022] | Includes index.
Identifiers: LCCN 2021060810 (print) | LCCN 2021060811 (ebook) | ISBN 978-0-8071-7801-0 (cloth) | ISBN 978-0-8071-7834-8 (pdf) | ISBN 978-0-8071-7833-1 (epub)
Subjects: LCSH: Craft, Lamar 1928–1951 | Barnes, Hattie Lee. | Justifiable Homicide—Mississippi—Pike County—Case studies. | Racism against Black people—Mississippi—Pike County—Case studies. | Racism in criminal justice administration—Mississippi—Pike County—Case studies. | Pike County (Miss.)—Race relations.
Classification: LCC HV6533.M7 B76 2022 (print) | LCC HV6533.M7 (ebook) | DDC 364.15209762—dc23/eng/20220131
LC record available at https://lccn.loc.gov/2021060810
LC ebook record available at https://lccn.loc.gov/2021060811

For Joan Wylie Hall

CONTENTS

ACKNOWLEDGMENTS

FIRST, THANKS TO THE Louisiana State University Press. It has been a great pleasure to work with Press director Alisa Plant's team again. As usual, Rand Dotson was patient and supportive as this project took shape. Thanks very much to Susan Murray for her careful copyediting of the manuscript. Also providing vital assistance for this book were Denise Carlson, who compiled the index, and Mary Lee Eggart, who created the map. To both of them, thank you.

Once again, this is a Mississippi story, and many Mississippi people offered support. In Tylertown, a significant place in this book, Elise Pittman encouraged my work, answered all kinds of questions, and helped me track down photographs. In the Walthall County Circuit Clerk's office, Kamie Bacot and Vanessa Walker provided copies of documents I needed. In the Marion County Circuit Clerk's office, Arvin Broom went beyond the call of duty in his search for records from the two Columbia trials that figure in this book. In Pike County, Gwen Nunnery answered a query about tax records and Circuit Clerk Roger Graves and his staff offered cordial help, as they always do. At the Mississippi Department of Corrections, Tammy Wood provided me with records on inmates from the 1950s and offered encouraging words. Finally, and also as usual, thanks to the staff at the Mississippi Department of Archives and History, an unmatched resource working daily to tell the story of Mississippi's people.

Thanks to Jack Ryan at the *Enterprise-Journal* and Carolyn Dillon at the *Tylertown Times.* Mac Gordon and Nancy Gordon Lazenby were generous in offering information on their father and life in McComb in the 1950s and 1960s.

Charles Dunagin shared his recollections of Charles Gordon and work on the *Enterprise-Journal* in the 1960s. In McComb, Ronald Whittington welcomed me to his office and discussed his interest in the Hattie Lee Barnes case with me.

IN MISSOURI, COUNTY RECORDERS in Pemiscot, Dunklin, and New Madrid Counties provided very helpful assistance. Thanks especially to Vanessa Darnell and Connie Green. Miranda Loesch offered sound advice on legal matters that figure in this book. At Missouri S&T, Linda Sands always asks how my Mississippi stories are coming along. One of the things that I missed most during 2020 was not seeing her in the office. Thanks also to my department chair, Kris Swenson, and Shannon Fogg in the CASB dean's office for support.

Other friends and colleagues answered questions or encouraged my work on this book, including Stephanie Rolph, Darlin' Neal, Steve Reich, and Jack Morgan. A special thanks to Vance Poole, whose friendship is one of the things that I can count on. My mother, Rita Watts, always provides a warm welcome when my research brings me home, which is one of the reasons I keep looking for Mississippi subjects.

For this book, written mainly during the eventful year of 2020, I tried not to bother my family very much. Because of my habits of rising early and producing a first draft on a typewriter (a 1949 Royal KMG), we all found my basement office a good place for me to work. My twenty-first-century children, Jack and Ellie, have grown up with a father whose head is usually in 1950s and 1960s Mississippi. My wife, Jennifer, puts up with my fascination with my native state. She also listens to my continued promises to try harder and do better.

Finally, during my undergraduate days at the University of Mississippi, it was my good fortune to meet Dr. Joan Wylie Hall. Everyone should have such a teacher. The book's dedication represents my thanks to her for all the long conversations, wise counsel, warm greetings, and generous spirit over the years.

ROADHOUSE JUSTICE

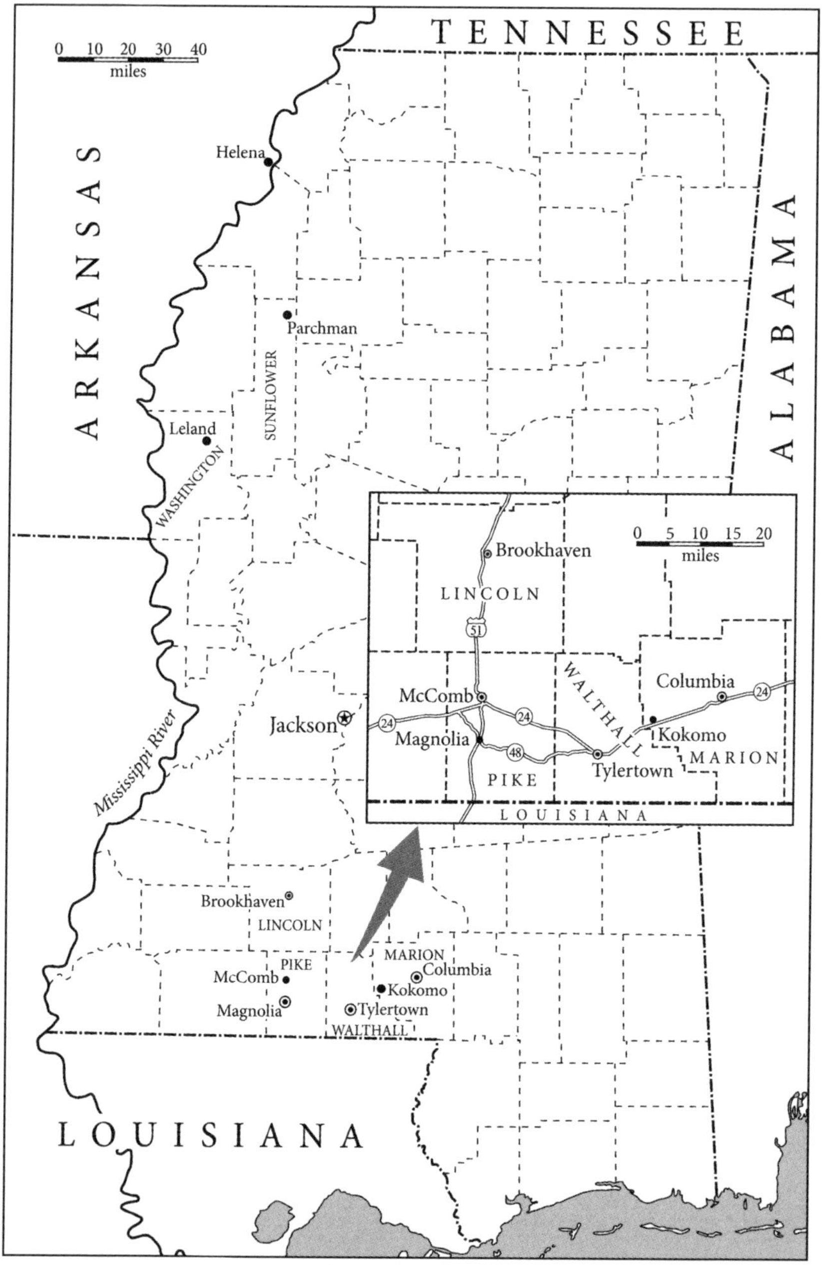

Southwestern Mississippi, with additional places central to the Hattie Lee Barnes story. Map by Mary Lee Eggart.

INTRODUCTION

IN THE EARLY HOURS of Tuesday, April 17, 1951, Lamar Craft, a twenty-two-year-old white man, was shot dead as he climbed through a window of Rob Lee's bar in rural Pike County, Mississippi.[1] "Lee's place," as people called it, was located about nine miles east of McComb, a town of 10,000 people in the deep southwestern part of the state. The bar stood beside state Highway 24, an east-west route; like many other Mississippi drinking establishments, it was near a county line. Earlier that evening, Craft, along with two companions, James Easterling and Oscar Hope, also young white men, were customers of Lee's, when they drank until closing time at midnight. An Air Force veteran, college student, and operator of a Pure Oil service station, Richard Lamar Craft was a native of Tylertown, a community of just over 1,300 people, located approximately ten miles east of the Pike County line in adjacent Walthall County. Craft had also been, the local newspaper reported, "a regular patron and close personal friend" of Lee's.[2]

After Rob Lee shut down his bar that night, Craft, Easterling, and Hope drove away, as did Lee himself. After a brief time, the young men returned. The trio were aware that Hattie Lee Barnes, a twenty-one-year-old African American woman, frequently stayed there overnight, working as a maid and caretaker.[3] It was for Barnes that the men, particularly Craft, returned. They anticipated some need for privacy, either from the law or from anyone else who might drive past the place at that hour. Parked out of clear sight of the road, Hope stood lookout, while Easterling assisted Craft as he attempted to enter the building.[4]

Unfortunately for Lamar Craft, Hattie Lee Barnes would present the greatest complication to his design. When she heard someone opening one of the building's rear windows, adjacent to the bed in which she slept, Barnes retrieved a Smith & Wesson .38 caliber revolver. As she later told authorities, Barnes fired twice "at a figure outlined in the window."[5] One bullet struck Craft in the chest, killing him nearly instantly. A second bullet went through the windshield and lodged in the upholstery of his car, parked behind the bar. It is not clear whether Barnes knew it was Craft at whom she shot. Subsequent accounts suggest that he called her name before trying the window. However, it would have taken no great stretch of Barnes's imagination to conclude what any man might want with her in the early-morning hours in a closed county-line beer joint.

Easterling and Hope fled the scene, not knowing whether Craft was dead or alive. Leaving his car where it sat, they walked about a mile to the house of Obid McCalip. Telling him that they had been in an automobile accident, they asked to use his telephone. Some men might have alerted the law or even consulted a friend for advice; these two called a cab from nearby McComb. Proceeding to the police station, they reported the incident. McComb police called Pike County sheriff Robert E. Lee, in whose jurisdiction the shooting had occurred. Sheriff Lee (not a relative of Rob Lee) asked that Easterling and Hope be brought back to Rob Lee's bar. McComb police patrolman S. M. Tarver did so, meeting the sheriff there.

Sheriff Lee, as it turns out, already knew something about the event. Hattie Lee Barnes herself had telephoned Lee, telling him that she had shot someone and asking him to come out to Rob Lee's place. In the meantime, Barnes had not left the roadhouse. She surrendered there to Sheriff Lee, who immediately jailed her in an "undisclosed" location, it was reported, a fact suggestive of the potential peril in which Barnes found herself for killing a white man. That same day, Pike County coroner Ray Cain ruled that Craft had come "to his death by pistol shot at the hands of Hattie Lee Barnes." Barnes's situation soon grew grimmer. Two days later, she was charged with murder. Conviction carried a possible death penalty under Mississippi law.[6]

The shots Hattie Lee Barnes fired not only killed Lamar Craft; they also served as the catalyst of events that developed across four years and more than a half dozen Mississippi and Arkansas counties. The dangers Barnes faced came not only from the hands of the Mississippi law. Before Barnes was tried in the fall of 1951 for Craft's murder, she was shot and nearly killed by bar owner Rob Lee and an accomplice, Walter Watson. After Craft's shooting and both before and after her own, Barnes was interrogated—both formally by law enforcement and informally by Lamar Craft's family and their attorney—and held under irregular, legally questionable conditions. Craft's family worked for years—through a variety of means—to shape not only the narrative surrounding the death of Craft but also the fate of Hattie Lee Barnes and other people involved in the events that constitute this story.

Barnes withstood her extended ordeal largely because of her own sheer determination. Acquitted at her trial for the murder of Lamar Craft, she also testified at the two trials of the men who shot her. Barnes told—multiple times—the story of what had happened to her in Rob Lee's bar and in the period that followed as she resisted pressures to change that story to fit others' agendas. But she also owed her freedom and perhaps her life to the principled representation of an unusually diligent court-appointed attorney and the dogged reporting of a southwestern Mississippi newspaperman. Over time, she also enlisted the sympathies and assistance of other area people who believed that her treatment was somehow wrong. The larger story demonstrates the precarious status of African American lives in that time and place. It also reveals the importance of chance, contingency, and personal influence over the Mississippi system of law and the courts. This book seeks to show some of those broader patterns and to explain how Hattie Lee Barnes survived.

ROADHOUSE JUSTICE: Hattie Lee Barnes and the Killing of a White Man in 1950s Mississippi unfolds in many small towns and cities, both in southwestern Mississippi and points beyond, in places such as Tylertown, Columbia, McComb, Brookhaven, Jackson, Magnolia, and Leland, with part of the story as well in Helena, Arkansas. It takes place in Mississippi hamlets such as Kokomo in Marion County and in other unincorporated areas, and along miles of Mississippi county roads and highways. Events here take us from some of the state's most rural areas to the capital city of Jackson. Its settings include county courthouses and jails, roadhouses, juke joints, small-town cafés, and other places where alcohol was bought and sold, and ultimately to the Mississippi Supreme Court.

This book recounts criminal acts that occurred in multiple Mississippi counties. Many of the people involved admitted certain facts: Hattie Lee Barnes said she shot Lamar Craft; Walter Watson said that he and Rob Lee shot Hattie Lee Barnes; numerous people described their sale and consumption of distilled liquor, a crime under Mississippi law; Lamar Craft's friends told of their role in helping him to break into Lee's bar. Watson and Barnes, both African Americans, testified multiple times to what they had done. Other people, specifically bar owner Rob Lee, a white man, availed himself of his constitutional privilege not to appear as a witness in his own trial for shooting Barnes. He also exercised an extralegal privilege not to appear for various other hearings and trials. However, except for some testimony that appears perjured, the reconstruction of this story is not challenged by basic uncertainties about who shot whom or who was at a given place at a given time. The more fundamental challenge is to learn why some of the people did what they did and to explain how broader social and institutional forces shaped and constrained their actions.

One exception to the general agreement about what happened in the early hours of April 17, 1951, is the position taken by Lamar Craft's family and their advocate, Tylertown attorney Breed Mounger. Craft's shooter, they maintained, was not Hattie Lee Barnes. The real murderer, they insisted, was never tried in a Mississippi court. The Crafts spent years and a considerable amount of money in attorney's fees attempting to control the public story of Lamar Craft's death. But their reasons for this effort seem less rooted in a search for the truth than in their desire to defend the family reputation against what they considered a fundamental humiliation. Edd Craft, Lamar's father, recoiled from the idea that his son, a "fine young man," as a judge termed him, had his life extinguished while trying to rape an African American woman.[7]

Despite the Craft family's attempts to obscure the role of Hattie Lee Barnes, this story—from the April 1951 shooting at Lee's bar through the disposition of the last legal matter in 1955—is usefully viewed as an extended narrative played out upon the body of an African American woman. Hattie Lee Barnes understood that Lamar Craft intended violence against her. She resisted with lethal force. In those last moments of his life, Craft might have been puzzled, had he the chance to reflect upon it, that his longing for Barnes could not be fulfilled. His judgment clouded by alcohol or not, he had come of age in a society in which Black people's bodies were often regarded by white people as objects for their use. That habit of thought—reflected not only in law and in economic practices but also in everyday speech—had roots in slavery, with its attempts to deny the agency and basic humanity of Mississippi's Black population. It is not accurate to say that white Mississippians in the 1950s thought of Black people as chattels. But it is not too much to say that many of them cared little what Black people thought or wanted, when their will conflicted with white people's interests or desires.

African American bodies were long seen by white Mississippians in terms of what they could do for white people. The state's broader culture and institutions reflected a good deal of thought as well about what those bodies might do to white people, if the Black bodies were not regulated. The prohibition of alcohol; the structure and use of the state penitentiary at Parchman; the crimes defined as felony under state law; the state's separate but unequal education system; the effective disfranchisement of Black voters—all these matters and more reflected the white majority's determination to control Black people. Black bodies were long deemed indispensable for certain tasks—in many parts of Mississippi, to produce cotton, both during and after slavery. Again, law and economic practices reflected the practical necessity, as white people saw it, to control the labor of Black people. With the mechanization and then the waning of the state's cotton economy, that labor gradually became expendable. And then those Black bodies, too, became expendable.[8]

The story that branches out from the 1951 shooting in Rob Lee's bar involves a large cast of men and women, Black and white. Many of them were little known beyond their own localities; others had considerable area or even statewide reputation. At least one of them, Judge Thomas P. Brady, on the bench at Barnes's murder trial, became by the mid-1950s familiar to at least some elements of a national audience as a spokesman for the Citizens' Council, a segregationist organization of considerable power in the Deep South. Many of the white characters in this story left traces in the public record for reasons other than their role in the Barnes saga: in newspaper coverage of various aspects of their lives; in subsequent legal entanglements; in records of military service; or in campaigns for office. Some of these people came to types of attention they surely did not wish to draw, at the time or in later years. First among these is Lamar Craft, whose death in Rob Lee's bar was both ignominious and literally a matter of public record. For most of us, our lives contain episodes we wish never to be known. Some people described in these pages had the resources to limit or overcome any scandal that became attached to their names; others did not. Some people who figure in this story, however, deliberately lived much more public lives than others. They sought attention—and our subsequent scrutiny—through interviews, statements to the press, writings, or in other utterances for the record. In those cases, their words and actions have left a broader canvas whose examination they essentially have invited.

The African American figures in this book led less-documented lives. That lack of documentation stems in part from white institutions' indifference: the birth, baptism, schooling, employment, and burial of Black Mississippians in this era was generally not deemed newsworthy, even if ties of acquaintance made their white neighbors aware of these matters. The Black Mississippians in this story did not own the land or the businesses where they worked and accumulated little in the way of material goods to show for a lifetime of labor, leaving light traces in county chancery court records. However, the state was most certainly interested in these and other Black Mississippians when they ran afoul of the law, as the state circuit courts' dockets and other records amply reveal.

The relative absence of these African American lives from the public record sometimes represents their rejection of white authority. Black Mississippians knew that attention from white people could bring unfavorable consequences. Some of them, like their white neighbors, spent a lifetime in or near their birthplace. But since the end of slavery, hundreds of thousands of Black Mississippians exercised one option available to them, mobility. Some moved frequently, both within the state and out of the state, seeking better conditions. That mobility, for whatever reasons and with whatever consequences, sometimes brought at least a measure of privacy.

Some Black Mississippians, including Hattie Lee Barnes herself, occasionally did not use certain elements of the state's legal system, a further reason for their absence from public records. Marriage and divorce were sometimes observed without strict legal accounting. One might not be able to afford representation for a divorce or the fee for a marriage license. At other times, the decision to marry or divorce off the record might be less a matter of cost than of pragmatism. One's husband might leave. After a time, considering that departure in effect a divorce seemed the expedient thing to do, as Barnes told a Mississippi court. Seeking to recover these lives, as historian Françoise Hamlin notes, carries not only documentary challenges but also ethical ones.[9] If people choose to live without unwelcomed scrutiny, what obligation does the historian have to respect their privacy? Throughout this book, I have tried to be mindful that at base it is a story about Hattie Lee Barnes's desire to control her body and her freedom.

Hattie Lee Barnes moved through a world in which her sexuality was a matter of white speculation and sometimes derision, and of regular threats to her ability to protect herself against white men's concupiscence. Labor in white people's homes or places of business represented one source of income for some Black Mississippi women but also a potential danger. By the 1970s, when alternative forms of employment became available, most Black women left those white people's homes, despite the claims of many white Mississippians that they viewed "the help" essentially as family. In the trials and hearings between 1951 and 1955, Barnes was never hypersexualized, as Black male defendants sometimes were. Indeed, references to her sexuality were muted. Newspaper coverage says little about her physical appearance beyond her color. Only two photographs of her were published. Only one witness, Walter Watson, one of the men who shot her, referred specifically to her appearance. When Lamar Craft's drinking companions testified, they either initially denied or seemed reluctant to say that Craft desired Barnes's body. Coverage of the case did not initially refer to the matter as a sex crime. However, judging by Lamar Craft's apparent intention, that is precisely what it was.

What white Mississippians said about interracial sex reflected what they thought of Black people. In some contexts, a white man's desire for a Black woman seemed natural, even a species of entitlement. To Lamar Craft's family, this was an occasion when that desire seemed shameful—one to be concealed from the public record. Because of the Craft family's wish to deny Lamar Craft's intention to assault Hattie Lee Barnes, and his friends' initial reluctance to admit it, these trials do not feature an examination of Barnes's sexual reputation. In that period, and for years to come, women in Barnes's position in Mississippi courts (and most American courts) would have found their reputations subject to critical examination, very often to excuse the violence against them.

But in this story, Hattie Lee Barnes's body was more than an object of wrangling over a white man's reputation. In 1951 and again in 1953, she was taken into custody by Mississippi law enforcement officials. She was also moved from place to place—by those officials and by her employer, Rob Lee—in the name of protecting her. At other times she was held without the rationalization that it was done for her own good. Instead, the only justification was that the State of Mississippi might have some use for her.

A consistent thread in this story is Barnes's determination to tell the truth and win her freedom. She was enmeshed in a system that was by design opaque to her. She was asked to give statements, sign documents, and submit to the authority of sheriff's deputies—all in a society in which the notion of explaining her rights to her, or respecting those rights, seemed unnecessary. The documents that shaped her fate were ones she could not read, a fact that would have seemed irrelevant to many white Mississippians. When she had her chances to depart, she took them, leaving Mississippi for Arkansas, although her mother's continued residence in Mississippi, as well as the hand of the Mississippi legal system, made it difficult to leave the state entirely. Unlike Rob Lee, she never literally fled the law. She herself contacted them, submitted to them, and awaited her fate. She was more than passive, however. From her jail cell, she spoke to a sympathetic reporter, cooperated with her attorney, and availed herself of the assistance and support she could muster.

Along with Barnes, two other characters figure centrally in this book. One is Joe Pigott, a McComb attorney who had practiced less than two years when appointed by the Pike County Circuit Court to defend Hattie Lee Barnes. His sense of duty and justice carried him far beyond a *pro forma* defense of his indigent client. Another is Charles Gordon, a reporter for the *McComb Enterprise-Journal*, the town's daily newspaper. Gordon, like most small-town newspapermen, covered every sort of story during his career. But during many months of coverage and many thousands of words on this story, he was more than a reporter; he became Barnes's advocate. Without Pigott and Gordon, it is unlikely that Barnes's fate would have been significantly different from that of other Black defendants in her position.

Barnes occupied the most unenviable rung in the ladder of a society marked by caste of race, social class, and expectations of gendered behavior. As historian Danielle McGuire wrote: "From slavery through most of the twentieth century, white Americans denied African-American women the most basic citizenship and human rights, especially the right to ownership and control of their own bodies."[10] But Barnes was a woman of grit. Under pressures that would have crushed many people, she resolved to survive. She did not merely endure, to borrow from Faulkner; in the end, she prevailed. In Mississippi of that era, for an African American woman to have faced charges of murdering a white man and to escape punishment must be accounted a victory.

As a recent study of Black Mississippi women before the bar of justice puts it, "African American women felt none of the protection or shelter that white men, and in some instances, white women might have received due to the ideas regarding how white southerners believed they should treat black women."[11] Throughout this story, Barnes's treatment reflects white notions about acceptable treatment of Black women. Other contemporary cases from Pike County, two of which I discuss in the pages below, indicate the sense of some white men that Black women's lives in significant ways did not matter. But this story also complicates common impressions of the pattern of race and justice in twentieth-century Mississippi. A betting person in Pike County in 1951, reading that Barnes had killed a white man, would not have concluded that she had a good chance of escaping punishment. That she did, however, is not primarily a credit to the quality of Mississippi justice. It is rather a testimony to the will and skill of some of the principal actors here, as well as the possibilities open to Barnes and her advocates in this particular time.

It might be said that Barnes was fortunate in the timing of her 1951 shooting of Lamar Craft. A few years later, white Mississippi felt increasingly under siege, becoming more aggressive in defense of Jim Crow. The 1954 *Brown* decision, national reaction to the Emmett Till murder, and rising evidence of Black discontent galvanized white public opinion.[12] Politics, from which race had never been absent, became seemingly a contest over who was best able to defend the "Mississippi way of life," as racial segregation was commonly termed. By the early 1960s, some white Mississippians concluded that state efforts were not enough, turning to a revived Ku Klux Klan and other terror organizations to maintain order, as they saw it. Had Barnes shot Craft a few years later, then, either the court or private forces might have felt a greater need to make an example of her. Had she shot Craft earlier, say in the 1930s or 1940s, the state would perhaps have chewed up Barnes without a trace. Some stories of southern legal atrocities, such as the Scottsboro case, came to national attention in that period. But it took a particularly egregious case of southern injustice in the years of Depression and war to command such attention. One Black woman's shooting of a white man and her punishment for it probably would not have been one of those stories.

The early 1950s represented a period in which it was possible for attorney Joe Pigott and reporter Charles Gordon to advocate Barnes's cause in strenuous ways. Historian Pete Daniel sees the South in the 1950s as years that were ripe with possibilities for change.[13] Without exaggerating those possibilities, especially in Mississippi, the state perhaps most defensive of Jim Crow, one can say that in the early 1950s, some things were possible that might not have been either earlier or later. Pigott and Gordon could see Barnes's case as one involving constitutional rights and fair play. They advocated her cause without meeting either indifference or accusations that they were attacking the Mississippi way of life. Barnes could speak the truth, no matter that some parties there wished to silence her, without the legal system seeing the need to make an example of her. But in the summer of 1951, this context and this reassurance would have offered little comfort to Barnes as she faced the possibility of death in Mississippi's electric chair. Nor would matters have seemed much more favorable to her by 1953, as she languished in one Mississippi jail cell or another without being charged with any crime.

1

A ROADHOUSE SHOOTING AND ITS CONTEXT

ON THE EVENING OF April 16, 1951, the last full day of his life, Lamar Craft and his friends decided to visit Rob Lee's bar. All things considered, it was not a bad day to enjoy a cold beer. That afternoon President Harry Truman, a southpaw, threw out the opening pitch in Washington's Griffith Stadium as the Senators hosted the Yankees to open the baseball season. In Pike or Walthall County, where one heard sports on stations such as McComb's WAPF, April 16 was a fine if somewhat cool spring day, with no rain and a high temperature of 71 degrees; low temperature on the evening that Craft and his friends went out was 48 degrees. The moon, three-quarters full, provided some light, as the sky was clear.[1] Even with Mississippi's mild winters, spring was a treat, with trees and many flowers long in bloom by mid-April. Like other Americans, local people anticipated the full opening day of the baseball season, April 17. The area's Falstaff beer distributor advised fans to have plenty of that beverage on hand to enjoy the games, while the Coca-Cola bottling company reminded people that their offering cost only a nickel a bottle—a carton of six for a quarter. On April 17, the National League's St. Louis Cardinals, most area people's favorite team, as they were geographically the most southern Major League Baseball franchise, dropped a 5–4 decision to the Pittsburgh Pirates.[2] Lamar Craft, however, did not live to hear the results of that game.

The Mississippi lives altered by the shooting at Rob Lee's roadhouse in the early hours of April 17, 1951, were lived within overlapping contexts. Events ranging from the international to the local and purely personal occupied their attention, as they do for all people. For one thing, there was a war, in effect even if termed a "police action." Craft and his friends Hope and Easterling were certainly aware that fighting in Korea had heated up. Some of their friends and relatives were in uniform; the draft continued to draw in more men their age. However, Craft grew up in an era when being "in the service" seemed a male rite of passage. Still, news from Korea continued to be complicated. The country that spring reacted to President Truman's firing of Gen. Douglas MacArthur. On the last day of Lamar Craft's life, the local daily newspaper weighed in with its editorial judgment: "Truman was right."[3]

In these months, the nation also witnessed what soon would be termed the Red Scare, with the House Committee on Un-American Activities turning its attention, among other places, to subversion within the film industry. The search for Hollywood Communists did not dim local people's taste for the movies. In McComb, where Pike and Walthall County residents came for shopping and entertainment, there were two downtown theaters, the State and the Palace, and a drive-in, the Ren. Business was good, as television was still a novelty for the rich. One could purchase a Motorola set with a seventeen-inch screen (black-and-white, of course) from Jack Mashburn downtown on North Broadway. But that television would set you back $339.95, the equivalent of almost $3,400 today.[4] On one of those televisions, viewers could have tuned in to one of the spring's top attractions, the Kefauver Committee's hearings on organized crime. Mississippians, like other Americans, heard a good deal that year and the next about corruption, in and out of government. But most of them—most white citizens, certainly—would not have thought of local affairs or local government as corrupt.

Area law enforcement had a quiet few days before the Craft shooting, although Pike County sheriff Robert E. Lee had helped recover a 1951 Mercury automobile abandoned by a man-and-wife pair of jail escapees from nearby Franklinton, Louisiana. Local Methodist men could have attended a lecture by Judge Tom Brady, who would figure significantly in several cases associated with the Barnes saga. Brady addressed the Methodists on the broad subject of law and order, assuring them that God's law was or should be the basis of law and government, a judgment they surely found to their taste.[5] Matters of race were a perennial feature of public interest and discourse. Readers of the McComb newspaper on April 16 learned that a 250-man posse had captured a Black man accused of fatally shooting a white constable in Hinds County, just over an hour away. And in a story with potential relevance for the Barnes case that was about to unfold, the Mississippi Supreme Court held that there were limits to what might be done to a suspect in custody—even a Black suspect. An African American man won an appeal of his 1949 murder conviction on the grounds that his confession had been extracted under torture in a padded jail cell.[6] Still, few area residents, Black or white, would have felt that anything fundamental was likely to change soon in the system of Jim Crow justice or the broader patterns of racial segregation in which they lived their lives.

By the 1960s, southwestern Mississippi became a violent battleground of the civil rights movement.[7] The tier of counties in which this story takes place—Pike, Walthall, and Marion—developed a reputation as a hard place in what many people considered the nation's most recalcitrant state. Even so, southwestern Mississippi has not drawn full scholarly treatment, as those counties lack book-length studies. Initially, historians of the civil rights movement concentrated on national policy, figures of broad reputation, and highly reported places of conflict such as Little Rock, Arkansas; Birmingham, Alabama; and Oxford, Mississippi. Further work showed how long-standing African American activism in the South's rural areas and small towns shaped events of the 1960s.[8] Recent examinations of movement activity at the county level in Mississippi and other southern states have revealed a good deal more about the forces that drove and impeded the movement for social change.[9]

With some significant exceptions, such as the Emmett Till murder, events of the 1950s in Mississippi remain less studied than those of the 1960s, despite historians' efforts to cast the civil rights movement as an event of long duration.[10] None of the figures here—Lamar Craft, Hattie Lee Barnes, Rob Lee, Joe Pigott, or Charles Gordon—would have thought of themselves as actors in an episode prefiguring Mississippi's civil rights movement. To cast them in that role is to fit them too neatly into a story that anticipates the sweeping challenges of the 1960s. Barnes and the other characters in this story, like all people, lived lives of complexity, nuance, and certainly also of contradiction. Ties of family and kin, economic obligation, and the pursuit of happiness, such as they defined it, mark their lives. But one does not have to treat the years of this story—those of 1951 to 1955—as a precursor to view the Barnes saga as a story about civil rights in Mississippi.

No matter how one defines the civil rights movement in Mississippi, the Hattie Lee Barnes case is literally a story about civil rights—one that demonstrates at a local and personal level how questions of law and other kinds of power worked. Barnes understood several things very well. She lived in a state where basic elements of civil rights were by design withheld from her. From 1951 to 1953, she saw that her freedom and perhaps even her life were being weighed in Mississippi's courts. Her attorney, Joe Pigott, probably would not have seen his advocacy for Barnes as "civil rights work." But he clearly believed that the case turned on matters of basic rights: that of guilt or innocence as defined under Mississippi law. At one point, Pigott sought to free Barnes from a jail cell via a habeas corpus petition, about as fundamental a matter of civil rights as one might find. The area's main daily newspaper, in several strongly worded editorials, argued that the treatment of Hattie Lee Barnes was not only a matter of fair play but also very much a matter of rights and the Constitution, and also a case that would show whether Mississippi believed in the rule of law or not.

In the lives of the people in this story, questions of race, law, and power figured centrally, as they had done throughout Mississippi's history. But those matters were inflected through a variety of other social and economic practices and institutions. Put less abstractly, the Hattie Lee Barnes saga unfolds in places other than courts of law. For instance, alcohol sale and consumption loom large in this story. In spots along those Mississippi roads and highways traveled by Hattie Lee Barnes, Rob Lee, and Lamar Craft, one could buy beer legally in town cafés and at county-line roadhouses, some of which were rough places, familiar to Mississippi law before and after the events of this story. Some of those bars had a patronage strictly segregated by race, whereas others did not. Whiskey, illegal under state law, also flowed abundantly.

Rural Mississippians bought necessities other than alcohol at the country stores that peppered the South in those days. In them, one found cheese, crackers, milk, canned goods, tobacco, clothing, hardware, sewing notions, and practically anything else.[11] As readers of Faulkner will recall, these institutions also served as information clearinghouses. They were good places to spend time on the front porch drinking a Coca-Cola and greeting one's neighbors. They were locally owned and operated. But the Deep South was tied, as it had long been, to broader economic markets, evident in this story through the production of staple crops, the Craft family's operation of a Pure Oil franchise service station, and in people's consumption of automobiles, whiskey, and recorded music.[12]

Other than the attorneys and judges, most of the people in this book were directly associated with the agricultural economy that still dominated Mississippi. Some farmed, either their own land or that of others. Others were small businessmen, dealing in gasoline, groceries, legal beer, or illegal whiskey. Much of their trade, however, would have been with people connected with the land. In school and court terms, church revivals, and a multitude of other ways, Mississippi life was still shaped by agricultural rhythms.

Still, Mississippi's state government and local citizens had attempted since the 1930s to attract outside investment in the form of factories. Local people pointed out the advantages of the state's business climate, with its combination of low taxes, light regulation, incentives for factory location or relocation, and a general antipathy toward unions that promised low payrolls as well.[13] By the early 1950s, those efforts to attract industry to southwestern Mississippi had been mixed. In the 1930s, Brookhaven lured a Stahl-Urban garment manufacturing plant from Indiana after union activity spooked owners there. McComb had several light manufacturing concerns, including one that produced ladies' undergarments. Local women found in these plants what seemed an attractive alternative to other sources of wage labor.

While the economy brought fat years and lean ones, often lean ones for many people in the area, the law was an abiding presence. Mississippi courthouses were literally and figuratively the center of their county seats. These courthouses represented one of the most visible, potent symbols of government. In them, people paid their taxes, registered to vote, recorded their buying and selling of land, their marriages and occasional divorces, and the final disposition of their property. There they also served on juries and occasionally stood trial. Unlike many states, Mississippi had no courts of appeal standing between county courthouses and the state's supreme court, and would have no such intermediary courts of appeal until late in the twentieth century.[14] The law reflected the white majority's insistence upon the maintenance of a segregated social order. Black Mississippians understood the law and courts as dangerous institutions, even if they would not have used those words before white listeners. Many white Mississippians would not perhaps have thought in those terms, most of them believing that the Jim Crow order was simply a matter of common sense or perhaps a reflection of practices that existed long before their memory.

The courthouses in Pike, Walthall, and Marion Counties, mostly modest buildings, were only a half century old by the 1950s. All three were built of brick; all stood in a square in the center of their small towns. All were surrounded by law offices and by business districts where country people still came on Saturdays to conduct their trade. Practically anything local people needed of goods, supplies, and services could be obtained nearby. The courtrooms themselves, especially when crowded for trials, smelled of cigarette smoke and sweat, of starched clothes wilting in the Mississippi heat, and no doubt also of some anxiety and despair. Figuratively if not literally, one could also sense the whiskey that was illegal in the state, but that could be readily purchased by anyone who wanted it. The business conducted in those courthouses seemed to most Mississippians to be white men's business, whether they liked that fact or not. And so it was, in the sense that the judges, attorneys, circuit and chancery clerks, police officers and sheriff's deputies, and registrars of voters all were white men. Within a generation, some of those matters would change, a result of the civil rights movement that broke upon the region. But when Hattie Lee Barnes entered those courthouses, neither she nor anyone else had the expectation that anything would soon be much different than it was.

The year 1951 was also an election year. Politics remained one of Mississippi's most popular sports. McComb newspaper editor Oliver Emmerich told readers that voting "is like a marriage ceremony. Think it over now, speak out on the ballot or forever hold your peace."[15] No one needed reminding that voting was white people's business. The Black population of the state was approximately 45 percent; only 5 percent of Black Mississippians were registered to vote, a figure unchanged until the mid-1960s.[16] The state voted for its governors in odd-numbered years; the slate filled for the August primary, from the top office through constables and the powerful county supervisors. Mississippi was overwhelmingly a Democratic state, despite bolting to the Dixiecrats in the presidential race of 1948. People understood that voices in the national Democratic Party, such as Minnesota's Hubert Humphrey, had hard things to say about the southern way of life. But these were the days in which the seniority system in Congress remained in force. The state's two US senators, James O. Eastland and John C. Stennis, held powerful committee chairmanships, a source of pride and comfort. At the state and county levels, the Democratic Party seemed unshakable, with victory in the August primary "tantamount to election," as people put it.

Pike, Walthall, and Marion Counties, where Hattie Lee Barnes, Rob Lee, and Lamar Craft lived and worked, and in whose courthouses elements of this saga were tried, lay in the southwestern corner of Mississippi; the counties bordered Louisiana. Walthall County in 1950 had a population of 15,563 residents, and during the 1940s experienced a population decline of more than 11 percent.[17] Tylertown, the county seat, was the only town of any size, with a 1950 population of 1,331.[18] Most Walthall County people worked in agriculture, a majority of them tenant farmers. In the 1930s and 1940s, there was little manufacturing in the county, with only eighty industrial workers recorded in the 1930 US Census.[19] Unlike the flat, fertile Delta, Walthall County held no vast cotton plantations. Farmers raised dairy cattle, corn, hogs, and a limited amount of cotton. The white population slightly outnumbered the Black. Practically no one had been born outside the United States. The 1930 census showed that its population included one person born in France, one in England, and two in Greece.[20]

Pike County was slightly larger and older than Walthall, the latter county created only in 1914, carved from Pike and Marion Counties. In 1950, Pike County held 35,137 residents, a figure essentially unchanged through the 1940s. With just over 10,000 residents, McComb was by far the largest town, but it was not the county seat. Magnolia was, so it was there that Hattie Lee Barnes was tried in 1951 for the murder of Lamar Craft.[21] Ties between Pike and Walthall—ties of commerce and kin—were close. "At least two-thirds of [Walthall] once belonged to Pike County and the early histories of the two counties are so closely interwoven that they are difficult to separate," a local source points out.[22] Those ties shaped and still shape the lives of area people. For many decades, those old county affiliations remained markers of identity, with obituaries recording that a person had been born in "Old Pike County."[23]

Marion County is less central to this story. Had Rob Lee not owned property just over the Walthall-Marion county line, property on which he and Walter Watson shot Hattie Lee Barnes, it would not figure at all. In 1950, the county had a population of about 25,000 people. Columbia, the county seat, larger than Tylertown but smaller than McComb, had about 5,000 residents. The county itself, about two-thirds white and one-third Black, had a slightly more diversified economy than neighboring Walthall County. Along with small farming operations, county residents could work in textile, wood, or furniture manufacturing, or in the small oil operations that had begun to deliver at the end of World War II.[24]

These county populations and town sizes show that Mississippi in 1950 was still a rural state with a small population.[25] This book spends considerable time in the towns of these counties, mainly because those were the seats of justice. However, many of the principal characters—the Crafts, Rob Lee, and Hattie Lee Barnes—were rural people. The main events here—the shootings, the liquor trade, and the emergence of grudges between Rob Lee and the Crafts—were rural stories. Much as they preferred, the actions of most Pike and Walthall residents generally did not rise to the level of public knowledge. People worked, went to school when they were able and church when they wished, and avoided the law and the county courthouse whenever they could.

A few daily and several weekly newspapers chronicled the lives and times of these communities, although African Americans generally saw their names (if they could read them, given Mississippi's stance on Black education) in those papers only if they were charged with a crime. As the year 1951 began in Pike County, *Enterprise-Journal* editor Oliver Emmerich told his readers, as he would many hundreds of times over the following decades, that "it's a privilege to live in McComb."[26] Emmerich's readers opened the year with a local episode connected with one of the state's most salacious recent cases. Ruth Thompson Dickins of Leland was convicted of the 1948 murder of her mother, Idella Thompson. Dickins, who killed her mother with a pair of garden shears, insisted that a Black man was responsible, a perennially favorite southern tactic. She identified one likely candidate: Charlie Ferguson, a sixteen-year-old held in the state mental hospital at Whitfield. Reporter Charles Gordon, who would diligently report the Hattie Lee Barnes case, pointed out that Ferguson was surely not the killer. At the time of the Thompson murder, Gordon discovered, Ferguson was not even in Leland but was instead in McComb with his grandmother; he was then a fugitive from Whitfield.[27]

In Pike and Walthall Counties, however, early 1951 was not a particularly violent period, at least measured in terms of fatalities. Pike County sheriff Robert E. Lee noted with relief that the March grand jury returned only eight indictments—none for manslaughter or murder.[28] The April killing of Lamar Craft seems to have been the area's first reported murder of the year. For that reason, and because of the race of Craft and Barnes, it was a noteworthy story. The spring of 1951 did witness the grim resolution of one of the state's most notorious recent cases. On May 8, despite significant national and even international outcry, Willie McGee, a Black man, was executed for the 1945 rape of a married white woman. Within a few years, with the Emmett Till murder and the emergence of the civil rights movement, Mississippi justice would more frequently become national news. But as Hattie Lee Barnes awaited trial, that development was yet another matter that few people would have anticipated.[29]

Despite abiding patterns in Pike, Walthall, and Marion Counties, life in Mississippi was not unchanged from the early twentieth century, as national journalists in the 1960s sometimes asserted. One well-noted change was the continued African American migration out of these counties and toward better opportunities in the North. Another development with consequences for the way this story unfolded was the war. Everyone in the area understood "the war" not to mean the Civil War or even the current fighting in Korea but rather World War II. The Second World War, as historians have long noted, brought significant economic changes to the Deep South. A change that is harder to quantify is that of attitude. Many young men, such as Joe Pigott, the attorney representing Barnes, returned from the war with a willingness to entertain the possibility of reform in their native state. Some African American veterans came home determined to work for the freedoms that they believed that they had fought for in Europe and in the Pacific; others, like all veterans, thought primarily of making better lives for their children in material terms.[30] In the late 1940s and early 1950s, a significant number of these veterans entered public life, either as elected officials, in the professions, or in civil rights work. A younger generation of politicians seemed poised to emerge in those years. Some of them held views that were progressive, certainly by the standards of the time. Changes in attitudes and institutions, however, proceeded unevenly.

If one wished to believe that things would never change, in the year 1951 that was still possible.

Few white southwestern Mississippi residents seemed anxious about matters of race. Far from it, in fact. Despite rumblings from Washington, the state's Jim Crow system seemed secure. If one were white, it was possible to believe in the early 1950s that there was no civil rights activity in Mississippi. The Barnes case, then, would not seem one of those matters that needed handling in such a way as to demonstrate to Black Mississippians anything about who really was in charge. Those years would come later, in the mid-1950s through the mid-1960s. Mississippi remained, in most ways that mattered, a conservative place, certainly if one measures conservatism by the white majority's attitude toward social change. Along with racial segregation, there were considerable continuities between past and present in the area, among them ties of kinship, proximity, and shared experiences and values. In that context, then, Hattie Lee Barnes, an African American woman, faced trial and possible execution for the murder of a white man. She would have understood the length of the odds against her.

2

THE CASE AGAINST HATTIE LEE BARNES

NOT ONLY HAD Hattie Lee Barnes killed a white man, but one of local prominence. Events of the next few years would demonstrate both the power and the limits of the Craft family's influence. Joining Pike County sheriff Robert E. Lee at Rob Lee's roadhouse in the early hours of April 17, 1951, was Lamar Craft's father, Edd Craft, a candidate for sheriff of Walthall County in that summer's Democratic primary.[1] A man with deep roots and connections in Walthall County, Edd Tunison Craft was born there in 1901. More precisely, he was born in "Old Pike County," as people still called it, before Walthall was created in 1914. A member of both the Shriners and the Masons, Craft was an officer in the latter organization in the late 1920s.[2] Craft farmed. By the 1930s he, like some other Mississippians, vexed by the vicissitudes of the cotton market, looked for alternatives to that staple. In 1938 he harvested a "fine spinach crop." Involved in various ways in the life of Walthall County, he was in 1938 one of the "transporters" of children to school in the western community of Mesa. Craft himself was a high school graduate, not an inconsiderable achievement in that time and place.[3] By 1940, Craft, age thirty-nine, his wife, Gertrude, and their children lived on a farm that he owned.[4] Along with raising cattle, by 1950 his business interests included the service station in Tylertown where his son worked, the "Purol S.S.," affiliated with the Pure Oil Company.[5] Although it might not seem appropriate by today's standards for a homicide victim's father to be at the crime scene, Edd Craft was determined. In any case, Walthall and Pike Counties were places in which personal connections led to cooperation and assistance. From the beginning, Edd Craft wished to learn what happened to his son, a natural impulse. He also resolved to do more than wait as area authorities moved the case toward trial.

Later that day of April 17, Lamar Craft's companions, James Easterling and Oscar Hope, were taken into custody and held at the Pike County Jail, pending further investigation into the shooting. The three men's motives for returning to the roadhouse were unclear—at least that is what the public would have heard. Had they intended to burglarize Lee's bar? Whether or not that was their plan, Easterling and Hope were held on burglary-related charges. According to reporter Charles Gordon, the two men said that the trio decided to return to the establishment after it closed, enter it, and "then carry out whatever design might suggest itself."[6] For a long time, neither Easterling nor Hope were forthcoming about their—or more precisely Craft's—motives for returning to Rob Lee's place. That reticence was surely motivated by the desire not to incriminate themselves. It seems also to have been driven by what they felt they owed to the memory of their late friend.

Pike County had no reason to believe that anyone other than Barnes was responsible for Craft's death. She said as much initially to Sheriff Lee.[7] Pending a hearing and formal charges, Barnes was held in the Pike County Jail, the initially "undisclosed location" and the same jail occupied by Easterling and Hope.[8] Barnes had the right to waive that initial hearing, should she choose. But Barnes was a woman of modest means, without the resources to hire legal counsel and surely uncertain of her rights and options. Without doubt, though, Barnes recognized the dangers she faced. Initially, charges were expected to be filed against Barnes in a preliminary hearing before Judge C. D. Rayborn, justice of the peace of Pike County's Third District, in which the shooting had occurred.[9] Instead, hearings for all three—Barnes, Hope, and Easterling—were held in the Pike County Circuit Court on Thursday, April 19, before Judge W. F. Jackson. Pike County prosecuting attorney R. B. Reeves filed murder charges against Barnes, who was held on $1,000 bond. Easterling and Hope, charged with breaking and entering, were held under $1,000 bond as well.[10]

On Wednesday, April 18, the day before Barnes was charged with his murder and the day after his body was discovered in Rob Lee's roadhouse, Lamar Craft was buried. After a 2:00 p.m. funeral at the Methodist Church, officiated by Rev. Swep Harkey, Craft's body was interred at the Tylertown Cemetery. Along with his father, Craft was survived by his stepmother, Katie Harvey Craft. His mother, Gertrude Tynes Craft, had died in 1941.[11] Other survivors included one sister and five brothers.[12] Several of his brothers, along with his father, did more than grieve. They planned action both to protect their family's reputation and to strike against the person they felt was responsible for Craft's death.

Lamar Craft's obituary in the *Tylertown Times* referred to him as a "tragedy victim," a view certainly shared by his family and other members of the community. Events of that April evening at Rob Lee's place were a tragedy, if not in the literary sense, at least in the common usage of the term. Not only Lamar Craft's family but also Hattie Lee Barnes surely rued the consequences of Craft's decision.[13] The photograph accompanying his obituary shows a smiling, fit young man wearing a striped sports shirt. His light-colored hair is thick and wavy. Obituaries, like eulogies, have their conventions, and Craft's, like those of most people who are not notorious, paints him in favorable terms. He was "popular" and the son of a "prominent" man. The "great throng of friends" at his funeral services attested to "the high esteem with which the youth was held." The "sad rites" that "paid tribute" to Craft featured a "profusion of flowers." As a service station operator, he was "most affable" as well as an "efficient businessman." Eight "intimate friends" served as Craft's pallbearers. Not among them were James Easterling or Oscar Hope, who were, even if their services might have been desired by the family, still locked up in the Pike County Jail. Of the circumstances of his death, readers would have learned only that Craft "was killed Monday night," although few people in the area would not have heard something more about that event, through gossip, if not from some nearer-hand source.[14]

Craft was a US Air Force veteran, having served three years immediately after his 1947 graduation from Tylertown High School, where he had played football, as did so many small-town Mississippi boys. He had begun studies at Mississippi Southern College in Hattiesburg, about fifty-five miles west of Tylertown on Highway 98. Fellow members of the Pi Kappa Alpha social fraternity attended his funeral. Three of his brothers still lived in Tylertown, along with a sister, a stepsister, his father, and his stepmother. Of the two other brothers then in military service, one was stationed in Florida and the other in South Carolina.[15]

Also among the mourners, one presumes, but whether she attended the funeral is unclear, was Lucy Scott of Gulfport. She was engaged to be married to Craft; the ceremony had been scheduled for June. One may wonder what Scott knew about the circumstances of Craft's death and what she might have learned later, how she learned of his death, and what memories and feelings she carried over the ensuing years. Of these matters, it is impossible to say. But it surely is the case that the Craft family's actions over the next few years in seeking to deny that young Craft was shot while trying to assault an African American woman were motivated by more than the desire to spare Lucy Scott from heartache or embarrassment. It is not hard to imagine, even in the absence of any evidence, that Scott must have felt both these emotions. Less than three months after the burial of her own fiancé, Scott sang at the wedding of a friend.[16]

What Hattie Lee Barnes might have felt about Lamar Craft is also one of those matters for which there is no evidence. But in the last weeks of April 1951, she had other matters on her mind, matters of her own freedom and ultimate fate. Given the circumstances of the shooting, particularly the breaking-and-entering charges filed against Craft's two companions, why was Barnes charged with murder rather than some lesser offense, such as manslaughter? The McComb newspaper reported without amplification that "it was pointed out by county officials that the charge of murder against the Negress was the only feasible move in the situation and that it would result in a hearing into the fatal occurrence in a competent and fully qualified court which could then rule on the evidence presented."[17] A legal hearing would provide a forum for hearing evidence in the case. Barnes had admitted to firing the shot that killed Craft. But that the location of Barnes's jailing was initially undisclosed suggests a grimmer possibility: Pike County authorities charged Barnes with murder perhaps to forestall any inclination among local whites to take justice into their own hands. By the early 1950s, vigilante justice against Black Mississippians was no longer as common as it had been a decade or two earlier. But the threat of white violence remained real, as events in the state from the mid-1950s through the mid-1960s would demonstrate. African American prisoners were still commonly moved out of the county in which they were charged with authorities explicitly stating that such moves prevented mob action.

Even if Pike and Walthall Counties had been relatively quiet early in 1951, Mississippi was a state in which murders were not rare. Crime statistics for

1950, released by the Federal Bureau of Investigation, showed that the state experienced 12.4 murders per one hundred thousand people, a rate higher than in the neighboring states of Louisiana and Arkansas and well over twice the national average of 5.11 murders per one hundred thousand citizens.[18] Traditionally, Mississippi law had taken a more serious view of Black-on-white violence than it did other forms of crime; and it still did. The pattern of Mississippi justice in the twentieth century also reveals that violence against African Americans was seen as a less serious matter, whether the perpetrator was white or Black. Still, notorious cases like the Till murder notwithstanding, white people could not expect to kill Black people with complete impunity. By the 1950s, white people were commonly sentenced to the state penitentiary for such crimes. But sheriffs and their deputies and local police officers enjoyed wide latitude in employing violence against Black citizens and were rarely called before the bar, either of justice or public opinion, to answer for it.

By law and custom, local authorities had a good deal of discretion over the treatment of prisoners and not a great deal of oversight or accountability. Treatment of Black prisoners within the state's jails or while in the custody of sheriff or police was capricious, often dependent on the personality or whims of a law enforcement officer or jailer, and thus potentially perilous. Some of these men acted with fundamental decency; others did not. Hattie Lee Barnes would have known this fact, as would any Black Mississippian. Some of the state's peace officers were among the most determined of its citizens to maintain racial order, as they saw it, and would remain so well after the events of this story. In a 1936 case, *Brown v. Mississippi,* one that reached the US Supreme Court, a Mississippi deputy considered the beating of Black prisoners to be so accepted a practice that he described it in testimony carefully and without apparent embarrassment.[19] In the 1960s, some law local enforcement agencies seemed almost an adjunct of the Ku Klux Klan, providing information to them and in some cases working closely with them.

Barnes consistently said that she was never physically mistreated by law enforcement authorities. Perhaps that is true. But being held under sometimes-undefined conditions, being moved from place to place without clear explanation, and the anxiety Barnes no doubt felt as she faced a potential capital charge all weighed heavily upon her. The fact that she said in various hearings that she had not been mistreated should not be taken as the last word, given what Barnes surely realized about the consequences of saying more than she needed to say. Her testimony at hearings and trials, explored in later chapters here, suggests a woman wearing down emotionally and physically under stress.

In that Thursday, April 19, hearing in the Pike County Courthouse, a fuller picture emerged of what happened early Tuesday morning at Lee's roadhouse. Some of that information came from Easterling and Hope, some from Barnes, and still more from law enforcement officers. One clarification, offered from the manager of the funeral home that handled Craft's body, corrected earlier reports that Craft had been shot in the mouth. Instead, said Floyd Freeman, the fatal bullet struck Craft in the right shoulder, "followed a rib into his chest and plunged downward until it lodged in the lower part of the man's spine." The initial confusion about the location of the wound, testified Sheriff Lee, stemmed from the amount of blood present on Craft's body. His chest wound caused him to bleed from the mouth as his body hung in the window through which he had attempted to enter the bar.[20]

Oscar Hope and James Easterling offered detail about the evening. Hope said that the three men left the bar in Craft's car shortly after midnight, driving east toward Tylertown, but then decided to turn around and head back toward Lee's place. En route, they passed both Rob and Ruth Lee, joint operators of the business, each driving a separate car. Reaching the tavern, they parked behind it. They knocked on both the front and the rear doors before Craft determined to enter via a window. Easterling said he held open the window as Craft climbed in. A shot rang out; Craft groaned. Easterling let go of the window and ran. Hope, standing in front of the tavern, fled as well when he heard shots. Neither Easterling nor Hope said then why they had returned to Lee's place after closing time.[21]

Sheriff Robert E. Lee testified that Barnes herself called him at his home to report the shooting, using the business's telephone. Barnes told him that she had shot someone and would wait there for Sheriff Lee to arrive. When he did arrive, said Lee, he "had a difficult time making the woman . . . understand who he was so she would let him enter." That day's testimony also featured the first mention of Barnes's stepfather, Dan Magee, who lived so close to Lee's bar that he could hear Barnes hail him from the business. She yelled to her stepfather that she had shot a man and that other men were still on the scene. Magee fired several shots into the air to attempt to frighten the intruders away.[22]

The state's case would be handled by county prosecuting attorney R. B. "Breezy" Reeves and district attorney L. S. McLaren.[23] Craft's family retained an attorney, Breed Mounger of Tylertown, to see to their interests; he was present at this initial hearing. What formal part Mounger might take in the legal proceedings was initially unclear, but he would turn out to play a large role, both formal and informal, in the Barnes trial and in many related pieces of the increasingly complex case. Hattie Lee Barnes now was represented by court-appointed attorney Joe Pigott of McComb.

Area authorities apparently had an eye on Rob Lee's place, as well as other Highway 24 roadhouses, for some time. The shooting allowed the state to move against Lee's bar and two other establishments, which were padlocked and closed for business as of April 18. County Prosecuting Attorney Reeves had earlier filed a complaint, heard by Chancery Judge Charles F. Engle of Natchez, that the bars constituted a violation of the law and a threat to public order. First, said Reeves, the offending bars all served "both white and colored patrons." That disregard of Mississippi law and custom was practiced and occasionally tolerated at many roadhouses and cafés. Here, as in many other instances, the practice of racial segregation in the state could vary significantly from locale to locale.[24] A pattern of interracial drinking that might have been allowed under some circumstances could excite official attention when the bar came to public notice for some other reason, such as the shooting of a white man by a Black woman.

At Lee's place, which did maintain separate if not equal Black and white bars, the complaint noted that "intoxicating liquor is stored and sold and . . . drinking is permitted, sanctioned, and condoned," a fact that would not have surprised anyone in either Pike or Walthall Counties. Mississippi was under statewide prohibition of alcohol during this period and would remain so until 1966, the last state to repeal its Prohibition laws.[25] The state's attitude toward alcohol was complicated, however, and deeply conflicted. From 1944, the state had levied a 10 percent tax on alcohol sales. In many parts of the state, including the Delta and the Gulf Coast, alcohol flowed freely and was essentially openly sold. Nearly everywhere in the state, one could find it for sale without a great deal of trouble, whether from a local bootlegger or at wide-open operations such as the Highway 24 establishments Reeves wished to shut down.

With the state officially under Prohibition, how were roadhouses like Lee's allowed openly to operate at all? To some Mississippians, "alcohol" meant distilled spirits, generally whiskey. Beer could be a different matter in public attitude and also under the state's confusing alcohol policy. As early as the 1930s, Pike County, in which Rob Lee's taverns operated, was a "wet" county in which beer was sold, while Lincoln County to the north was "dry." Predictably, some Lincoln County residents routinely enjoyed beer in Pike County, whereas others complained that the availability of beer there disturbed its "law and order."[26] From the 1930s, a Brewers and Mississippi Beer Distributors Committee operated in Jackson, directed by W. W. Pierce and headquartered in the Millsaps Building. That committee saw a real difference between upstanding establishments and "beer joints."[27] Beer advocates argued for years in Mississippi, as they had in other parts of the United States, that beer was a moderate beverage, the consumption of which would decrease the thirst of customers for whiskey and other hard liquor. Area preachers and other abstinence people disagreed.

Many people in Pike and Walthall Counties wanted their alcohol, but the men who supplied it, such as Rob Lee, carried in some eyes at least an unsavory reputation. Whether that reputation stemmed from the sale of alcohol itself, the mixing of white and Black patrons in their establishments, or other disturbances of the peace, such as gambling or fighting, that often occurred there, is difficult to say. What is absent from the Barnes case is any suggestion that Lee's establishments or the other juke joints and roadhouses at which the people here drank dealt or allowed people to deal in narcotics or drugs other than alcohol. Neither public discourse nor the dockets of the county courts would provide much evidence of that vice until the 1960s.

In 1949, McComb held a "beer election," as both sides called it, to decide whether to continue legal sales of the beverage.[28] Local arguments over alcohol had been a hardy perennial of Mississippi political discourse since the national repeal of Prohibition of 1933; they would remain so for decades, continuing well into the twenty-first century. Such debates were almost always conducted with an eye to the moral and religious ramifications of the issue. Considerations of basic law and order were generally to the fore as well. In the background, one occasionally heard discussion of alcohol, race, and social control, such as had been featured in the South since the nineteenth century.

McComb reporter Charles Gordon noted in 1949, in words that speak to conditions that one would see across the Barnes case, that "Walthall County and Tylertown are just exactly as dry as it is possible for a section to get . . . [T]hey make up a prohibitionist's dream, or do they?" Gordon cited with evident pleasure a story from the Tylertown newspaper; a man building a chicken house in a rural area was interrupted fourteen times by callers who thought he was a bootlegger putting up a new dive.[29] That spring, the grand jury in Magnolia reported that the sale of beer in Pike County "attracts many undesirable characters, many of whom come from adjoining counties."[30] In advance of the beer election, a Mississippi beer trade group weighed in, framing the consumption of alcohol simply as a matter of respecting differences of opinion and the other fellow's ability to exercise his rights, essentially the same thing as "his right to earn a living" or "his right to cast his vote against your candidate." Just as much a right was a man's ability "to enjoy a moderate, friendly glass of beer or ale—if and when he chooses. Let's keep it that way!" Pike County voters seemed to agree.[31]

From the 1930s through the 1960s, roadhouses such as Rob Lee's establishments were notorious for violence as well as drinking. The lifting of statewide Prohibition in 1966 allowed drinking in many parts of Mississippi to come out of the shadows and into the light. Mississippi remained ambivalent about alcohol, even while many state residents consumed it with destructive gusto. Area newspapers and court dockets regularly featured stories originating in these county-line "joints," as many people called them. Pike and Lincoln County residents of a certain age still recall such bars as the Hi-Hat Café and the Briar Patch as "rough as hell," as one former patron told me. In a 1964 shooting at the latter place, a patron shot another with a .38, as "the raucous strains of a hillbilly band filled the air."[32]

In the 1950s, then, for a bar such as Lee's to be shut down, it had to do more than simply offer alcohol for sale. It also had to rise to the level of a public nuisance. Sometimes that nuisance took the form of the owner's not maintaining good relations with the sheriff or deputies in whose jurisdiction the business operated. In other cases, the nuisance might come from the business owner's catering too openly to other vices, such as gambling. In these cases, said Reeves in his 1951 argument for shuttering the three Highway 24 bars, the roadhouses also operated slot machines. In still other cases, a place might become notorious for violence to such a degree that the local authorities could no longer countenance it. Such seems also to have been the case with the bars

Reeves targeted. Along with Craft's shooting at Lee's bar, another roadhouse was a place "where fights occur and recently parties in an intoxicated condition attacked an officer, a public official of Pike County."[33]

Rob Lee's beer joint was probably not a good deal worse than many others in the area.[34] Hattie Lee Barnes had no previous criminal record in the Pike or Walthall county courts. As Lamar Craft's obituary suggests, local people likely did think of him as a promising young man. But the combination here of alcohol sales and a white man's shooting by a Black woman gave authorities a reason to shut down Lee's place. The fact that the shooting was linked to Rob Lee's bar and an African American woman also represented both an embarrassment and an opportunity for Edd Craft and his family. It gave them an incentive and an opening to shape the investigation of the case and to seek their own species of justice. Hattie Lee Barnes tried from the beginning simply to tell what happened to her that evening. Some people in southwestern Mississippi, like the Crafts, determined that Barnes would say what they wanted her to say. Others, like Rob Lee, decided that she should not have the opportunity to speak at all.

3

TWO ATTEMPTED MURDERS

FROM THE MOMENT Hattie Lee Barnes heard someone at the window of Rob Lee's bar, she confronted significant danger. Shortly after her Thursday, April 19, hearing, now facing a murder charge, Barnes met new threats from still other quarters. That same day, she was moved from Pike County to Tylertown in Walthall County. Her detention was described as "protective custody," although how being held in the Crafts' hometown could be protection was unclear, certainly not to Barnes herself. In Tylertown, however, Breed Mounger, the Crafts' attorney, had access to Barnes. Mounger and the Crafts wanted her to change the story she told Pike County authorities. Early that evening, Mounger brought Barnes to his office for a lengthy meeting conducted under no clear legal authority. Initially present, along with Mounger, were Craft's father and brothers, joined later in the evening, around 9:30 p.m., by district attorney L. S. McLaren. McLaren listened to Barnes present an account fundamentally at odds with her previous statements. In Mounger's office, Barnes implicated bar owner Rob Lee in Craft's shooting. Less than two months later, Lee, weighing the threat that Barnes's changed account might present to him, shot her multiple times and left her for dead.[1]

During her time in Mounger's office and then in the Walthall County Jail, Barnes "was persuaded," according to *Enterprise-Journal* reporter Charles Gordon, to change her account of what happened to Lamar Craft. Rob Lee, she now said, shot Craft. Released from the Tylertown jail and also from Breed

Mounger on Monday, April 23, Barnes returned to Pike County. Gordon, who had filed the first published story on the case the previous week, interviewed Barnes that evening. To Gordon, however, Barnes disavowed her changed story, insisting that the version she told Pike County authorities the previous week was true. She, not Rob Lee, fired the shot that killed Craft. Barnes's instincts told her to trust Gordon, or at least to speak freely to him. Gordon's instincts told him that something not only newsworthy, but also fundamentally wrong, was happening to Hattie Lee Barnes. For the next two years, he followed the case closely because he knew it was a compelling story. But he also saw Barnes's treatment at the hands of Mississippi justice as a fundamental matter of right and wrong and insisted that his readers see what was happening to her at the hands of local people and institutions.[2]

Barnes was not the only person in and then quickly out of jail in Pike County. Craft's companions James Easterling and Oscar Hope had been charged with breaking and entering and held under $1,000 bond from the Pike County Circuit Court. Both were soon released. But Easterling almost immediately found himself jailed in Walthall County on what the newspaper called "a charge no one has defined here." How did Barnes and Easterling find themselves in jail in Walthall County for charges stemming from a case in Pike County? For Barnes, her Walthall County custody was orchestrated by the Craft family, via their attorney, Breed Mounger, to allow them access to her. But Mounger and the Crafts also wanted Easterling. They wished to hear what he had to say, but more important, they wanted to pressure him also into telling a story that suited them.

How were all three freed from Pike County custody? Immediately after the Thursday hearing, both Easterling and Hope were released on a promise that they would each secure the $1,000 bond levied by the judge, a generous construction of typical bond requirements. Barnes's posting bond was more complicated and more revealing of the dangers she faced. Barnes, apparently with no immediate hope to make bond, was taken across the street from the Pike County Courthouse in Magnolia to the jail. She did not remain there for more than a few hours. At 4:30 p.m., J. C. Henson, a Walthall County man, appeared at the courthouse with the $1,000 bond for Barnes.[3] Barnes was summoned from her cell; she and Henson signed bond papers. Neither the sheriff nor other county officers were present. It is not clear if they knew Barnes would make bond. Nor is it clear when they learned she had been released. Nothing in Barnes's later accounts suggests that she expected to be bonded out or that she knew Henson. But sheriff's office deputy Mrs. Nettie Holmes, satisfied that the bond was in order, released Barnes, who left Magnolia with Henson.[4]

Then, Henson, Barnes, and "a Jackson private detective named Roberts" began driving the short distance north toward McComb. There, near the intersection of Highways 51 and 24, the latter the route toward Tylertown, the men stopped; one of them made a telephone call to Tylertown. The distance from McComb to Tylertown was about twenty miles. The distance from McComb to Barnes's house, located near Rob Lee's roadhouse, was about half that distance. At they neared her house, Barnes asked to be taken home. The men refused, saying they intended to take her to Tylertown. Arriving at Breed Mounger's law office, Barnes encountered a frightening scene without benefit of legal counsel. She faced Edd Craft, several of Lamar Craft's brothers, and other Craft relatives. As Barnes told reporter Charles Gordon a few days later, those men interrogated her for hours about the death of Craft, repeatedly warning her that she could be "electrocuted" for the crime—unless, of course, she changed her story about what had happened to Craft.[5]

Neither Hattie Lee Barnes nor any other Black Mississippian would have considered the threat of execution to be an idle one. Mississippi did use electrocution as its means of execution in this period. Until 1940, the state executed by hanging. Then, from 1940 until 1954, the state's oak electric chair was moved from county to county as needed. Should one wish to see that device, it is still on display at the Mississippi Law Enforcement Training Academy. The electric chair was first used in September 1940 on a man convicted of murdering his wife. The state's executioner assured everyone that the murderer had died "with tears in his eyes for the efficient care I took to give him a good clean burning." Prior to 1951, the State of Mississippi had conducted more than seven hundred legal executions. The first of them was in 1818, the year after admission to the union, for the crime of "stealing a Negro." Of those executed, the majority were Black men. No white woman had been executed by the state, but some African American women had been.[6]

The interrogation at Mounger's office lasted through the night, ending only around 4:00 a.m. the following morning. As a result of the threats and questioning, Barnes told Charles Gordon, she changed the story that she had given in court earlier on Thursday and "told them anything they wanted me to say." Sometime that evening, the men also took Barnes to Marion County, to the east of Walthall County, to look for a man who someone in the office suggested might have had a hand in Craft's slaying: "a second Negro, one Leroy Collins." Near midnight, Pike County prosecuting attorney R. B. Reeves was summoned as well to Tylertown to learn the new and unfolding developments.[7]

Within certain limits, there was no strict legal prohibition against the Craft family and Breed Mounger trying to learn what they could about the shooting of Lamar Craft. But there is also no apparent reason why the authorities of two counties cooperated with Mounger in answering his summons to his office and bringing witnesses for him to interview. No reason, that is, except for the patterns of cooperation that had developed between Mounger and these other attorneys and law enforcement officials, testimony to the ways in which a good deal of business was done in that era. James Easterling, released on bond from Pike County earlier that day, was brought to Mounger's law office that evening, where he was interrogated by this quasi-legal body. Easterling, a white man, like the room full of those questioning him, apparently stood his ground and gave very much the same account as he had done earlier to Pike County sheriff Lee. Much later, however, Easterling and Edd Craft gave conflicting accounts of what Easterling said that evening.[8]

During her long interrogation, Barnes told reporter Charles Gordon that she was not physically abused but that she was "scared to death," an eminently reasonable response. Nothing suggests that she was able to consult Joe Pigott, her court-appointed attorney, or that Pigott was even aware that his client had been released from the Pike County Jail and removed to Tylertown. There is little doubt that the men interrogating Barnes did not explain her rights to her or suggest that she had no legal obligation to cooperate with them. Held for the better part of a day in Breed Mounger's office, and then held in the Tylertown jail over the weekend, Barnes was freed on Monday afternoon. Walthall County sheriff Marshall Bullock drove Barnes to the Pike-Walthall county line, where by arrangement he met Pike County sheriff Robert E. Lee, to whom he released Barnes, further evidence of the cooperation of two counties in the Mounger-Craft detention and interrogation of Barnes.[9]

According to a case timeline later created by Barnes's attorney Joe Pigott, "Sheriff Bullock had Hattie Lee to keep her head down in his car so she could not be seen and he brought her to the county line where Sheriff Robert Lee of Pike County took her to a place to stay on Summit Street in McComb."[10] Summit Street was a center of Black McComb, an area of stores and cafés, of churches and residences. Why Sheriff Lee took her there; under what authority, if any, he took her from Bullock's into his custody; or what Barnes understood about the status of her arrest and detention at that time: all these matters are unclear. What was clear to Barnes was that the Craft family was determined to blame Rob Lee for shooting Lamar Craft. Under duress, Barnes had agreed to their version of events. Under the circumstances, there seemed no safer option for her than to agree. But then she recanted that story, first to Charles Gordon and then in multiple subsequent public forums. Some people in Barnes's position might have been willing to cooperate in this new story implicating Rob Lee, if only to try to save themselves from the electric chair or from further dealings with the Craft family. But Barnes seemed determined to tell the truth.

Soon, Barnes would see just how dangerous the Crafts could be, as they took investigation and punishment further into their own hands. On May 9, 1951, two of Lamar Craft's brothers, Vennon and Milo, attempted to assassinate Rob Lee near his home on the Walthall-Marion county line.[11] At approximately 8:00 p.m., as Lee was "in the act of entering his pickup truck," a Ford F-3, the brothers sprayed Lee's truck with gunfire: "shotguns roared and buckshot riddled both sides of the truck's cab."[12] The shooting occurred just within Marion County, so the sheriff's department and court there would have jurisdiction. Marion County sheriff J. C. Broom reported that "the car was shot up . . . it really was." County authorities later counted "42 places on the truck" struck by the gunfire.[13]

Lee, attempting to avoid the gunfire, fell to the floorboard; his quick reaction probably saved his life. Not struck by any of the shotgun pellets, Lee was wounded in the left eye by glass splinters. "He may not be able to see out of one eye," reported Sheriff Broom, but the injuries were not life-threatening. Taken to the Tylertown hospital, Lee stayed there for a few days, undergoing an operation to remove the glass splinter from his eye. Both Vennon and Milo Craft were arrested and charged with "assault and battery with intent to kill." The brothers were taken into custody in Walthall County on Marion County warrants. Each man posted a $2,000 bond and was released. Both were due in court the following month.[14]

After returning to Pike County from her extralegal detention in Walthall County, Barnes, apparently fearing for her safety, left Pike County in late May. She went to Leland in the Delta county of Washington, more than two hundred miles north of Tylertown. Barnes's decision to go to Leland was fateful, and more dangerous than she realized. For this movement was directed by Rob Lee and for Lee's own purposes; he had concluded that Barnes was a threat to him, and he wanted her dead. Barnes obviously did not know Lee's plans. Her immediate concern seems to have been to steer clear of Mississippi law enforcement and also the Crafts. She could not have known what the Crafts were thinking, but she did know that they were capable of potentially murderous violence after their attempt on Lee's life. Whether or not she believed that the danger to her in southwestern Mississippi had fully passed, she agreed to return home in June, when Lee went to Leland to retrieve her. After an eventful journey with Lee and his accomplice, an African American man named Walter Watson, Barnes was taken by Lee and Watson to a "tenant cabin" located on Rob Lee's land in "Marion County, just above the Walthall County line."[15] The property was in the unincorporated community of Kokomo, approximately ten miles east of Tylertown.[16]

There, on June 14, Barnes became the next victim in the increasingly complex story of revenge and attempted silencing. Around 6:30 p.m., Lee and Watson shot her multiple times and left her for dead. Struck in the head, arm, shoulder, and abdomen, Barnes crawled toward the highway, seeking assistance. There, Mrs. Rob Lee saw her and took her to the hospital in Tylertown. From her hospital room, just before being taken into surgery, Barnes identified Lee and Watson as her would-be murderers to Walthall County sheriff Bullock.[17] Lee, she said, had shot her three times "with a snub-nosed pistol" before walking away. Lee was assisted, Barnes said, by Walter Watson, "a Negro." As she lay on the ground, wounded, Barnes begged Watson to leave her alone. In response, he shot her in the face, this time "with Lee's 'regular' pistol." Barnes made this statement before Walthall County sheriff Bullock and several other "Pike, Walthall, and Marion County officials." The presence of these men reflects in part the complex, multicounty nature of these rapidly developing cases. It also indicates some of the informal patterns of mutual assistance these departments rendered to each other. Other displays of collaboration were present as well, for also present in Barnes's hospital room was

Tylertown attorney Breed Mounger, in whose office she had been held and interrogated. He was presumably there, as he had been from the time of Lamar Craft's shooting, to see to Craft family interests.[18]

District Attorney McLaren promised a continuing investigation of the shooting, pending Barnes's ability to assist him.[19] A hospital statement noted that her condition was perilous but that she was "responding to treatment." The next seventy-two hours, they predicted, would determine whether she would survive.[20] Barnes survived the weekend and would in fact provide the state both assistance and testimony when her assailants came to trial. By Friday, June 15, both Lee and Watson were in custody. Marion County charged the pair with "battery and intent to murder." Lee was held in the Marion County Jail and Watson in "an unannounced jail," according to Marion County sheriff J. C. Broom. Watson, it turned out, was in fact jailed with Lee in Columbia, the Marion County seat. Broom was evasive about Watson's location because over the weekend, one of Broom's deputies, J. T. Duckworth, drove Watson some thirty-five miles and two counties to the east to take Watson's statement about matters leading to his arrest.[21] Whether or not it was explicitly Sheriff Broom's intention, removing Watson to Hattiesburg in Forrest County to take that statement not only insulated him from the intimidating Lee but also distanced him from the Craft family and their attorney, Breed Mounger.

In the Forrest County sheriff's department in Hattiesburg on June 16, Watson offered a version of the events that led to the shooting of Barnes. That statement was introduced as evidence at his trial ten days later. One senses here the pressures facing Watson, who was questioned by Marion County deputy sheriff Duckworth. Duckworth asked Watson if he had been "threatened in any way." Without hesitation, Watson replied, "Yes, sir." But that was not the answer Duckworth wanted, wishing instead for Watson to state that he had not been threatened by officers in Marion or Forrest Counties. Perhaps Watson had not, at least in any overt way; he may well have been speaking of Rob Lee rather than any officer of the law. Still, Watson then affirmed that while in custody, he had not been threatened, mistreated, or promised anything in order to persuade him to make his statement.[22]

Watson described events from the Leland excursion through the shooting of Barnes by Lee and Watson at Lee's property in Kokomo. Watson's statement is specific on many matters, but often less so on geography and chronology, as well as the reasons he, Lee, and Barnes went the places they did. "They was sitting there at a table that night," said Watson of Rob Lee and Hattie Lee Barnes. One cannot tell in what building or what county they were, although Watson likely refers to a café in downtown Leland. Watson claimed that he did not then know Barnes by name, describing her as a "tall, dark girl with two gold teeth in her mouth." Watson, aware that the statement he gave would be used in court, gave no indication of malice against Barnes, which in fact he may not have felt. He gave practically no indication why he did any of the things he did, except that Rob Lee had insisted upon them. In Watson's telling, Lee was a volatile, violent man, a seemingly fair assessment.[23]

After returning to Walthall County from Leland, Lee, Barnes, and Watson went to a "juke joint" near Tylertown for more whiskey, as Watson and Barnes probably saw it, but as far as Lee was concerned, apparently in preparation for his assassination of a woman being pressured into implicating him in Lamar Craft's shooting. At the juke joint, they purchased half pints of Early Times whiskey, testimony to the availability of name-brand liquor in a nominally dry state. Barnes grew alarmed at the whiskey consumption and clearly suspicious of where it might lead. She took one of the bottles behind the juke joint and "busted that half pint," said Watson.[24]

In the meantime, Watson entertained himself by listening to the jukebox, a "Seaburg machine." A man with good judgment in music, if not companions, Watson played "Rocket 88" (1951) by Jackie Brenston & His Delta Cats, regarded by some aficionados as the first rock-and-roll record. His enjoyment was likely compromised by overhearing Rob Lee say to Barnes, "I will blow your damn brains out." To a man sitting next to him, Watson asked, "Recon [*sic*] he will do it?" "Yes," the man replied, "he will do it." The man who offered the judgment of Lee's intentions was a "nub legged negro." Perhaps because of the driving and drinking, Watson could not identify that juke joint, except to say that it was off the highway, on a gravel road, and was "a red house sitting up there on a road." It was run by a lady who had three or four children and was again "in the family way."[25]

Watson insisted that he had asked the one-legged man to dissuade Lee from violence against Barnes, with Watson himself saying to Lee, "Mr. Rob, no need bothering that girl." Conversation or not, the men purchased more Early Times and drove on, with Barnes in the car. They stopped at a house owned by

Rob Lee. Barnes went behind the house; Lee followed her. Watson heard three shots, as Barnes cried out, "Oh, Lord!" In response, said Watson, "what I was fixing to do was to get away from there." But Lee insisted that Watson take one of his pistols and shoot Barnes. "When he did," said Watson, "I shot. I wasn't trying to hit her. And then she shut up." Both men drove away, with Lee at the wheel. "You got her," said Lee. "We are coming back about dark," he added, "and if you didn't get her I will get you." Watson told Lee, "I got to get out" of the car. When he did, Watson escaped Lee: "I kept going, and I slept in a corn field that night." The next day, he caught a train to Columbia. There, he took a cab to a "colored hotel," paid for the room, and gave the proprietor a pistol to hold for safekeeping. At the hotel, he was arrested and taken to jail, where Rob Lee was a fellow prisoner. Respecting Mississippi patterns of racial segregation as well as good sense, the men were not held in the same cell, but still in one close enough for Lee to maintain ominous communication, punctuated by threats, with Watson throughout the night.[26]

In Watson's telling, Lee's anger stemmed from Watson's inability to finish the job of killing Barnes. Why did Lee enlist Watson in the shooting, a matter that Lee himself could have managed? Watson never said why; perhaps Lee imagined that having a Black man upon whom he might pin the killing would be a useful thing to hold in his back pocket. Watson felt that Lee would now turn his anger upon him, if he had the opportunity. "Walter," Lee told him, "you messed me up and messed yourself up—you sho' got to go." "All through the night," remembered Watson, "he would call me and say the same thing." The deputy assured Watson that he "need not be scared of Mr. Rob," an assurance that likely did not give him much comfort. Then the deputy asked Watson a reasonable question—why Lee had wanted Barnes dead. Watson replied: "he said he [*sic*] was going to mess him up." "About the Craft killing in Pike County?," said the deputy. "I guess so," replied Watson. It certainly had messed things up for Lee when Barnes implicated him in the killing, a fact Lee would have known simply by reading the newspaper. But in all his remarks about the time in Leland, the trip back to Walthall County, and the period up to the shooting of Barnes, Watson never said that he heard Lee say anything to Barnes about the Craft shooting. The statement concludes with suggestive remarks in which Watson said that Barnes had talked to him about what had happened in Pike County; what Barnes told him, Watson did not say.[27]

Walter Watson, an African American man without legal counsel in the hands of Mississippi law enforcement, rightly feared Rob Lee and had no reason to trust the deputy sheriff when he gave that statement. Watson's affirmation that he had not been mistreated is precisely what the deputy would have wished the record to include. While there is no evidence that the statement was physically coerced, coercion comes in many forms. Fundamentally, there is no reason to believe that Watson did anything other than to say what he felt that he needed to say, without having a full understanding of his rights. Judging from Barnes's own later testimony, Watson's statement seems to have been true, so far as it went.

Charles Gordon's reporting reflected Barnes's continuing communication with him and also Gordon's determination to tell his readers just what was happening to her. Among other things, Gordon's story on the shooting provides some explanation of why Mrs. Rob Lee assisted Barnes after Lee and Watson shot her. Ruth Lee was in fact Rob Lee's "estranged wife," another layer of complexity in the story. Readers learned as well other facts that highlighted the dangers Barnes faced. After her return to Pike County from Walthall County earlier that spring, the Monday after she shot Craft and had been detained for interrogation in Tylertown, Barnes intended to stay with friends in Baertown, an African American section of McComb. In Baertown, according to Gordon, a group of unidentified Walthall County residents appeared at the house where Barnes was staying and "asked for Hattie Lee." She was not present when the men appeared. When she returned to the house and learned of that visit, she was "whisked away." By whom she was "whisked away," Gordon did not specify. Sensing danger, Barnes then accepted Rob Lee's offer to leave southwestern Mississippi for Leland in the Delta, where she remained for weeks until Lee determined to retrieve and murder her.[28]

An area weekly newspaper, the *Tylertown Times,* referred to the 1951 shootings, those of Craft, Lee, and Barnes, as elements of a "mystery-shrouded case," although central features of the story, such as who shot whom, were not obvious mysteries.[29] Still, what did appear puzzling, unless one had followed Charles Gordon's stories in the *McComb Enterprise-Journal,* was what Barnes precisely had said and where she had gone during the last two months. "Immediately upon being released under bond, she was returned to Walthall county and held for several days." Readers of the Tylertown newspaper would not have been aware that she was "held" there under ill-defined authority. Nor would they have read that her statement implicating Rob Lee had been extracted in Breed Mounger's office. Readers might well have been confused, then, to learn that "she is alleged to have changed her original story to make it appear she was not even present when the bullet was fired killing Craft." Without knowing the circumstances of that statement, one might indeed be suspicious about this "mystery-shrouded case." "She was returned," the account continues, "to Pike County and then disappeared." Again, why she was returned, by whom, and into whose custody or why, in fact, in custody at all if she had made bond, would have been unclear. "This led to rumors of her death or being sent away by one or another of interested parties."[30]

Because of the locations of the various shootings, legal proceedings unfolded in two Mississippi county courts, Pike and Marion. Barnes's trial for murder in Pike County still awaited the fall term, should she survive to see it. Two other cases, the ones against Rob Lee and Walter Watson for assault and battery with intent to kill Barnes, and that of Vennon and Milo Craft for assault and battery with intent to kill Rob Lee, would be heard in Marion County before Judge Sebe Dale. In mid-June, both of those cases were expected to go before the grand jury. In his charge to that grand jury, a Mississippi tradition then and later, Judge Sebe Dale denounced the county's rampant lawlessness. Of Marion County, "the crime sore spot of South Mississippi," Judge Dale said that if "you take the population of Marion County and compare it to the population of Chicago during Al Capone's reign you will find that the homicide rate in Marion County is higher than that of Chicago." Who was to blame? "You and I," asserted Dale, "have not done our duty as officials and citizens."[31]

Judge Dale said that the liquor trade, a calling that area newspapers consistently reported was followed by Rob Lee, was at the root of much of this crime. Reminding the jury of a recent murder conviction, Dale argued that the man who sold the murderer whiskey before the killing "was just as guilty," a moral if not entirely legal judgment.[32] Using a homely metaphor, Dale continued: "A pig doesn't stay a pig but grows up to be a hog . . . We have winked at liquor violations so long it grow [*sic*] up to be a hog." In a further caution, one that ran counter to long-standing white Mississippi assertions that liquor moved Black people to criminal acts, Dale urged law enforcement to look elsewhere for the problem. He told investigators "not to go down to the Negro quarters and jump on a bunch of Negroes." Instead, he said, "Get the citizens who ride in big cars, flout the law, and get rich at it," a description that might be said to apply to Rob Lee. While Lee might not have been rich, he did do well enough from his taverns, and violence did seem to follow in his wake.

Lee's problematic reputation or Judge Dale's characterization of the real sources of Walthall County violence, however, would not have done much to ease Barnes's mind. In a matter of weeks, she had shot a man who intended to rape her, was charged with murder, and then survived an attempted murder at the hands of Rob Lee and his accomplice, Walter Watson. The grim shadow of the state's electric chair still loomed, as she had been told in Tylertown. Those following the case in southwestern Mississippi had a good deal to consider. Would Barnes be convicted of murdering a white man? Would she live to see that trial? Why had Lee and Watson shot Barnes? Mississippi courts tended to operate quickly. The story of her own shooting would be told in Walthall County in less than two weeks.

4

THE TRIAL OF WALTER WATSON

ON JUNE 21, 1951, seven days after they shot Hattie Lee Barnes, Rob Lee and Walter Watson were indicted in the Marion County Courthouse in Columbia for "assault and battery with intent to kill and murder." The trial of Watson ("colored," as court documents indicate) was scheduled for Tuesday, June 26, at 8:30 a.m.; Lee's trial was set for Wednesday, June 27, also at 8:30 a.m.[1] The pair remained in custody in the Marion County Jail. In the Tylertown hospital, Barnes was recovering from five gunshot wounds. Depending upon her health, she might testify. Rob Lee's attorneys filed a motion to quash his indictment on the grounds that Barnes had not appeared before the grand jury. Judge Sebe Dale denied that motion; Lee's trial was expected to continue as scheduled. The trial of Walter Watson offers a detailed picture of the circumstances leading to Barnes's shooting. But testimony at that trial also reveals two other fundamental matters. Along with Hattie Lee Barnes, Walter Watson, as a Black Mississippian, navigated a society shaped by broader imperatives of racial segregation. Even assisting in an attempted murder followed Jim Crow etiquette. Watson's trial also demonstrates continuing efforts by the Craft family to insist that the shooting of Lamar Craft, not Hattie Lee Barnes, was the real story here, and that Rob Lee was the central actor in that shooting.[2]

Indictments of Lee and Watson were among twelve returned by that Marion County grand jury. Other cases ranged from manslaughter to grand larceny to drunk driving to sale of whiskey to unlawfully cutting timber, a typical slate of work in a southern Mississippi county.[3] Not among the indicted, however, were the Craft brothers, Milo and Vennon, still free on bond after their May shooting of Rob Lee. Area speculation was that charges against the two men might be dropped.[4] And, in fact, the men were never tried for the shooting. Charges were not dismissed. The district attorney simply never secured an indictment.[5] Why the Craft brothers were not indicted for what a layperson might see as attempted murder is unclear. Sometimes a prosecutor determines that a case is not strong enough to pursue. In some instances, a shooting victim like Rob Lee chooses not to cooperate with prosecutors. But there is no evidence of that happening here. Whatever accounts for the disappearance of the matter, it is difficult not to suspect the influence of Edd Craft, perhaps assisted again by attorney Breed Mounger.

Walter Watson's trial began on schedule the morning of Tuesday, June 26, 1951, some twelve days after Hattie Lee Barnes's shooting. After making the trip of just over twenty-two miles from Tylertown to Columbia, Barnes limped into court wearing a bandage on her face and arm. Dressed in a patterned skirt, white slip-on shoes, and a light, short-sleeved blouse, Barnes appears in a newspaper photograph seated in a wooden chair. Tired and worn, Barnes looks directly at the camera with what one might call either an expression of determination or exasperation.[6]

District attorney Robert Livingston and Marion County prosecuting attorney Philip Singley argued the state's case; Watson was represented by Hattiesburg attorney Claude Pittman.[7] Watson's one-day trial featured only five witnesses. The state called Hattie Lee Barnes; Ernestine James, a juke joint operator; Ben Stringer, the police officer who had arrested Watson in Columbia; and Jim Duckworth, the deputy sheriff to whom Watson gave his statement in Hattiesburg. The defense called only Watson himself.

Barnes offered detailed testimony. Barnes ("colored," as the transcript indicates) said that though she customarily lived in Walthall County, for approximately one month before the trip back to southern Mississippi and her shooting, she lived in Leland. Why Leland? Initially, she said only that Rob Lee took her there "for protection." In Leland, she first met Walter Watson "around the joints where the colored people go." There on Tuesday, June 12, the two men met her, with Lee promising to take her home to see her mother. On that ride south, both men were armed with .38 caliber pistols. Instead of Walthall

County, however, Lee and Watson drove instead to Columbia in Marion County. Well after midnight, the trio arrived at Rob Lee's son's house. Lee went inside; Watson and Barnes slept in the car, one in the front seat and the other in the back. The following day, Wednesday, the three of them drove the area, with neither Lee nor Watson explaining to Barnes why they were not taking her home. But Lee had errands on his mind. One stop was to look for Leroy Collins. Although Barnes did not mention it here, in April during her interrogation in Breed Mounger's office, someone suggested that Collins might have had a hand in Lamar Craft's death. Another stop was at Floyd Duncan's place to see Ernestine James about more whiskey.[8]

Duncan was a Walthall County farmer; he also operated a business, like Lee's, open to the public for drinking.[9] There, Barnes, Lee, and Watson met the one-legged man and pregnant woman described in Walter Watson's statement. From their meeting in Leland on Tuesday through all the following day, Barnes was never long out of sight of Watson and Lee. While drinking at Duncan's place, Lee and Watson brought out their pistols, shooting cans and bottles in the yard: "they called themselves practicing, I guess." The guns and the drinking alarmed Barnes. "I was afraid of them. They were about drunk." So she destroyed a bottle of whiskey the men bought at Duncan's. Lee was not finished, however, either with drinking or with his real errand, so they bought more whiskey and drove on.[10]

Leaving Duncan's, Lee again promised Barnes to take her to her mother's house. But he did not. They stopped instead at one of Lee's properties. Lee said he wished to introduce them to his dog, chained near the front door. The time was near 4:00 p.m. Barnes exited the car and went around the back of the building to relieve herself. Turning, she saw Lee. "I told you," he said, "I was going to do it," and began shooting.[11] Wounded, Barnes cried out, asking Lee to take her to a doctor. Incredibly, Lee agreed: "I'm going to send Walter around here in the car to pick you up." She waited two or three minutes. Watson appeared, but not on an errand of mercy. "I was going to ask him to take me to the Doctor and I didn't get it out before he shot me." Contradicting Watson's statement that he had not attempted to hit her, Barnes maintained that Watson came "pretty close," indeed "almost over me," before shooting her in the face. She asked for no more help from either man: "I was afraid that I would get shot again."[12]

Barnes said that as Watson shot her, Lee remained at the front of the building, standing by the car. Because the building was raised and because she was lying on the ground, she could see him. Watson walked back to Lee: "We got her." The men drove away, presumably to leave her to die. Disappointing their plans, Barnes, suffering five bullet wounds, made her way to the highway to seek help. Ruth Lee, Rob Lee's ex-wife, took Barnes to the Tylertown hospital. It had been two weeks since her shooting; she had been in the hospital all that time. She concluded by saying that Rob Lee never told her why he shot her, nor did Walter Watson.[13]

The defense seemed less interested in Walter Watson than it was in Rob Lee. In cross-examination of Barnes, one might in fact wonder who was on trial, Watson or Lee. Claude Pittman, Watson's attorney, first tried to tell the jury not about the shooting of Barnes but that of Lamar Craft. Barnes said she had known Rob Lee for two years, working "out at his colored saloon in Pike County." Pittman wished to explore alcohol sales at Lee's place. The state objected to the relevance of that testimony; the judge agreed. Barnes had not yet faced trial for Craft's murder. But Pittman wanted to discuss that charge "to show why Rob Lee wanted to get rid of this girl." Judge Dale would not have it: "That is in an entirely different County and this Defendant is not charged with it . . . Rob Lee is not on trial here." Watson's attorney, like Edd Craft and his attorney, Breed Mounger, seemed fixed on Craft's shooting, not Barnes's, as the heart of this complex matter. At the center, they seemed determined to show, was Rob Lee.[14]

In her initial testimony, Barnes said she went to Leland for "protection." In cross-examination, she said that Lee told her that she faced possible retaliation from the Craft brothers. However, Lee himself, not Barnes, had been the literal target of the Craft brothers' ire. Pittman then asked Barnes if she told Pike County officers that she killed Lamar Craft. She said that she had, but that the statement was not true. From the time of the April shooting of Craft, Barnes had maintained—except for a statement made in Tylertown and then retracted—that she had killed Lamar Craft. Here, however, for whatever reason, Barnes seemed poised again to change her story and potentially to finger Rob Lee. Pittman attempted to continue this line of questioning: "I will ask you, Hattie Lee, who actually did kill young Craft?" Barnes began to offer an answer: "Mr. ——," but Judge Dale interrupted: "The Court will rule that has no place in this trial . . . Anything further in reference to it I think would be inadmissible on the trial of this case." It is impossible to know why Barnes said here that she had not killed Craft. She was being led—essentially if not in a legal sense—by an attorney's questioning. Perhaps her pending murder trial had caused her to think more about the electric chair and a possible means of escaping it. After this statement, however, in her own trial and in later forums, Barnes did not waver from the story that she killed Lamar Craft.[15]

Thwarted in his attempt to tell the jury more about Lamar Craft's shooting, defense attorney Pittman continued to introduce material about Rob Lee, wishing to show that Lee rather than Watson was the guilty party in Barnes's shooting. The prosecution and judge attempted to keep the focus on Watson. Barnes repeated her account of the drive from Leland back to southern Mississippi, during which the trio stopped "at various places" to buy whiskey. Here, Barnes said more about Lee's interest in finding Leroy Collins, "a colored boy that use to help him around the place." Pittman asked Barnes what Lee might have wanted with Collins. "He said he was going to kill him," replied Barnes. Again, Judge Dale cut off this line of questioning, which he said had no direct relevance in the trial of Walter Watson.[16]

What Barnes's testimony makes clear is that Rob Lee's actions through the spring and early summer of 1951 were driven by his anxieties over what the Craft family might do to him, particularly if their pressures on Barnes to change her story were successful. As soon as they returned from Leland to Walthall County, she said, Lee "stopped and asked about the Craft boys." He asked a night watchman if the Craft brothers "were still looking for him." According to Barnes, Lee told that watchman: "I just wanted to know; I come to finish it out with them." Pittman again asked Barnes if she knew of any reason why Lee might wish to kill her. She replied: "Well, when I made my statement about Mr. Craft." The defense attorney did not follow up on this statement, nor did Barnes amplify it. Again, Judge Dale, respecting the law if not the curiosity of many people in the courtroom, would not allow it.[17]

Judge Dale was concerned that a great deal of this testimony had introduced matters having "no part in the trial of this defendant." Sending out the jury, he took up the question with the attorneys. Defense attorney Pittman said that he wanted the jury to hear about the Lamar Craft slaying because it bore directly on Barnes's shooting. Lee, he argued, killed Craft. He planned to "hire" or "coerce" Barnes into taking the blame for that shooting, then to eliminate Barnes. Where did Watson fit into this plot? Lee enlisted Watson's aid in shooting Barnes so that Watson "would not be a witness against him," a peculiar line of reasoning never explored in any other testimony. The state replied that it had no objection to the material about the Craft slaying, as it spoke to the motivation of Watson in shooting Barnes. Judge Dale concluded that, in order to "protect the every interest of the defendant on trial of this crime," the material as introduced should stand, but that neither the state nor the defense should go any further into the Pike County shooting of Craft.[18]

For the remainder of the trial, however, both the state and the defense focused more closely on Watson's shooting of Barnes. The state's next witness was Ernestine James, who worked for Floyd Duncan, at whose place Lee and Watson stopped to replenish their whiskey supply and to practice their marksmanship. On Thursday, at about 2:30 or 3:00 p.m., according to James, a party consisting of Lee, Barnes, Watson, and Homer Regan arrived. Lee and Watson were armed. Out of the presence of Barnes, said James, Lee told her that "Hattie Lee and Leroy Collins had to go." Lee produced his pistol, placing it on the counter. Watson's remained in his pocket as he stood selecting music from the jukebox. Neither man said explicitly what he intended to do with his gun.[19]

James had not spoken with Barnes, other than to sell her "a mess of collard greens." Lee purchased Early Times whiskey. The party remained at James's until 5:00 or 5:30 p.m., she said, with Watson and Lee shooting in the yard while she and Barnes stayed inside. The next morning, she said, she heard that Barnes had been shot. In cross-examination, she clarified the identity of Homer Regan, who had arrived with the other three but did not stay long. He left "right after his wife come and got him." Again, the defense blamed Rob Lee for the assassination plot and the shooting. James repeated that she had heard Lee threaten the lives of Leroy Collins and Hattie Lee Barnes, but that she had not heard Watson make any threatening statements against anyone.[20]

After the defense's unsuccessful motion to exclude all previous testimony and to peremptorily find Watson not guilty, Watson took the stand. Watson said he was a resident of Leland, where he had lived for five years, having been born there in Washington County. He had known Rob Lee only two months and only learned his name when Watson came with Lee and Barnes to south Mississippi just before the Barnes shooting. Showing Watson his two roadhouses, one for white patrons and the other for Black, Lee said, "Yonder is my name there now; that's my two places." Watson did not know Barnes's name either until he was in jail; he read her name in the newspaper.[21]

What accounts for Watson's willingness to travel with and shoot a person whose name he did not know? While Watson did not blame alcohol for his predicament, his relationship with both Lee and Barnes was rooted in whiskey. How did Watson meet Lee?, the defense attorney asked. "Well," replied Watson, "I saw him drinking whiskey and I love it, and he would give it to me and I went to drinking with him." Watson first met Barnes in Leland, he said, at a café operated by Herbert Fergerson, which Barnes and Lee frequented. At Fergerson's, said Watson, Lee and Barnes "bought some whiskey and set down at a table drinking it and offered me some and I drunk some of it, and we played the juke box." During the period that Barnes lived in Leland, Watson saw her drinking regularly at Fergerson's place, "talking to the other girls."[22]

The drinking at Fergerson's underscores a fact that troubled many white Mississippians: alcohol and juke joints did not always respect the culture of segregation. Alcohol sometimes proved a solvent of lines that many white Mississippians wished to maintain. Defense attorney Pittman led Watson through a detailed retelling of the trip from Leland to southern Mississippi. Although Watson did not precisely recall the June date of the beginning of the trip, he did remember going into the Day & Night Café in Leland. There, he saw Lee and Barnes at a table drinking. Lee hailed him, "Well, there's old Walt." Lee said, "How about driving me tonight?" Lee explained that he was making a quick trip down to his home and then back the next day. They made preparations; both Watson and Barnes needed fresh clothes. Watson lived "in front of the café," an explanation for his familiarity with the place. Barnes lived, he said, "in the new addition." Watson returned to the café wearing a pair of tweed pants. After checking their road supply of whiskey, they filled the gas tank at a Gulf station and headed south, arriving at Lee's son's house about 3:00 a.m. Fetching more whiskey, Lee shared it with Barnes and Watson before the three of them retired for the rest of the evening. Both Watson and Barnes woke up a few hours later, thirsty. Lee's son's wife provided them with ice water.[23]

On Thursday, the drinking began early and continued through the day. Lee's son gave them more whiskey, followed by bottles of Pabst Blue Ribbon beer. Lee was in the mood for more driving. Off they went to a "colored juke,"

Floyd Duncan's place. One loses track of the number of bottles of whiskey bought and consumed on this road trip. Watson again wished to show that he was not really responsible for Barnes's shooting. Sitting in the car, said Watson, "I heard the pistol fire three times." He also heard Barnes cry out, "Oh, Lord." Lee returned to the car, telling Watson, "Walt, I didn't get her . . . Go around there and finish her; if you don't I will finish you." Replied Watson, "Yes, sir." Only under duress, said Watson, had he followed Lee's instructions, with Lee watching from the corner of the building. "I didn't try to hit her," he maintained. But why, asked Watson's attorney, did you shoot? "I was afraid he would shoot me and that is why I shot her." Watson never denied shooting Barnes—or at least shooting at her. But his explanation was always that in the face of Lee's threats, "I was afraid of him." Well indeed he might have been, given Lee's alleged words to him as the two men left the scene of the shooting: "I'm going back when it's dark and if she ain't gone you've got to go."[24]

On cross-examination, district attorney Livingston tried to show the jury that Watson's story was incredible. Why would Watson have agreed to drive Rob Lee, a man he hardly knew, across the state with a woman he scarcely knew any better, and against whom he bore no ill will, and shoot her at Lee's direction? Something was missing, suggested Livingston. Watson said that Lee, sitting in the café, said, "How about driving me tonight?" The distance from Leland to Kokomo was more than two hundred miles, and this in a day before interstate highways. Such a trip at a moment's notice for a man he hardly knew seemed highly suspicious, Livingston suggested, especially when Watson added, "He didn't offer me any money at all." Incredulous, Livingston replied, "You mean you were driving this man you'd only seen two times in your life and there was no agreement as to what he was to pay you?" "No, sir," replied Watson. But "I thought maybe he would" pay him. Watson disagreed with Livingston's contention that Lee had promised to pay Watson fifty dollars for "work for you to do down here." "He never give me a penny," said Watson.[25]

Livingston is correct that something is missing here, not least a fuller explanation of what Lee had said to Watson to enlist his cooperation. At what point did Lee develop the idea that Watson would be useful to him in his plan to eliminate Barnes? Did Watson make the extended trip for no reason other than the hope that this white man turned drinking companion might pay him? There were ways in which a white man like Lee might coerce a Black man like Watson, but other than in the shooting itself, Watson offered no indication that he acted under coercion. Watson again told of the shooting and then his escape from Lee into the cornfield. The district attorney suggested that the men were actually planning a later rendezvous and return trip to Leland. Watson denied that suggestion, claiming that his only plan was to get away from Lee, whom he continued to fear and of whose advance plans he had had no knowledge.

But why, asked Livingston, would a man like you, weighing 207 pounds and possessing a loaded pistol, be afraid of Lee? And why would you have given no thought to "the little negro girl shot down there behind that house bleeding to death?" Replied Watson, "I was afraid to and I didn't have time." Were you not worried about her because you thought you had killed her? "I didn't think I hit her." But why did you tell Lee she was dead? "I told him that so we could get away from there." "Didn't your conscience bother you," continued the district attorney, "about that little old colored girl lying out there stiff and stark behind that house?" Watson offered, "I was hoping she wouldn't die." And with that exchange, the state ended its cross-examination of Watson.[26]

Both sides rested their case. The matter went to the jury of twelve white men. As was typical, the jury received instructions from the court, the state, and the defense. The court's first instruction to the jury, the one that in the end shaped their verdict, said that "a person is not authorized to attempt to take the life of another person at the command of a third person, whether he is in fear of such third person or not." That argument—that Watson had shot Barnes out of fear of Lee—was the central one that Watson's attorney had presented, and the jury was told that it was not an acceptable legal defense. Amplifying the point, the instruction reminded the jury further that even if the evidence seemed convincing that Watson had been "ordered and compelled by one Rob Lee," it was nevertheless "your sworn duty," if the evidence otherwise showed Watson to have been the shooter, "to find him guilty as charged."

The defense offered instructions, some of which the judge allowed and some he did not. If they believed Watson did not intend to "kill and murder" Barnes, then their verdict should be not guilty. While it was not necessary for the state to prove a motive, the defense was allowed to instruct the jury that the failure of the state to show a motive could be "a circumstance in fact of the defendant's innocence." But on the defense's seemingly major point, the argument that Watson had been compelled either directly by Lee or by Watson's fear of Lee, the judge would not allow the jury to receive the defense's instruction that Watson's own "fear of bodily harm" was a reason to find him not guilty.[27]

The jury deliberated briefly and returned a guilty verdict. Before sentencing, Watson was allowed to speak to the court, if he wished; he did not. Judge Dale sentenced him to ten years in the Mississippi State Penitentiary at Parchman. Watson appeared calm as Judge Dale read that verdict and pronounced sentence.[28] Watson, a dark-skinned man with a firm build, looked grim, naturally enough, as he was led from the courthouse by deputy sheriff Jim Duckworth. Unlike defendants of a later era, Watson did not wear either jailhouse orange or a lawyer-suggested suit and tie. Instead, he is dressed in light-colored trousers and an open-collared short-sleeved casual shirt with a print of lively design; those clothes may well be the ones that he wore when he was arrested earlier in the month.[29]

Watson's attorney, Claude Pittman, immediately filed an appeal in the Marion County Circuit Court. The appeal was denied. Then he prepared an appeal to the Mississippi Supreme Court. Pittman argued: "This is a very unusual case, and the appellant has a most unusual defense, still the fact is that the act of the appellant in shooting the said Hattie Lee Barnes amounts to an act of self defense" in the face of his fear of Rob Lee, "a notorious bootlegger and saloon keeper," who had been drinking and "exhibiting his pistols" for two days and who was altogether a "dangerous man." The nub of his defense and his appeal, replied the court, was Watson's contention that he acted with "Rob Lee holding a gun on him, compelling him to do so." As a matter of law, however, Watson "had no right whatsoever to take the life of an innocent person because of the fear of bodily injury to himself." Over the course of the multi-day road trip, said the court, Watson had opportunities to get away from Lee, especially on the night he slept unsupervised outside Lee's son's house. When it came to the shooting of Barnes, said the court, Watson himself was armed. He had the opportunity to escape or to protect his life as well as that of Barnes. Indeed, Watson "probably" would have been justified in shooting Lee.[30]

So to Parchman Watson went, and there he remained. "Parchman" was officially the Mississippi State Penitentiary. Located in Sunflower County, neighbor to Watson's home county, Washington, Parchman sprawled over twenty-five thousand acres of Delta land, "level as a floor and as fertile as the Valley of the Nile," as a 1912 report termed it. From its origins at the beginning of the twentieth century, Parchman intended to get good work out of bad men; it was essentially a vast cotton plantation, for a time providing the State of Mississippi "with its greatest source of income other than tax revenues." By the 1950s, the decline in the cotton economy made Parchman less of a golden goose for the state than it had been. It remained a bleak place, dreaded by generations of Mississippians, particularly African American men, for whom Parchman had been especially designed and built. From conjugal visits and the Midnight Special train that brought women to the inmates, to corporal punishment with Black Annie, to moonshine rations produced by "hooch boys," to the work songs recorded by folklorist Alan Lomax, Parchman in the twentieth century seemed one of the most southern places on earth.[31]

Their work with Watson done, the Marion County Circuit Court prepared to hear the case against Rob Lee the following day, June 27. Lee, however, had other ideas. He had been arrested on June 15 and initially jailed without bond, but he was released when Barnes appeared likely to survive her shooting.[32] Free on $2,500 bond, a bond secured in part by his brother, John W. Lee, Rob Lee failed to appear on the morning of June 27. Judge Dale ordered a forfeiture of the bond, issued a bench warrant for Lee's arrest, and ordered a new bond of $10,000 in the event of Lee's capture. With no other outstanding cases, Judge Dale adjourned court, ending the spring term of work.[33] As reporter Charles Gordon had predicted, one matter that the grand jury never did take up was the shooting of Rob Lee by Lamar Craft's brothers, Vennon and Milo. "This was taken here," said the Tylertown newspaper, "as meaning that the case had been dropped against these young men."[34]

Where was Lee? He had been in the courthouse the previous day to watch the trial of Watson, in which he was not called as a witness. Returning to his Kokomo home after satisfying himself about Watson's situation, and certainly calculating his own odds, Lee decided to leave, not in his Ford pickup truck, but in a "light blue, 2-door Mercury automobile," for which local authorities and the highway patrol were watching.[35] The Mississippi State Highway Patrol alerted other state police of Lee's flight from bond, as well as the US Border Patrol, should Lee's travel plans include a trip to Mexico.[36]

After more than two weeks on the lam, Rob Lee surrendered to Marion County deputy sheriff Neville Patterson on Saturday, July 14. He posted the

$10,000 bond set by Judge Dale after his flight and was released. The amount of the bond was substantial, but given Lee's demonstrated flight risk, it is surprising that it was granted at all. At his surrender that Saturday, he told the deputy that he had never left the county, leaving one to wonder just where and how hard local authorities had searched for the fugitive.[37] It is possible that Lee was not truthful with the deputy. He had a habit of ranging far and wide within the state when he had business to attend to, including the business of staying one or two steps ahead of the law.

Rob Lee's trial, part of what reporter Charles Gordon rightly called this "many-sided case," would presumably occur in the fall term of court in Marion County.[38] In the meantime, Lee did not stay put in southern Mississippi to await his fate. Out of jail on Saturday, Lee was on the move again the next day. While Lee's marriage to Ruth Lee may have been finished, he maintained working relations with his ex-brother-in-law, Jimmy Martin. The two of them left Marion County in Lee's Mercury and headed for Arkansas, where Lee was interested, according to Gordon, in "buying a new place." The men did not make it that far, however. On Sunday evening near the Delta town of Belzoni in Humphreys County, with Martin behind the wheel, the men "topped a hill" and were "confronted with a wrecked machine belonging to Negroes." Attempting to avoid the other vehicle, Martin steered Lee's Mercury away from that danger but quickly went down an embankment, badly damaging Lee's car. Lee suffered cuts and bruises as well as a broken left leg, "just above the knee," which, as Gordon put it, was just the "latest 'break' in the chain of news stories."[39] Lee was taken to the hospital in Belzoni; Martin was not injured. Investigators for the state highway patrol concluded that the accident was unavoidable. No driver was at fault. The accident was one of the few elements of this story in which no one was shot and for which there were no legal consequences for anyone involved.

5

THE TRIAL OF HATTIE LEE BARNES

IN A MATTER OF WEEKS, from mid-April through mid-June of 1951, Hattie Lee Barnes survived attempted rape and attempted murder. Detained legally and extralegally, she traveled from one end of the state to the other and back. She faced great pressure to alter her account of Lamar Craft's shooting to place blame on her employer, Rob Lee. Testifying against one of her would-be killers, Walter Watson, she saw him convicted. The most perilous ordeal, however, still stood before Barnes. She faced trial for the murder of Craft; conviction carried a possible death penalty. Her fate would be in the hands of a white, male jury in Pike County. But Joe Pigott, one of her court-appointed attorneys, determined not to see Barnes railroaded to a long sentence at Parchman or to the electric chair. His strategy was to avoid putting Barnes's fate in the hands of a jury at all, appealing instead to the judge presiding over the trial, a man who would in a few years be known throughout the South as one of the region's most ardent defenders of racial segregation. Of the many ironies in this story—to this point and to come—perhaps the greatest is this: Hattie Lee Barnes told and retold the story of what happened to her in Rob Lee's roadhouse many times, but in her own trial, Barnes did not speak, except through her court-appointed attorneys. Perhaps to her surprise, however, and no doubt to her great relief, Pigott's strategy was successful.

In the 1950s, Mississippi's circuit courts, in which most criminal matters were heard, held two terms per year, one each in the spring and the fall. Each opened with a grand jury, which returned indictments for that term's work. The grand jury that met at the Pike County Courthouse in October 1951, returned indictments on twenty charges, among them three murders, assault with attempt to rape, grand larceny, embezzlement, and disturbing an election. All three murder indictments were against African Americans, one of them a man accused of murdering his wife, another of a woman accused of killing her baby by throwing the child from a kitchen window. The third of those indictments was against Hattie Lee Barnes for the murder of Lamar Craft.[1]

The Pike County Courthouse was located in Magnolia, the county seat, with the courtroom on the upper floor of the building. The Pike County Jail sat next to it. Like Judge Sebe Dale in Marion County, Judge Tom Brady delivered a charge to the grand jury. Also like Dale, Brady lay the blame for much of the court's work at the feet of alcohol. Judge Brady asked these Pike County citizens carefully to note the number of cases (one of them the Barnes case, although he did not mention it specifically) that had their roots in alcohol. Yes, Brady realized, many Mississippians believed that laws prohibiting the sale of alcohol were "unenforceable," but they should nevertheless come down hard on bootleggers. "In the wake of the bootlegger," counseled Brady, "we always find the gambler, the prostitute, the pimp and petty racketeer, the thief and the murderer."[2]

Hattie Lee Barnes was arraigned on Thursday, October 4; she entered a plea of not guilty. Judge Brady appointed two attorneys to represent Barnes: Joe Pigott from the McComb firm of Cassidy, McLain, and Alford; and George Winston Cutrer, of Magnolia. Pigott's representation of Barnes had, however, begun earlier, dating from her arrest that spring. Cutrer, like Pigott, was a young man. He was twenty-six years old; Pigott was only twenty-five. A Magnolia native, Cutrer was the son of a longtime judge, Richard Cutrer. Like Pigott, he was a World War II veteran, with Coast Guard duty including action in the Pacific. Also like Pigott, Cutrer held a law degree from the University of Mississippi.[3] But the court could hardly have found two less-experienced attorneys to defend Barnes. In that period, Mississippi counties had no public defender's office. There was no clearly defined, or at least publicly announced, system for matching attorneys with indigent clients. One should not, however, imagine in this instance a front-porch visit between judge and attorney such as one sees in *To Kill a Mockingbird.* Most area attorneys simply took their turn with such representation, although it seems not to have fallen as regularly upon long-established attorneys with a busy practice as it did upon young men like Pigott and Cutrer.[4]

Of that term's work, the trial of Barnes was "expected to draw most interest," noted the local newspaper, because it was the only one involving an interracial killing and also because of the unusual twists and turns the story had taken during the spring and early summer. Barnes's case was set for call for the following day, Friday, October 5, but no one anticipated that the trial would begin that quickly. There was indeed a delay in Barnes's trial, stemming partly from the heavy docket. Also complicating matters was Judge Brady's unexpected absence. His son Bruce, a student at New Jersey's private Lawrenceville School, as Judge Brady himself had been, fell ill, requiring Judge Brady to leave Mississippi to attend to his son. Young Brady developed a life-threatening case of peritonitis after an emergency appendectomy. Trials had been expected to start on October 15, but the delay would last at least until October 22.[5]

Judge Brady's son recovered; the judge and his wife were expected back in the area soon. Court could then proceed. Barnes's case was expected then to be the "first order of business." It was, noted reporter Charles Gordon, "one of the most warmly-debated murder cases in recent Pike County history."[6] Gordon did not specify exactly what was so "debated" about the case. It certainly would have been much discussed, but just which elements were debatable, unless one were a member of the Craft family, is not clear. What might have been most hotly debated was whether an African American woman could shoot and kill a white man and escape punishment.

By mid-October, the Pike County Circuit Court was back on track. A grand jury again assembled to finish consideration of that term's indictments. A list of thirty-six potential jurors was drawn from all five county supervisors' districts. All of the names were those of white men. There would be no African American jurors in Mississippi until the 1960s, and no women jurors of any race until 1968. Practically everyone that Barnes encountered in these legal proceedings was a white man. Other than the longtime court reporter, Miss Tommye Thomas, every person in any position of authority in the Pike County Courthouse was a white man. The only African American faces that Barnes would have seen were those of fellow defendants or witnesses. Not all white men were equally privileged under the law, no doubt, but all African Americans were equally second-class citizens under it.

Barnes's trial began on Wednesday, October 24, with jury selection. Both Barnes's attorney, Joe Pigott, and district attorney L. S. McLaren asked potential jurors if the fact that the defendant, a Black woman, was charged with killing a white man would influence their ability to hear evidence. Such a question was a typical feature of jury screening, then and later. All members of the jury pool assured the court that nothing of the sort would sway their judgment. Some potential jurors were excused, as usual, but no one for answering that he would be unduly influenced by the racial nature of the case.[7]

The prosecution consisted of district attorney L. S. McLaren, county prosecuting attorney R. B. Reeves, and, incredibly, Breed Mounger, the Tylertown attorney in whose office Barnes had undergone her extralegal interrogation back in the spring. Mounger was not an elected prosecutor in Pike County or in Walthall County, where he lived. But he was, in fact, "working with the prosecution on behalf of the dead man's family," Charles Gordon reported. Exactly why he was tapped to join the prosecution team is not clear, except perhaps as a reflection of the influence of the Craft family. Mounger certainly had as much information about the case as any area attorney or law enforcement official.[8] The jury sworn in at 10:30 a.m., the district attorney read the indictment of murder against Barnes. Joe Pigott replied that Barnes pled not guilty.[9]

The state's case seemed solid. There was no question of venue, as everyone other than the Craft family seemed confident that Lamar Craft met his death in Rob Lee's Pike County roadhouse. Barnes herself said that she had shot Craft. In that pre-*Miranda* era, there would be no argument about that statement's inadmissibility on the grounds that she had not been informed of her rights before giving it. The jury heard first from Pike County sheriff Robert E. Lee, whose account was generally consistent with his statement at the spring's preliminary hearing. Lee said that he was awakened at his home by a telephone call about 1:15 a.m. on Tuesday, April 17. The McComb Police Department told him they had received a call from Rob Lee's roadhouse on Highway 24. "A Negro woman" told police that she shot a white man who was attempting to break into the closed bar. Lee drove from his house in Holmesville in eastern Pike County to Rob Lee's place, a distance of approximately one and a half miles. There he found Barnes, with the .38 caliber revolver, fired twice, that she used against the intruder. Also, Lee saw the body of Craft, whom he recognized, lying across the bed in which Barnes had intended to sleep that night. Lee did not say that the McComb Police Department had also been informed of the incident by the arrival of Easterling and Hope at their headquarters. It is unclear why Hope, Easterling, and Barnes contacted McComb police or why Lee did not mention that Barnes herself had called him as well, which he had said in the spring hearing. Perhaps she called both the sheriff's department and the police department. One can imagine that under the circumstances, Hope, Easterling, and Barnes would not have thought carefully about matters of jurisdiction as they considered whom to contact. Too, area sheriffs and police departments consistently cooperated without strict consideration of jurisdictional lines.[10] Despite this ambiguity about whom Barnes called and when, one matter is clear: she made no attempt either to evade law enforcement or to deny at that time that she shot Craft.

The next witness was Oscar Hope, twenty-two, one of Craft's drinking companions on the fatal evening.[11] He and James Easterling began their Monday night by drinking in a café in Tylertown, joined by Craft about 8:30 p.m. Craft proposed that the men continue drinking at Rob Lee's place. The three arrived at Lee's about 9:00 p.m., Hope said, and there they remained until closing time, "drinking beer and whiskey until after midnight." When the bar closed, the only person left there, as far as Hope knew, was Hattie Lee Barnes.[12] The three men left, said Hope, but then decided "to go back and see Hattie Lee," one of several variant stories Hope and Easterling would tell of why the men returned to the roadhouse. Hope did not explain why the men wanted to see Barnes, although it is not difficult to conclude what three drunk white men might have wanted from a young African American woman.[13]

Hope's description of their return to the bar made him sound less responsible than anyone else for what happened next. He walked to the front of the building to serve as a "look-out" as the other two considered how best to gain entry. Hope saw into the building "as he peered through a crack." Inside was Barnes, illuminated by a light in her bedroom. Both he and Easterling, Hope assured the court, counseled Craft not to enter the bar. But Craft was determined. From his post, Hope heard shots. Running to the back of the building, he did not see Craft, but he did see Easterling. Choosing not to investigate for himself, Hope fled with Easterling. Hope concluded by saying that he never saw anyone else inside or around the tavern at that hour, other than Barnes, Easterling, and Craft.[14]

After a recess, the state called other witnesses, including James Easterling, Craft and Hope's drinking companion. Easterling gave much the same story as he had done in the April 19 preliminary hearing, one that corroborated Hope's testimony. Easterling, like Hope, told of an evening of steady drinking, first in Tylertown and then at Rob Lee's place. The three men left Lee's place at closing time, only to return very shortly thereafter "to see Hattie Lee." After the shooting, said Easterling, the men "were forced to flee in terror and confusion."[15]

The state also called Hattie Lee Barnes's stepfather, Dan Magee, and her mother, Lizzie Magee.[16] Her stepfather was a longtime Walthall County resident. Born in 1896 in Warnerton, Louisiana, Magee was a laborer and farmer with a second-grade education. In 1940, he and a previous wife, Maggie, had lived in Walthall County for at least five years. That year they had a one-year-old daughter living with them, but that child was not Hattie Lee Barnes.[17] By 1951, Dan Magee had married Hattie Lee's mother, Lizzie. The testimony of the Magees, Barnes's stepfather and mother, shed little light on what happened before and immediately following the shooting. Both said that they heard no gunshots, a surprising fact given that they were some one hundred yards from Lee's bar when the shooting occurred. What their testimony did make clear is another basic element of segregated life in Mississippi. Lee operated two establishments, one for white people and the other, "Rob Lee's Negro joint," where they both worked. Neither of the Magees could testify that they had seen anyone trying to break into Lee's place or that they had seen Hattie Lee Barnes fire any shots.[18]

Pike County coroner Ray Cain offered testimony as well. Mississippi coroners were not trained medical professionals. Until quite recently, a high school diploma was not required for the job.[19] Their job was simply to verify that a person was dead and to conduct a basic investigation into what appeared to be the cause of death. The task here was not difficult. Craft had been killed with a bullet to the right side of his chest.[20] Cain, Pike County's coroner since 1936, was a decorated veteran of World War I service in Europe, where he earned a Purple Heart. After the war, he worked for the Illinois Central Railroad for fifteen years. That job ended in 1934 after Cain stumbled while walking across train tracks and was run over, his right arm amputated just below the elbow.[21] In his campaign for coroner the next month, he reminded voters of his war service and recent injury; he sought the office "as an aid in earning a livelihood for himself and family." Then and later, coroners worked by assembling a jury to confirm a cause of death. At no stage was an autopsy or testimony of a physician required. In this case, however, no medical expertise seemed necessary to establish Craft's cause of death.[22]

With these six witnesses heard, the state rested its case. The trial of Hattie Lee Barnes, unlike that of Walter Watson, featured no attempt to place Rob Lee at the center of the story, or anywhere at all. Despite the Craft family's desire to blame Lee for Lamar Craft's death, the case presented by the State of Mississippi offered jurors no option, it seemed, other than to conclude that Barnes herself killed Craft.[23] Had the prosecution convinced the jury, however, that the shooting constituted a murder? As a basic matter of law, the burden of proof was on the prosecution, and their obligation was to prove Barnes's guilt beyond a reasonable doubt. Had they done so? The testimony of the state's witnesses took the better part of the day, concluding around 3:30 p.m. Most trials in Pike County, even murder trials, were quick affairs, many of them conducted in less than a day. However, this one appeared likely to stretch longer than that.[24] The defense had not presented its case. Barnes had not testified. But the trial of Hattie Lee Barnes was in fact concluded in one day, and in a manner that few people in the courthouse would have anticipated.

What manner of defense had Barnes's attorneys, Pigott and Cutrer, prepared? They never filed for a change of venue, in later years a very common occurrence in potentially inflammatory cases such as this one. But motions for changes of venue were rare in Pike, Walthall, and Marion Counties in those days. Court dockets for the period show that almost everyone was tried (and tried quickly) in the county in which the case originated. Because the circuit court case file seems no longer to exist, one cannot tell if the defense summoned any witnesses. If they did, they did not call them. Had the defense prepared Barnes for possible testimony through a discussion of points they wished to raise or that they anticipated the state would raise? Such preparation, then and now, is standard legal practice. If they did prepare Barnes, there is no indication of it. Perhaps Joe Pigott had concluded well before October that putting Barnes on the stand would not be prudent. Because these decisions between an attorney and client are no part of the formal legal record, no surviving evidence throws light on Barnes's preparation for trial.

Pigott had counseled Barnes since her April hearing. Cutrer appears to have had no hand in the defense until his October appointment by Judge Brady. Both men participated in the voir dire process of jury selection. Once the trial began, which of the attorneys spoke before the court? Nothing in the surviving record indicates whether Pigott or Cutrer offered the opening statement. Generally, one of the two attorneys would have acted as lead in the case, but it is possible that each one could have delivered a portion of the opening statement during their allotted time. Neither man cross-examined the state's witnesses, because the defense strategy apparently called for no examination of state's witnesses or presentation of their own.

Pigott and Cutrer did not dispute that Barnes shot Craft. In their opening statement to the court, however, they argued that Barnes's shooting of Craft was not murder but instead a justifiable, legal reaction to Craft's breaking into the bar. Barnes's attorneys said that she had been sleeping overnight in Lee's place for "several weeks," "thereby setting it up as her 'home,'" as Charles Gordon reported. Whatever caused the three men to return to the roadhouse and attempt to enter was illegitimate: "they had no valid reason to be where they were." So Barnes, they maintained, feared for her safety and had every right to defend herself.[25] But the jury did not hear Barnes tell of protecting her home against a menacing intruder. No defendant is compelled to testify. But the defense strategy was a calculated risk, as many juries, in Mississippi and elsewhere, wish to hear a defendant's testimony.

But Joe Pigott, almost certainly the chief defense strategist, did not wish to place Barnes's fate in the hands of that jury at all. That afternoon, he offered a motion to Judge Tom Brady that the jury be peremptorily instructed to find Barnes not guilty. The tactic was common. A competent defense uses all the tools at hand, filing motions from the beginning of a case through the end, including ones to request that the court dismiss the case against their client or to ask that the judge instruct the jury to return a not guilty verdict. But there is no indication that this motion was simply one part of the defense strategy. Beyond the offering of an opening statement, it seems to have been the entire defense strategy. There is no evidence of what Pigott or Cutrer would have been prepared to argue or present should Judge Brady have ruled unfavorably on that motion.[26]

No extant record describes precisely what happened after the state rested its case. Various motions, including the motion for a directed verdict, are listed in the court's docket, but no contemporary copy or even an account of the motion itself seems to exist. Such motions, however, were not generally presented in written form but instead as an argument to the judge. A court reporter would have taken down the words. If a trial transcript was prepared, the language of the motion would have appeared there. But there is no known copy of the trial transcript, nor is there reason to believe that one was ever prepared, as the case resulted in an acquittal. What almost certainly happened in this instance is that Joe Pigott would have indicated to Judge Brady that he intended to offer a motion. The judge would have sent out the jury and entertained that motion in open court, with spectators, court reporter, attorneys, and other officers of the court present to hear it. No one in the courtroom would have been surprised by the fact that the motion Pigott wished to offer was one for a dismissal or a directed verdict.[27]

The fact that Pigott moved for a directed verdict is documented both by newspaper coverage of the trial and by the docket book of the Pike County Circuit Court. Pigott's argument would have been based largely on Mississippi statute and precedent. Under state law, murder was a killing "willful, felonious, and with malice aforethought." However, Pigott argued, Barnes acted in self-defense, resisting an attempt to kill her or cause her great bodily harm. Under the circumstances, then, with Craft climbing through the window into her "bedroom," Barnes had "reasonable ground" to believe that she was in "imminent danger" and was justified in shooting him.[28]

Whatever Joe Pigott said to Judge Brady, it worked. Brady told the jury that while such circumstances as these, in which a "fine young man" such as Craft "had met an untimely death," were to be "regretted," the law was the law and the court was bound by it, including the nature of the evidence presented to the court. The old standard of a man's home being his castle applied here, said Brady, and the defense had sufficiently established that Rob Lee's place was Barnes's castle, such as it was. In those circumstances, said Brady, "the law does not expect any person to take chances when his or her premises are being invaded." Therefore, said Brady, he sustained the defense motion, which was, according to reporter Charles Gordon, "equal to discharging Hattie Lee Barnes as acquitted." Brady ordered the jury to retire briefly and to return with a not guilty verdict, which they did.[29]

Joe Pigott's work on behalf of Barnes was noteworthy and principled. The obligations of a court-appointed attorney notwithstanding, taking the side of a Black woman in the killing of a white man would not have seemed in the eyes of many area people a laudable stand. Some men in Pigott's position would have taken their small fee and counseled their client to accept a plea deal. A less diligent or hardworking attorney might have explained to Barnes that if convicted of murder, she could face the death penalty, and so a manslaughter plea, even with a lengthy prison term attached, might be a wise option. It is not clear what Barnes's other court-appointed attorney, George Cutrer, did in her behalf. Less than Pigott, it would appear. For their defense of Barnes, Pigott and Cutrer received $150, almost certainly split equally between the two men.[30]

Because of the complexity and nature of the case, the Hattie Lee Barnes trial drew attention beyond the local press. The *Jackson Clarion-Ledger,* the state's only newspaper read from one end of the state to the other, covered the story. In those days, matters of race increasingly consumed that paper's editors. Even by regional standards, the editorial policy of the *Clarion-Ledger,* reflected on all its pages, viewed matters through a segregationist lens. Readers were told that a "Negro woman" was freed in the death of a white man by an "all-white jury."[31] The Hattiesburg newspaper as well told readers of Barnes's acquittal by an "all-white jury."[32] The case drew limited attention outside Mississippi, with an Alabama newspaper noting the acquittal of a Black woman for killing a white man, and informing its readers that Barnes's defense counsel consisted of "two white court-appointed attorneys."[33] None of this coverage, however, reflects outrage or even surprise at the decision. The trial of Barnes received almost no national notice. Had she been convicted and sentenced to death, perhaps it would have drawn more publicity. *Jet,* the Chicago-based "Weekly Negro News Magazine," ran a brief notice of Barnes's acquittal. Her case, it said, was heard before an "all-white jury." She was defended by "two white lawyers."[34] Readers of *Jet* might have been struck by the novelty of Barnes's fate, but nothing in the magazine's brief story hints at the complexity of the matter.

Judge Tom Brady's decision to sustain Joe Pigott's motion for a directed verdict becomes more dramatic given later developments in his career. In 1951, Brady did not have a name that resonated much beyond Mississippi. Soon he would. Thomas Pickens Brady (1903–1973) was born in New Orleans to a Brookhaven, Mississippi, family. Brady took an undergraduate degree at Yale in 1927, and after a year at the law school of the University of Michigan, finished his law degree at the University of Mississippi in 1930. Brady practiced in Brookhaven from 1930 to 1950, when he was elected circuit judge for the Fourteenth District, a position he held until 1963. He was appointed then to a vacancy on the state supreme court following the death of a sitting justice. Subsequently elected to fill that unexpired term, in 1969 Brady was elected to a full term in his own right. He served as an associate justice until his death in 1973.[35]

Active in state and national Democratic politics, Brady attended his party's national convention from the 1930s through 1960. Like many white Mississippians, in 1948 Brady supported the States' Rights, or Dixiecrat, movement, an indication of their unease with the Democratic Party's evolving position on civil rights. In later years, again like many white Mississippians, Brady construed this discontent as a principled stand on government's reach. "The less control the Federal Government exercised over our . . . rights," he said in a 1972 interview, "the happier we would be."[36] Brady's reputation and legacy were determined by the course he took as the civil rights movement gained momentum. By the mid-1950s, he became the leading intellectual theorist of the Citizens' Council movement. His book *Black Monday* (1955) denounced the *Brown* decision and vigorously defended the southern way of life, defined largely as the maintenance of racial segregation.[37] The book gained Brady fame and, in later decades, notoriety. By the mid-1950s, few articles about Brady failed to mention the book. It is impossible to speak of him now without reference to it. *Black Monday* aims at a legalistic refutation of *Brown*. But the book also offers Brady's observations on the Black southerner, whom he claimed to have studied with care. Like the segregationist cause, the book has not aged well.

One legal historian noted of Mississippi jurists of the era: "Mississippi judges were torn between their desire to support the existing social order, and their distaste for the compromises they often had to make between legal ideals and the imperatives of racial supremacy."[38] In 1951, however, Brady would not have seen the Barnes case as a clash between idealism and imperatives. He did not need to. He regretted the fate that the promising young Craft had met, but the law was the law, especially as evidence showed that Craft had been shot breaking into a closed bar. Unlike cases Brady and other Mississippi judges would hear in the later 1950s and 1960s, the Barnes trial did not seem fundamentally about support for the existing social order, which would have seemed to Brady in 1951 to be secure, at least as viewed from the bench of the Pike County Circuit Court. Mississippi judges sometimes showed less regard for the rule of law than did Brady in 1951. Especially in a period when national scrutiny had not yet fallen on Mississippi in ways that it later would, it is not difficult to imagine another judge overruling Pigott's motion, sending the case to the jury, and being perfectly satisfied with his actions. Brady was and remained a segregationist, a man who thought of Black Mississippians as a lesser breed. But in this instance, he ruled properly.

After the trial of Barnes, reporter Charles Gordon reminded readers of the mayhem that had unfolded since April, including Barnes's shooting of Craft; that of Rob Lee by the Craft brothers; that of Barnes by Lee's accomplice Walter Watson, now convicted; and that of Barnes by Lee himself, whose trial was still presumably set to come. But, concluded Gordon, this chapter of the story seemed to have come to an end—"at least locally and presently." Such might have seemed the case to readers of the *Enterprise-Journal.* But the ordeal for Barnes was not ended—not by a long shot. Despite the dismissal of these charges against her, two more years would pass and more Mississippi jails awaited her before she was finally free.[39]

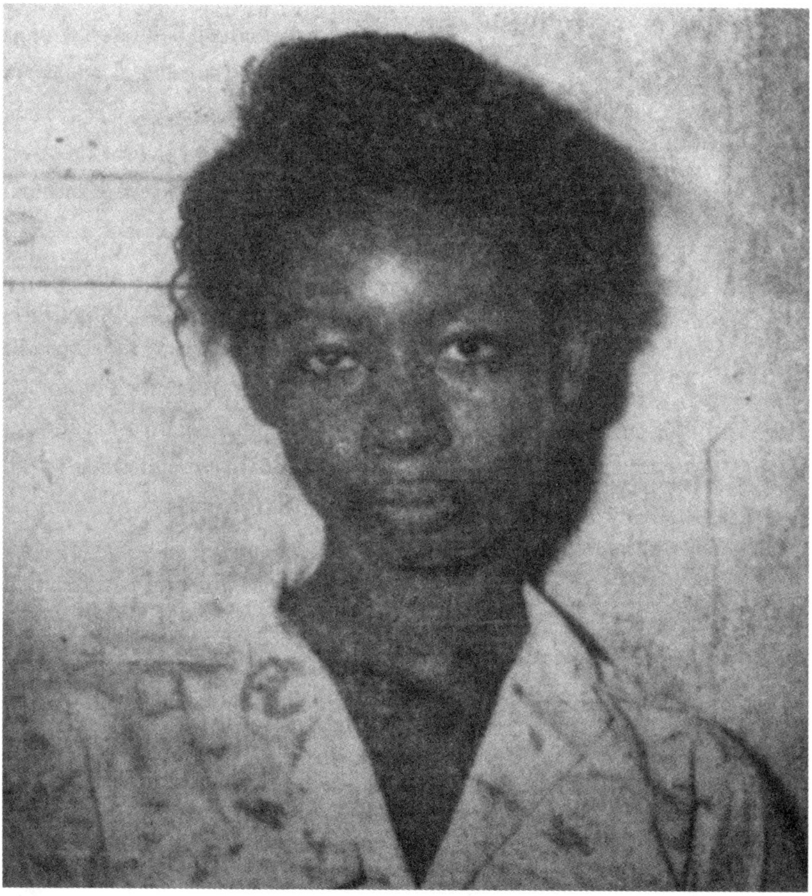

Hattie Lee Barnes.
Photo courtesy of *Enterprise-Journal*.

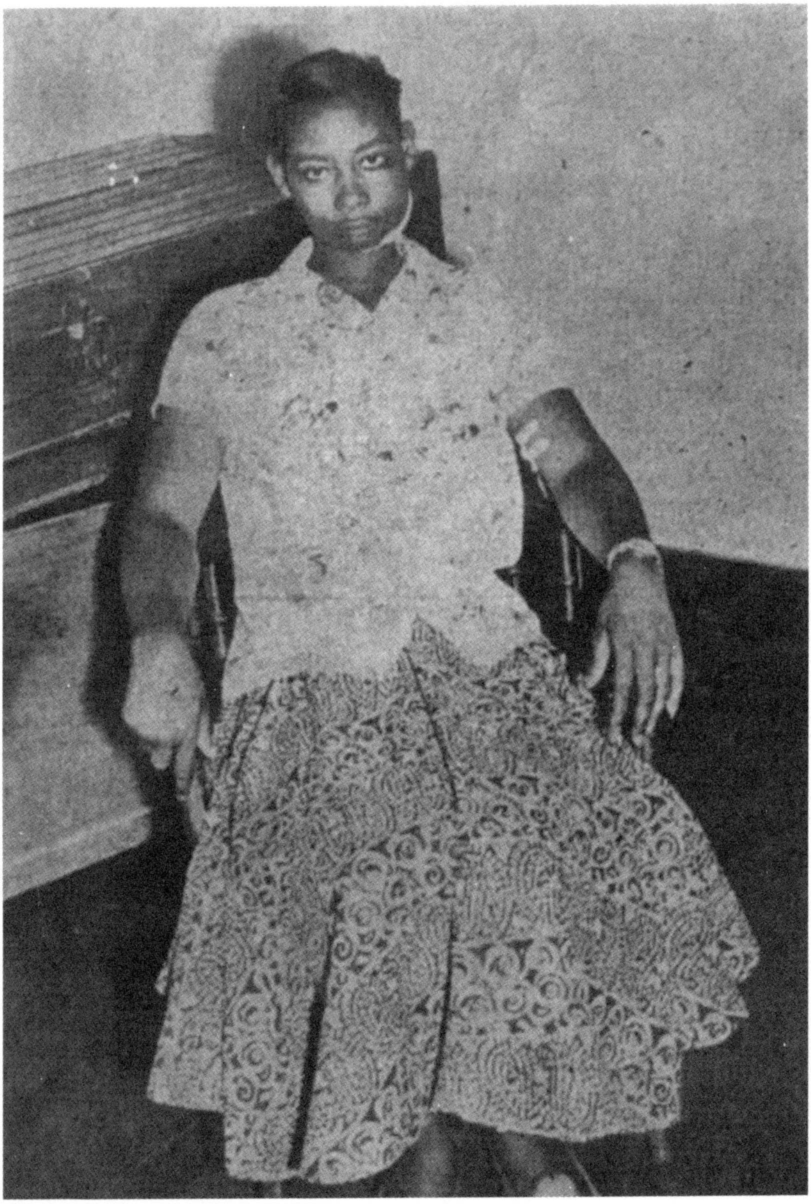

Hattie Lee Barnes.
Photo courtesy of *Tylertown Times*.

Lamar Craft.
Photo courtesy of *Tylertown Times.*

Joe Pigott.
Photo courtesy of *Enterprise-Journal.*

Charles Gordon.
Photo courtesy of Mac Gordon.

Edd Craft.
Photo courtesy of author.

Walter Watson (*right*) with Marion County deputy sheriff Jim Duckworth.
Photo courtesy of *Tylertown Times*.

Breed Mounger.
Photo © The *Clarion-Ledger*—
USA Today Network.

Judge Thomas P. Brady.
Photo courtesy of *Enterprise-Journal.*

6

THE TRIAL OF ROB LEE

AT THE END OF 1951, Rob Lee remained a free man, at liberty on $10,000 bond set by Marion County Circuit Judge Sebe Dale. His co-conspirator, Walter Watson, sentenced to ten years at Parchman, appealed to the Mississippi Supreme Court. In December, the court upheld Watson's conviction.[1] Watson argued that he had acted under duress. After shooting Hattie Lee Barnes multiple times, Rob Lee ordered Watson to "finish her off." Watson feared Lee, so he complied. The Mississippi Supreme Court held that "fear of another is no license to take the life of a person." Justice Olney Arrington wrote that even if Watson felt compelled to follow Lee's orders, "he is of course equally guilty as he would be, had he done it entirely of his own volition." Lee and Watson acted together, so "each was equally guilty regardless of who fired the fatal [*sic*] shot," a curious misstatement, for despite Lee and Watson's efforts, Barnes was still very much alive.[2]

The main reason Lee himself had not yet been tried, reported Charles Gordon, was "the Barnes woman's failure to appear as a witness."[3] Why would Barnes hesitate to testify against a man who attempted to murder her? There were reasonable grounds for Barnes's reluctance. She surely feared Rob Lee. Although Barnes had been acquitted of Lamar Craft's murder—and perhaps because she had been acquitted—Lee might imagine that she could still somehow implicate him in that crime. Too, Barnes saw that Mississippi could not pin down Lee and compel him to face trial. With Lee initially at large after skipping bond and now free on a new, heftier bond, Barnes could not feel confident of law enforcement authorities' protection, should Lee try again to kill her. And should the state bring him to trial, Barnes could not have been sure of a conviction. Her mother and stepfather remained in Walthall County, should anyone wish to retaliate against them for Barnes's testimony. Perhaps she wished simply to be free of Mississippi, trial of Lee or not. Other matters would become clearer when Lee did finally appear in Marion County Circuit Court—almost two years after he shot Barnes. The State of Mississippi convicted and ultimately sent to the penitentiary Rob Lee, a white man, for attempting to murder a Black woman. However, Barnes was wearing down under the weight of her ordeal. Before and after Lee's trial, Barnes herself would be jailed through months of bewildering delays as various county courts decided what to do with or to her. Once again, Joe Pigott stepped forward to assist Barnes, as Charles Gordon worked to tell his readers what she endured.

In the spring court term of 1952, Marion County intended to prosecute Lee, but Barnes's continuing reluctance to appear complicated those efforts. District attorney Vernon Broom said that Lee's was among four cases that might not come to trial that spring. His case would be continued until the November term "because of the continued absence of the woman." Why she was reluctant to appear, Broom did not say, if in fact he knew. Nor was it clear that anyone in the Marion County court system knew Barnes's whereabouts, or Lee's, either, for that matter. Of the trio present at Barnes's shooting, the location of only one of them was certain: Walter Watson, Lee's convicted co-gunman, continued to serve his ten-year sentence at Parchman.[4]

There would be no trial of Rob Lee in the fall 1952 court term, either. Not until the spring of 1953 did Marion County finally try Rob Lee. Lee's defense attorneys continued to press for a delay in the reckoning, filing motions for yet another continuance on the grounds that "certain key defense witnesses were 'missing.'"[5] Judge Sebe Dale denied that motion, and Lee's trial was set for Wednesday, June 17, 1953, at the courthouse in Columbia. Even then, matters did not get underway as scheduled. At 9:00 a.m., Lee's attorneys filed still another motion for a continuance. Clearly impatient, Judge Dale ordered the defense to have its witnesses ready to appear by 1:30 that afternoon. The defense had two years to prepare their case, Dale said; he would tolerate no further delays.[6]

The case against Lee, reported Charles Gordon, had been "carried from term to term" because Hattie Lee Barnes, "naturally the key witness in the prosecution of her former employer," could not be located. Now, Barnes and Walter Watson were prepared to testify. Both had been brought to the area—Watson from his prison cell in the Delta and Barnes from Arkansas, where she had moved—and were currently "held in undisclosed locations."[7] This undisclosed detention of Barnes indicates two things: One is a cavalier attitude about the rights of Black Mississippians, as there were no clear or announced reasons for Barnes's being held. The other is the potential danger facing Black Mississippians prepared to testify against a white man. Some of that danger might come from the Lees, a family with a demonstrated capacity for violence. In the period preceding the trial of Rob Lee, the Lee family were no strangers to the law in Marion County. His son Glenn Lee and his son's wife were arrested in the spring of 1953 "after a pitched gunbattle with the Marion County sheriff and his deputies who tried to search their home for bootleg whiskey." The lawmen "were driven from the house in a volley of gunfire." Taken into custody, Glenn Lee and his wife were free on bond at the time of the elder Lee's scheduled trial.[8]

Once they had Rob Lee in court, Marion County made quick work of him. In a trial of less than one day, a jury found him guilty of "assault and battery with intent to kill" Hattie Lee Barnes. As everyone had expected, Barnes was the prime witness against Lee. Her testimony, however, was not as crisp or precise as observers, including the district attorney, might have anticipated. On many matters, she seemed either short on detail, hesitant to speak, or perhaps simply worn down. Often, her testimony consisted of brief answers to the district attorney's questions, which if not leading questions in a legal sense, seem questions intended to draw out answers from a reluctant witness. Barnes told the court that she was twenty-three years old, born in Mississippi, but unsure of which county.[9] For the last year she had lived in Helena, Arkansas. District attorney Vernon Broom asked Barnes: "Do you know Mr. Rob Lee?" With understatement, Barnes replied: "I know of him." He led her through another telling of the trip from Leland to Marion County. Barnes seemed weary of telling the tale, saying to Broom that "there ain't much I can tell . . . All I remember is I got shot."[10]

Compared with her testimony in Watson's trial, Barnes's answers here are spare. She replied, "I don't know" or "I don't remember" to many of Broom's queries, including what she did when Lee shot her, what she did after Watson shot her, and how long it had taken her to secure assistance from Mrs. Ruth Lee and a ride to the hospital. Broom asked Barnes when she had next seen Lee. She replied that she had not. Asked when she had next seen Watson, she said that she had not. Not receiving the answers that he had expected, Broom asked if she had seen both men at Watson's trial in Marion County. Barnes offered no reply. Frustrated, Broom asked, "Are you the same Hattie Lee Barnes who testified in that trial?" Replied Barnes, "I hope I am." She did not remember seeing Lee at that trial but did remember seeing Watson. Seeking some reason for Barnes's hesitation, Broom asked, "Hattie Lee, are you afraid?" She did not reply, so he repeated the question. "No, sir," she eventually answered.[11]

To more questions, Barnes replied, "I don't know" or "I don't remember," including when after leaving Leland she had been shot, where she had slept on one of the nights of the road trip, whether she had bled after being shot, and how long she remained in the hospital. Her answers are remarkable for their tentativeness, given Barnes's tenacity at earlier stages. Even a question about her injuries provoked a cautious response. Broom said, "State whether it was necessary for doctors to treat you over there." Replied Barnes, "Yes, sir, I guess."[12]

Asked about witnesses Ernestine James and Robert James, who worked at Floyd Duncan's place where Barnes, Lee, and Watson had stopped to drink and buy more whiskey, Barnes replied that she "knew of" them. Are they in the courtroom? "I think they are." Were Lee and Watson armed at that point? "I don't know." Had you known Watson before he shot you? "I think I remember seeing him once." What kind of place was the James's residence? "I don't remember." Do you remember Lee saying anything to you before he shot you? "I don't." Defense counsel R. H. Dale did not question Barnes, and with that brief, tentative testimony, Barnes was dismissed.[13]

What accounts for the very different Barnes one sees here when compared with her assured behavior in her own trial in 1951 and that of Walter Watson the same year? Not mentioned in Lee's trial, by Barnes or anyone else, is that in 1953 Barnes had been extradited from Arkansas and held in undefined custody in jails in Marion County and then Lincoln County as she awaited use by the State of Mississippi. Lincoln County was directly north of Pike County. It was also a place with no apparent connection of residence or occurrence with any person or event in this case. For months, Lee had been free: out on bond, as a fugitive after skipping bond, and then released again on bond. But Barnes had been a prisoner. Surely she was dubious of the law and the courts in Mississippi; perhaps her reticence reflects a fear of Lee or simply an exhausted woman ready to be finished with her ordeal.

The trial moved briskly. The state's witnesses offered brief testimony; the defense seemed content to listen and wait. Robert James, a bootlegger, testified. He and his wife, Ernestine, were in business, he said, "selling a little whiskey and stuff." James knew Lee but had not previously met Watson. When Barnes, Lee, and Watson visited them for a fresh supply of whiskey, both men were armed with pistols. However, no "difficulty or fight" occurred during their visit of one or two hours. He witnessed no shooting and did not learn of Barnes's fate until the following day. The defense asked no questions of the witness. Then Ernestine James testified. She had known Rob Lee for about eleven years. Watson she had met only "one time." While she could not recall the exact day, she, too, remembered the visit of Lee, Watson, and Barnes. Like her husband, she said that both men were armed, no one caused any trouble there, and she only learned of Barnes's shooting the following day. Again, the defense had no questions.[14]

"Attired in his striped convict's uniform," Walter Watson testified, telling of the driving and drinking that he, Lee, and Barnes had done before the men's unsuccessful attempt to kill her.[15] He was forty-five years old, he said, and originally from Indianola in the Delta. He had known Barnes about a month before the shooting, meeting her on Magee Street in Leland, where Lee had brought Barnes after Lamar Craft's death. In his own trial, Watson claimed to have known Rob Lee only a brief time before the 1951 shooting of Barnes. Here, however, he said that he first met Lee in 1948, although he did not specify how or why. He renewed that acquaintance with Lee in Leland in 1951. Unlike Barnes's, Watson's recollection of dates and times was generally sharp. Contradicting his earlier testimony, he said that while there were two weapons in the car on the road trip, Barnes did not have one. In this version, there was no snub nose pistol in her handbag. At one of the trio's stops, at Rob Lee's son's "joint," he played the slot machine, an illegal activity, in addition to the jukebox. On the Wednesday of the shooting, he said, they were all "dirty and sweaty." So he "went to a store on the corner and got me a pair of pants, a suit of underwear, a shirt, some towels and soap, and tried to find a room to take a bath and couldn't find one." Instead, Rob Lee suggested that the two Black Mississippians bathe in a river.

Along with whiskey, they eventually needed food. At a crossroads store, they stopped for "some cheese and a quart of sweet milk" and filled the car with gasoline before driving on, stopping ostensibly to check on Lee's dog. The real plan, of course, was to kill Barnes.[16] On a fundamental point, Watson was adamant. He was not a willing shooter of Barnes. When Lee told him to "finish" Barnes, he said, "Oh, no, sir," acquiescing only when Lee threatened him. Escaping from Lee through a cornfield, he "caught the doodle bug train" to Columbia, where he asked a cab driver to take him "to the colored part of town." Finding a hotel, he paid the clerk two dollars, drank a beer, and napped before the police arrived to arrest him. Once again, the defense had no questions for the witness.[17]

Not only did the defense question none of the state's four witnesses, but they presented none of their own, including Rob Lee. Both sides then rested their case. As the jury retired, attorney Kelly Hammond, one of three representing Lee, moved for a mistrial based on the district attorney's having told the jury: "This case is not contested. You heard the evidence and nobody disputed it." Such a statement, said Hammond, was "highly prejudicial," an attack on Lee for not testifying, which was his right. By that point, however, the jury had returned with its verdict. Judge Dale told Hammond that the defense had not raised the issue of the potentially prejudicial remark before the jury retired, so he had no opportunity to direct the jury to disregard the statement, if in fact the statement had been improper. Now, Judge Dale instructed the defense to "embody it in a bill of exceptions" in case an appeal was necessary.[18]

The trial was quick work, even by Mississippi standards, partly because Lee's attorneys presented almost nothing beyond their opening statement and unsuccessful motion for a mistrial.[19] Judge Dale himself was surprised by the speed of the trial. Even jury selection had taken far less time than he expected. It was all over in a few hours. The jury hardly had time to sit down. They were back in five minutes with a verdict of guilty. Everything was completed before 5:00 p.m. on that Wednesday afternoon. In at least one facet of this case, Marion County justice seems to have been racially even-handed. Like Watson, Lee was sentenced to ten years in the state penitentiary.[20] *Jet* magazine, which had provided a brief story on Barnes's acquittal, also ran a brief story on Lee's conviction. "Miss. White Man," its readers learned, "Gets 10 Years for Shooting Negro," in a four-sentence notice of the trial.[21]

Lee's attorneys saved their real efforts for an appeal, immediately to the Marion County Circuit Court and then to the Mississippi Supreme Court.[22] Neither was successful. The appeal produced witnesses, not called at the trial, to provide an alibi for Lee. Both witnesses' testimony flatly contradicted Barnes and Watson. Homer Regan, a resident of Marion County and a man who had known Lee all his life, offered a story that placed Lee with him during the time Barnes was shot. That afternoon, Lee came to his house around 3:00 p.m. After a brief visit, Lee asked him if he wanted to go to "Duncan's juke," which he agreed to do. Regan remained for only an hour before his wife retrieved him. Later that afternoon, about 4:30 or 5:00 p.m., Lee returned to his house in a car with "that negro man and woman," Barnes and Watson, whom he did not know. But then those two left, leaving Lee to enjoy a visit with Regan, as Lee "set in the swing at my house," remaining until 5:30 or 6:00 p.m. When Watson returned for Lee, Watson was alone. Lee asked Watson, "Where is my woman?" Watson replied, "I carried her home." Watson left again, leaving Lee at Regan's. Lee waited for Watson, who never came back. Lee eventually left—precisely how, Regan did not say. Later that evening, about 10:00 p.m., Watson came back to Regan's. He awoke Regan and his wife to ask for a ride to Jackson, which Regan would not provide. He did, however, take him to Kokomo "to catch the bus." Rob Lee, asserted Regan, "couldn't" have shot Barnes because "he was at my house." Regan's story was rooted in some truth—the visit of Lee, Watson, and Barnes to his house the day that Barnes was shot. But it also seems likely that the details of Lee's remaining at Regan's during the window in which Barnes was shot and the strong implication that Watson alone had shot Barnes are manufactured, an instance of a man seeking to help a friend.[23]

The other appeal witness, William Garner, also a lifelong resident of Marion County and a longtime friend of Lee, offered an even more helpful story. Garner gave an eyewitness account of a shooting at which Lee was not present. On the afternoon Barnes was shot, Garner was driving from Tylertown back toward his home. Passing Lee's bar, he saw his friend's car and decided to stop. In an incidence of incredible timing, just as he turned off the road and pulled toward Lee's place, he "heard a noise down there." Stopping to investigate, Garner witnessed "two negroes behind the place—a negro man and a negro woman." Undeterred by the arrival of a white witness, "the negro man," who "had a gun," "started firing and 4 shots were fired, and the negro man turned and run and got in Rob Lee's car and headed toward Kokomo. I didn't know what happened, whether he'd killed her or not. I stayed there a minute or two and the negro woman got up and run around the joint and down the road toward Tylertown. She didn't look like she was hurt so I got in my car and went home." If Garner thought of alerting Lee to the shooting on his property, or perhaps even the law, he did not say. This tale of fortuitous coincidence is almost certainly another case of one Marion County man seeking to do a good turn for another one.[24]

In cross-examination of Garner, district attorney Broom revealed considerable skepticism. Garner said that the "negro man" appeared to have shot "the negro woman" with a pistol, but he was "a good piece off. I was about 50 yards off." Broom offered the possibility of someone else behind the building, someone Garner could not see. Garner disagreed: "I could see all around [the building]." "All 4 sides of it?" said Broom. "Three sides of it," admitted Garner. Broom also asked Garner why he stopped at Lee's place just in time to witness this shooting. "I seen Mr. Lee's car parked there," Garner replied. "He'd already got shot down there somewhere right around the same place and I didn't know but maybe he'd got shot again and might have been in the car, or something." Or something indeed. Garner admitted that despite Watson's trial for shooting Barnes, he never told any law enforcement officer of what he had witnessed. He himself had been in a bit of legal trouble before. About two years earlier—relatively close to the time of the shooting of Barnes, that is—Garner was convicted of selling whiskey "one time." He worked for Rob Lee's son. Both Regan and Garner readily allowed that they had been asked to appear as witnesses by Rob Lee, which might have surprised no one.[25]

In September 1953, the Mississippi Supreme Court upheld Rob Lee's conviction, noting the decision of his "able and astute counsel" not to offer witnesses at the initial Marion County trial or to cross-examine the state's witnesses. Like the Marion County prosecutors, the Supreme Court also observed the difference in character between Barnes's testimony against Walter Watson and hers against Lee: "It is obvious from reading the record in the case at bar that the prosecuting witness, a negro woman, did not testify as freely in the case at bar as she did in the Watson case, when one of her own color was being prosecuted . . . Her apparent reluctance to testify in the case at bar is obvious and needs no further elaboration in this brief."[26]

Where was Hattie Lee Barnes through these months? By the summer of 1953, "some very strange developments" had taken place, as reporter Charles Gordon put it with considerable understatement. Gordon had followed the case from the beginning, filing the first published story on the shooting of Lamar Craft in 1951. Gordon's reporting had been exemplary. He covered every detail of all the related cases that stemmed from the Craft shooting. But from mid-1953, his coverage reflected not only the instincts of a good reporter following a complex story but also those of a person convinced that something fundamentally unjust was happening to Hattie Lee Barnes. The "strange developments" during the summer of 1953 were essentially this: Hattie Lee Barnes was being held in one Mississippi jail or another for vague reasons. Once again, Joe Pigott came to Barnes's aid. Now, however, Pigott acted not as a court-appointed attorney but rather as a man motived to see justice done. He seems to have done all his work that year for Barnes not for pay but rather as a matter of duty and integrity.

Gordon's June 24, 1953, update on the Barnes story took unusual form, published not as a news article but rather in the "Highlights in the Headlines" sidebar in the *Enterprise-Journal,* usually reserved for chatty news commentary by editor Oliver Emmerich. It was unusual for anyone else's writing to appear in that space; Emmerich filed copy for it when he was out of the state or even the country. Gordon wrote that details of Barnes's status were not clear, again an understatement. On Tuesday, June 23, however, one week after Rob Lee's trial and conviction, Barnes had been taken from a jail cell in Marion County by two Pike County deputies, Meredith Carr and Lucian Hart, and transported to another jail, "presumably in Brookhaven," located in Lincoln County. What had Barnes done and why was she in jail? Pike County sheriff W. E. "Bucky" Moore was "out of the county today" and thus could not explain the charges against Barnes. But, continued Gordon, "possibly he doesn't know exactly, his orders to send and get and move her undoubtedly having come from a higher echelon in the judicial district's setup."[27]

Rumor had it, said Gordon, a man with a skill for sorting fact from rumor, that Barnes's custody stemmed from one of the oldest elements in the entire story: efforts to pressure her into saying that she did not fire the shots that killed Lamar Craft. Gordon heard that Barnes had recently signed a document, presumably in the Marion County Jail, saying just that. But, continued Gordon, why was Barnes in jail in Marion County in the first place? And why was she now being held in Brookhaven, if that report was true? "What else, if anything, is she accused of?" And "is the girl in what is known as 'protective custody'? If so, from or for whom?" These were all very good questions. Black Mississippians like Hattie Lee Barnes were commonly held and interrogated under a variety of circumstances. Few of their stories were told in a public forum like the *McComb Enterprise-Journal.* Without the work of Charles Gordon, it is likely that Barnes's story, too, would have been known only to her, her family, and the men who held her.

Gordon was correct. Barnes was in custody, and by early July, so she remained. She was also determined to gain her freedom. Barnes had been held initially in the Marion County Jail from approximately June 4—before Rob Lee's trial—until June 23, when she was transferred to jail in Lincoln County, this time as "a prisoner of Pike County."[28] On Barnes's behalf, Joe Pigott filed a petition for a writ of habeas corpus, an effort to compel the state to bring a prisoner to court to determine whether or not that person's detention is lawful. Whether Barnes reached out to Pigott or Pigott reached out to her is unclear. On July 7, Chancery Judge F. D. Hewitt set a hearing on that petition for July 14, ensuring that Barnes would spend another week in jail on charges that still had not been publicly revealed. Sheriff Moore of Pike County, the defendant in the habeas corpus action, would in theory be required to explain the charges on which Barnes was being held and why "she should not be discharged and set at liberty, or granted bail, and be advised of the reasons or causes, if any there be, for her confinement or for the necessity of bail."[29]

In that petition and hearing, and through Gordon's coverage, one learns a good deal more about what happened to Barnes between 1951 and 1953. Little of it would have given her much confidence in southern courts and law. It surely accounts in part for her hesitancy and reticence during Rob Lee's trial, a fact noted both by the district attorney and the Mississippi Supreme Court. Sometime after her 1951 acquittal, Barnes moved to Arkansas, and in 1952, using an assumed name, she married Leon Gardner in Caruthersville, Missouri.[30] How and when Barnes met Gardner is unclear. Nor are some facts about their marriage clear. The files of Pemiscot County, in which Caruthersville is located, contain no recorded marriage of Gardner and Barnes (or of Gardner and anyone else) for the years 1949 to 1953. It is possible that the officiant simply did not file the signed license with the county. It is also possible that the marriage was not, strictly speaking, a legal one.[31] Whatever the legal status of their marriage, she lived with her husband near Helena, Arkansas, working on a cotton plantation owned by former Arkansas governor Ben Laney. Helena, a small town in Phillips County, was separated from the Mississippi Delta less by history and culture than by the Mississippi River. Like the Mississippi Delta, the bread and butter of Helena was the production of cotton with African American labor. In the period just before Barnes lived there, Helena was also fertile land for the blues.[32] Aficionados of the genre know Helena as the longtime originating spot for the *King Biscuit Time* radio broadcast. Governor Laney had substantial holdings in at least three Arkansas counties. In 1951 he purchased four thousand acres of the Highland Lake plantation, likely the land on which Barnes and her husband worked. Almost certainly too they lived in one of the seventy-two tenant houses on that property.[33] It is unlikely that Governor Laney knew either of them by name or even perhaps by sight, and unlikely as well that he was aware of this legal entanglement of one of his tenants.

It was there at her Helena, Arkansas, home that on June 3, 1953, as Barnes chopped cotton on Laney's place, Sheriff Polk of Marion County, Mississippi, confronted her, claiming that he held an arrest warrant on charges of "obstructing justice." Two other men accompanied Laney, one a Marion County deputy and the other an Arkansas lawman, likely a sheriff's deputy as well. Taken by the men and "through and by false representations and promises," in the habeas corpus petition's formal language, Barnes was coerced into signing a document, a document she did not understand and that she was certainly not given the time to study, could she even have read it. Within a day, said Barnes, she found herself back in jail in Marion County. That signed document was a waiver of extradition. Barnes was held in Marion County from June 4 until approximately noon on June 23. On that date, Barnes's petition said, two Pike County deputies, Meredith Carr and Lucian Hart, came to Columbia and transported her to Brookhaven, where she was placed in the Lincoln County Jail. She was held there, her petition said, as "the prisoner of the Sheriff of Pike County, Mississippi." Why she was being held in Lincoln

County rather than Pike County, and why she was being held after the conclusion of Rob Lee's trial, she had no clear idea.[34]

How did Mississippi find Barnes in Arkansas? According to Charles Gordon, Lizzie Magee, Barnes's mother, who still lived in Walthall County, visited Barnes in Arkansas, allowing Mississippi authorities to track her down. Initially, Barnes might have been under the impression that she was brought back to Mississippi to serve as a state's witness in the trial of Rob Lee. In June, Barnes did testify, albeit hesitantly, and saw Lee convicted. Lee, however, remained free on bond pending appeal, whereas Barnes, the victim, was in jail. Why was Barnes still being held? Gordon, and again he was on the right track, wrote that she was considered a "material witness" in a case that "might or might not" be filed. Just as had happened in 1951, while in custody in 1953, Barnes had faced relentless interrogation, was accused of lying and otherwise making false statements, and had been pressured into signing a statement that she knew to be false. According to her petition, she signed that false statement because she was promised that if she did so, she would be released from Mississippi custody and allowed to return home to Arkansas. That statement once again implicated Rob Lee in the shooting of Lamar Craft, and the potential case to which Gordon referred was a prosecution of Lee for the murder of Craft.[35]

When the habeas corpus petition was heard, it would mark almost exactly two years since Lee and Watson had shot Barnes and only slightly longer than that since Barnes shot Craft. The hearing, to Hattie Lee Barnes a bid for her own freedom, represented for other parties a chance to revisit the Lamar Craft shooting to look for Rob Lee's hand. On July 14, 1953, before Pike County Chancery Judge F. D. Hewitt, Barnes held to the story she tried to tell since the beginning: she shot Lamar Craft.[36] At the end, however, Judge Hewitt denied Barnes's petition. Her confinement was lawful, he said, pending further investigation into the Craft shooting. He ordered bond for Barnes set at $2,500, a far higher figure than the $1,000 bond set for her after her 1951 arrest. Not seeming to account for the circumstances in which Barnes was held and interrogated, Hewitt professed grave concern at Barnes's "contradictory" statements about Lamar Craft's shooting. Especially troubling to Hewitt was that statement Barnes signed on June 18, while in jail in Marion County, "on the second day of visits and interrogation from 14th District Attorney E. C. Barlow and others." That statement, which Barnes's attorney Joe Pigott was not allowed to view "in full," said that Craft was shot by some party or parties at a location unknown to Barnes. But his body was transported to Rob Lee's place on Highway 24. There the corpse was discovered when law enforcement authorities were told of the killing.[37]

Joe Pigott represented Barnes at the hearing. Aware that Barnes's signed statement about Craft's shooting gave the state its best reason to detain her, he asked Barnes to explain the circumstances surrounding that statement. Barnes admitted signing it, but she said that she had done so only because she was "tired and afraid." Before Rob Lee's trial, she told the court, she was visited by a group of men, including district attorney Barlow, Marion County sheriff Polk and one of his deputies, Walthall County sheriff Rufus Dillon, and Edd Craft, Lamar Craft's father. Both sheriffs testified that Barnes told them, "I killed Lamar Craft." On June 18, the day Rob Lee was convicted of shooting Barnes, the sheriffs returned, as well as the district attorney and Barnes's husband, Leon Gardner. This time, Edd Craft was not present. Now, district attorney Barlow presented Barnes with a statement that Barlow had handwritten. He insisted that Barnes sign it. That statement said that she had not killed Craft. Instead, Rob Lee was the real killer. Barnes said that Barlow assured her that if she were to sign the document, she would be protected "by the power of the state of Mississippi" and that she would be freed and allowed to return home to Arkansas. She signed the document.[38]

But Barnes was not freed. Instead, she was taken by two Pike County deputies to the Lincoln County Jail in Brookhaven, and there she had remained. Throughout the process, Barnes had been told little more than it suited the immediate interests of local authorities to tell her. "Did they tell you why they were holding you?," asked Joe Pigott. "No, sir, they didn't exactly tell me," replied Barnes. "They brought that summons and I saw for myself what was on it . . . Mr. Edd Craft's name was on it and the American National Insurance Company." The summons to which Barnes referred was connected with another case, one involving a life insurance policy on Lamar Craft, as Pigott well knew, as he was counsel to one of the parties in that action. That suit, a civil rather than a criminal matter, had been filed in Walthall County in 1952. Pigott asked, "Is that the only reason they told you they were holding you?" Barnes replied, "Didn't nobody tell me exactly anything."[39] Here, finally, was the heart of the matter. Edd Craft had filed a civil suit attempting to cast the blame for his son's death onto Rob Lee. At the same time, he continued his efforts to persuade the district attorney to pursue criminal charges against Lee. In these efforts, he, local authorities, and certainly his attorney Breed Mounger had concluded that Hattie Lee Barnes might be useful to have on hand. Constitutional rights or not, they seemed to have determined that she would be kept in jail until needed.

But in those jails, area sheriffs insisted, Barnes had little about which to complain. Marion County sheriff Polk said that she had been well treated while in his custody.[40] "I saw that Hattie Lee had clothes; cigarettes; just about anything Hattie Lee asked for she got it and most of it came out of my pocket . . . [M]y wife and sister gave her some of their clothes and she had cigarettes and candy whenever she asked for it." Additionally, Walthall County sheriff Dillon testified that "Hattie Lee wasn't threatened in any manner whatever. She was treated just like she was a white woman." But Barnes maintained that no matter how well she might have been treated, the statement she gave was not true. She had been pressured by district attorney Barlow into signing the statement that Rob Lee was responsible for the death of Lamar Craft. She said that she had signed that statement only to secure her release from custody. Barlow, she said, told her that if she signed, "I could go and if I couldn't get no other way he would carry me in his own car."[41]

In the hearing, Barnes once more repeated the story of the shooting at Lee's bar, a practice of which by this time she must have been exhausted. Several matters of interest emerged in Pigott's questioning of Barnes, but nothing that changed her basic account. Barnes did not know Lamar Craft ("at the time") when he came to Rob Lee's bar. At closing time, Barnes found Rob and Ruth Lee and asked them to persuade Craft and his friends to leave so that she could close up. Shortly, a car returned to the scene, and "somebody came to the door with a bunch of keys and tried to open the door." She listened as someone tried to force entry first through the rear double doors and then "got a bucket or something" to try to enter through a window. Barnes found the gun that "stayed there every day." Afraid to go into the room where the intruder was attempting to gain entry, she "just stood by the door and held [the gun] up side the door and aimed it and shot." "What did you shoot at?" asked Pigott. "A man," replied Barnes. Firing once, the gun jammed. "I kept pulling on the trigger until it went off." Then she called the McComb police. "They asked me why I didn't get the sheriff and I told them I didn't know his number and so they give me his number and I called him."[42]

On cross-examination by district attorney Barlow, Barnes gave evidence of an unsettled life. Barlow's reactions reveal in turn a fundamental lack of understanding and sympathy, a consistent thread in Barnes's experiences in these years. He asked Barnes where she had been born. "In Mississippi," she replied. "In what part of Mississippi?" "I don't know where I was born." However, she had lived most of her life ("until I was grown") in Walthall County, as well as briefly in Pike County. Barlow asked her if she gave her name at her marriage to Gardner as Hattie Lee Magee. She said that she had not. "Who married you?" asked Barlow. "I couldn't tell you," she said, but the officiant was a preacher. She had married, she said, under the name of Ella Mae Smith. "Why?" asked Barlow. "I don't know why I did," she answered. However, she had been married before but did not know the current location of that man or if he was living or dead. "Did you ever get a divorce from him?" asked Barlow. "He got his own divorce." "Whereabouts?" "I don't know," said Barnes. "Don't know that either," replied Barlow.[43]

Finally, a Pike County justice of the peace, M. M. Berryhill, offered testimony that shed light on the potential criminal charge against Rob Lee, and thus one of the fundamental reasons why Barnes might be in jail and might well remain there. On June 17, 1953, district attorney Barlow, so dogged in his attempts to have Barnes repudiate her claim to have killed Lamar Craft, filed an affidavit in his court charging "Bob (alias Rob) Lee" with the killing of Craft. That affidavit was filed the day before Barlow and the other men appeared at Hattie Lee Barnes's cell with the handwritten statement for her to sign, the statement that implicated Lee; it was also the day before Lee's trial and conviction for shooting Barnes. As of this hearing, however, Lee was still free. It was now clear that it was as a "material witness" on this potential charge against Lee that Barnes was being held. Judge Tom Brady, who had in 1951 presided over Barnes's trial, ordered on June 18 that the Pike County sheriff go to Columbia, arrest Barnes, jail her under a $2,500 bond, and pending payment of that bond, hold her until the next meeting of the circuit court's grand jury. That order was carried out on June 23, and Barnes had been in jail in Brookhaven since that time, with no resources to post bond.[44]

Barnes said that all that she wanted was to go home to Arkansas. But she promised the court that she would return for any purposes for which the court might need her. Barnes added that she was not afraid of anyone involved in the case, a remarkable statement, given everything that had happened to her over the previous two years. Chancery Judge Hewitt was not persuaded. He maintained that Barnes willingly signed the waiver of extradition and returned to Mississippi to testify against Rob Lee "of her own free will." Moreover, he said, she had been well treated in all the jails in which she had been held and that nothing that had happened to her had violated her civil or constitutional rights. So, then, counter to Pigott's petition on her behalf, Hewitt ruled that Barnes was being "lawfully confined." The judge's order sustained Judge Brady's decision that Barnes should be held on $2,500 bond as a material witness in the case against the still-unindicted Rob Lee.[45] Thus, pending Barnes's ability to meet that bond, or a lower bond, which Hewitt announced that he was at liberty to set, she would remain in custody.

In mid-July, then, Barnes remained jailed in Lincoln County. Also briefly in jail once again was her former boss and convicted shooter, Rob Lee. Lee was arrested in Hattiesburg, Mississippi, on Sunday, July 19, charged with the April 17, 1951, murder of Lamar Craft. Unlike his colleague Walter Watson, Lee was not in the state penitentiary for his conviction of the attempted murder of Barnes but rather was free while that conviction was under appeal. Lee's Hattiesburg arrest occurred under that affidavit filed by district attorney E. C. Barlow with Pike County justice of the peace M. M. Berryhill. Lee was brought by Pike County deputies to the jail in Magnolia and held under a reported bond of $7,500. Early reports indicated that Lee would waive his right to a preliminary hearing on the charge. As of July 21, however, Lee had not posted bond.[46]

In the meantime, Joe Pigott prepared an appeal of Judge Hewitt's denial of Barnes's habeas corpus petition, and that appeal was headed to the Mississippi Supreme Court. Additionally, Barnes filed with the Supreme Court a "pauper's oath," a statement that she could not afford the court costs associated with the appeal. At the time of the appeal, the Supreme Court was not in session. But they could possibly, noted Charles Gordon, "return to consider an appeal in a habeas corpus hearing—regarded as one of the most important and significant actions that can be taken for a client under American law." Gordon could now inform his readers that Barnes was not in protective custody, as he had earlier wondered, but was in fact facing fresh charges, this time of "(a) 'obstructing justice' and (b) 'material witness.'" That custody demonstrates primarily the fierce continuing efforts by Edd Craft to find some court to say that Rob Lee rather than Hattie Lee Barnes had killed his son, as well as Craft's ability to project his influence into the courts of several counties.[47]

It was possible that charges against Lee might be heard in the next court term in Pike County, scheduled for October 1953. Late on Wednesday, July 22, however, Lee was out of jail again, having quickly posted his $7,500 bond.[48] A number of area men, including Ansel Thornhill, Ott Pool, Jack Spiers, Barney Bedwell, Earnest Gaddis, Hillary Thornhill, as well as Lee himself, had signed as guarantors of Lee's bond. These men were "well worth and then some" the amount of the bond, according to a statement on the document signed by Marion County sheriff J. V. Polk; the bond was approved as well by Pike County sheriff W. E. Moore. Hattie Lee Barnes Gardner had no access to men with considerable funds to guarantee her bond. The Supreme Court considered and denied her habeas corpus appeal. So unlike Lee, she remained unconvicted of any crime, but still jailed.[49]

7

DOUBLE INDEMNITY

An Insurance Suit and Lamar Craft's Reputation

AT HER HABEAS CORPUS hearing in July 1953, Hattie Lee Barnes told of the summons she received that had "Mr. Edd Craft's name . . . on it and the American National Insurance Company." Lamar Craft's life was insured for $1,000, with a double indemnity clause in the event of accidental death. American National agreed to pay beneficiary Edd Craft $1,000, but not $2,000, maintaining that Lamar Craft's death occurred under conditions that nullified the obligation for double indemnity. On July 8, 1952, Edd Craft filed suit against American National in the Walthall County Circuit Court. That suit sought—and cost—money. Craft also sought something else valuable, if less quantifiable: the redemption of his son's good name and the revelation of his son's true killer. Into 1953, that case had not come to trial.[1] The only simple matter in this element of the complex tale is that everyone agreed that Lamar Craft was dead. Once that suit did come to trial in the Walthall County Courthouse, Edd Craft made his most deliberate public effort to insist that his son was not shot while trying to rape an African American woman. Joe Pigott, representing the insurance company, demonstrated through dogged examination of witnesses that whatever Edd Craft might wish to assert, those were precisely the circumstances in which his son died.

In covering that trial, reporter Charles Gordon frankly noted that "the sexual angle" of the men's return to Lee's bar was apparent, as indicated in Barnes's 1951 trial. But "events in the case . . . have grown so profuse, and have grown so complicated, that keeping up with them is very difficult."[2] Three things, however, remained clear: Hattie Lee Barnes still insisted that she shot Lamar Craft; into the early fall of 1953, Barnes remained jailed in Lincoln County; and the Craft family continued to apply pressures to her and to the public record to clear their son's name, as they saw it. What remains opaque is the reason for their insistence that Rob Lee or someone acting on his behalf was the true killer of their son and brother, except perhaps as a more palatable alternative to the truth.

The trial of Edd Craft vs. American National Insurance Company was heard in Walthall County Circuit Court on August 12, 1953.[3] The cast involved in that trial demonstrates the relatively small world of law and the courts in southern Mississippi, as well as the interlocking nature of the various elements of the Barnes saga. Joe Pigott, Barnes's attorney in 1951 and again in 1953, represented American National. Breed Mounger, who assisted in the extralegal interrogation of Barnes in 1951 and also in her trial for murder later that year, represented Edd Craft. On the bench was Judge Tom P. Brady, who presided over the trial of Barnes in 1951 and ordered her held in 1953 as a material witness in a potential trial of Rob Lee for killing Lamar Craft.

For American National, the suit was business, a defense against what they regarded as an invalid claim. For the Craft family, the suit was not really about money but rather about salvaging the reputation of Lamar Craft. In 1951, newspaper coverage of Craft's shooting and the trial of Hattie Lee Barnes revealed that he had been killed by an African American woman in suggestive circumstances. From the time of the shooting, the Crafts contested that story. Family patriarch Edd Craft seems especially to have been grieved and embarrassed by this account. He wished in the American National suit to do what he could to change the public narrative of the death of "my boy."[4] The difference between the $1,000 that American National agreed to pay and the $2,000 that the civil suit sought was not the issue, even granting that in 1952 $1,000 was a substantial piece of money. However, the services of attorney Breed Mounger were not cheap. Although there is no way to know how much Edd Craft spent on attorney's fees, to him that was not the point.

Edd Craft was the beneficiary of a policy from the American National Insurance Company of Galveston, Texas, taken out on October 9, 1945. A copy of that policy was introduced as evidence. As is typical, the company qualified the circumstances under which the "double accidental death benefit" would be paid. On the copy of the policy in the court file, someone marked "clause f" of the exceptions; the benefit would not be paid if the injury was received "from engaging in an illegal occupation or attempting to commit an assault or felony." There was the crux of the insurance company's case. There also was the broader narrative of Lamar Craft's death that his father was attempting to contest.[5]

Upon his son's death, said Edd Craft, he sought payment from the company, supplying the undertaker with a form to verify that death. In response, he received a check for $1,000 from American National, marked "final settlement." But, "I didn't sign it. I mailed it back to them." If the company sent Craft any explanation of why the double death benefit would not be paid, he did not mention it. Nor is there any indication how American National might have learned that the double death benefit was one that they might not have to pay.[6]

As plaintiff in this civil trial, Edd Craft could serve as a witness in a way that would not have been possible in the earlier criminal trials of Watson, Barnes, and Lee. His attorney, Breed Mounger, could ask Edd Craft and others the questions Craft wanted to ask, as they attempted to shape the story they wished the public record to show. No earlier account of the April 1951 shooting indicated that Edd Craft had any firsthand knowledge of the death of his son. But here, Craft offered testimony that foregrounded his actions following his son's death. Edd Craft admitted that he did not of his "personal knowledge" know whether Lamar Craft had been killed on the night of April 16, 1951, or in the early hours of April 17. He had last seen his son alive about 9:00 p.m. on April 16. He next saw him dead at 3:30 or 4:00 a.m. on April 17. Lamar Craft exhibited, as Edd Craft's attorney, Breed Mounger, put it in a somewhat confusing locution, a gunshot wound "right on the left side of the right breast."[7]

Joe Pigott cross-examined Edd Craft. Craft saw his son's body "laying across the bed out here in a place they call Rob Lee's Tavern, I believe they call it—I call it." Exchanges between Pigott and Craft were chippy. In Barnes's 1951 trial, the heart of her defense was that Rob Lee's bar amounted to her home; she shot Craft as he attempted to enter her bedroom. Here, Edd Craft took issue with Pigott's characterization of the room on the back side of the bar as a bedroom: "I wouldn't call it a bed room. It was a juke joint." But there his son lay, on a single bed in that room, whatever one might prefer to call it, with "one foot over the foot of the bed." Pigott intended to establish that Lamar Craft was up to no good, at least as American National might define it, when he was shot. Was there, asked Pigott, a pint of Seagram's V.O. whiskey in that car?[8] Craft said there was nothing in the car when he arrived, which might well have been the case. But, said Pigott, did you not attend the Magnolia trial of Hattie Lee Barnes? Yes, said Craft. And there, said Pigott, did you not hear that there was a pint of whiskey in the car? Craft protested. What he heard then was that in the car was a half pint, brand unspecified.[9]

If Edd Craft worked here to establish a story for purposes beyond the dollars-and-cents matter of the insurance settlement, so too did Joe Pigott. Pigott was in the courtroom as American National's advocate. But he was also a man who had thought at great length, both in his defense of Hattie Lee Barnes in 1951 and his continued representation of her in 1953, about what Lamar Craft had done on the evening that he had been shot. He asked Craft, "Did you also hear testimony to the effect that your son was killed while climbing in the window?" Before Craft could answer, Breed Mounger objected. The attorneys sparred over Pigott's line of questioning. The court sustained Mounger's objection. Then Pigott asked Edd Craft whether Lamar Craft had any legitimate business in the bar after closing time. Edd Craft answered that to his knowledge, young Craft had no "right, title, or interest" in Lee's establishment.[10]

Pigott established that Edd Craft had no direct knowledge of the manner in which his son had met his death, again a point that speaks to the broader issue at stake for both men: Craft's attempt, as he would have put it, to tell the story of his son's true killer. Upon learning of the shooting, however, Edd Craft and his family rushed to Rob Lee's bar to learn what they could. In those early-morning hours of April 17, 1951, his sons Wendell, Vennon, and Milo accompanied him, along perhaps with Vennon's wife. Others there, Craft said, were interested friends and law enforcement officers, including Sheriff Marshall Bullock of Walthall County, Vance Harvey, J. C. Hinson, Madge Hinson, Georgie Kilcrease, and Pike County sheriff Robert Lee. Whether or not one-armed Pike County coroner Ray Cain was there, Craft could not recall. Tylertown physician A. B. Harvey, called as a plaintiff's witness, added nothing about the reason that Craft had a bullet in his body, only that he certainly did have one, "that entered on the right side of his chest and penetrated his lung and the big vessels of the heart on into the spine."[11]

These plaintiff's witnesses heard, Pigott moved for a preemptory judgment for the defendant, arguing that nothing so far merited American National's having to pay out double for Craft's death. As Pigott probably expected, his motion was overruled. He then brought witnesses who, unlike Craft's father, might have direct knowledge of what led to young Craft's being found dead on a bed in Rob Lee's bar. James Easterling, one of Craft's two companions on the fatal evening, testified. The other, Oscar Hope, "said now to be working in Wichita, Kansas," was not summoned for the trial. Easterling provided the most detailed, salacious version to that point of the three men's actions and intentions that night. On direct examination, Easterling said they had gone back to Lee's primarily because, according to Charles Gordon, they "knew Hattie Lee Barnes had been left there alone and that sexual designs were held for the negro girl."[12]

On the evening of the shooting, Easterling attended a movie in Tylertown, the "first show," afterward stopping at the City Café to "get a cup of coffee." There, he "run up on . . . the Hope boy." Soon, Lamar Craft arrived. "Somebody made the suggestion we go out and get a beer and we went out and drank beer and little later on drank whiskey." They went to Rob Lee's place in Craft's car, staying until it closed "between 12 and 12:30." At Lee's bar were the three men; Mrs. Lee and her daughter; Hattie Lee Barnes; and only one other customer, "the McCalip boy . . . he was in service at the time." McCalip left earlier than the other three patrons: "I think he was going back to Camp." At closing time, the men helped Mrs. Lee "close the windows and shutters." Rob Lee and Leroy Collins, "this colored fellow," then "come in from the colored place," Lee's other bar. Lee told the men to finish their beer, as closing time was midnight, "and the law would come there checking." Pigott asked Easterling if he noticed a bedroom in the place. Easterling said that he had, but he did not know who used it.[13]

Following a brief detour, said Easterling, they drove back to the bar. Craft "went to the door and knocked and called Hattie Lee a couple of times and called Leroy [Collins] and then he tried both back doors, I believe, calling and knocking and nobody didn't answer." To this point, Easterling had not said why they returned to Lee's place. But Lamar Craft clearly expected Barnes still to be there.[14] Easterling too was aware that "Hattie Lee . . . was night-watching the place." Craft directed Oscar Hope to the front of the building "to watch," while Craft "raised the window," saying that he "was going in there." Easterling begged Craft not to do it: "she has probably got a gun." Undeterred, Craft asked Easterling to hold open the window as he climbed inside. "He got just inside the window," said Easterling, "and was sitting on the window sill when the gun was fired." Said Easterling: "When the shot was fired, he grunted when the bullet hit him and he kinda fell forward like that (indicating) and the blood shot from his mouth, and that is when I caught him by the arm and called his name. He was bent over like this (indicating) sitting in the window. Well, he was falling forward then. About that time the second bullet was fired." What happened, then, asked Pigott? Easterling replied, "I run." Both Easterling the window-holder and Hope the lookout ran at the sound of gunfire, each one around a corner of the building, with the two men meeting on the side of the building. They continued to run "through the woods and out to the highway and up to Mr. McCalip's." Taking a cab to the McComb police station, the two men made their report. "They knew the place," he said.[15]

Breed Mounger then cross-examined Easterling. Like Pigott, Mounger represented a party in an insurance suit. Also like Pigott, he worked to construct a broader narrative of the shooting. He was counsel for the Craft family's interests, and their primary interest was to show that the story of Hattie Lee Barnes killing Lamar Craft was fiction. Mounger wished to demonstrate that Easterling was lying about fundamental matters. To begin with, even Easterling's current New Orleans residence was telling. Mounger asserted that Easterling had fled Mississippi after 1951. Just as important, Easterling's inconsistent accounts indicated a man attempting to hide the truth. Why, for instance, could not Easterling give a precise time of Craft's shooting? Why had he "carefully avoided" such specifics? But Easterling did not yield. He could not say at what time Craft was shot or when he called a cab because he was not wearing a watch and did not inquire of anyone about the time.[16]

The truth, continued Mounger, was that Easterling's account was a "story" that he and Hope "pre-arranged." Easterling replied, "We didn't arrange anything." Mounger countered that perhaps Easterling and Hope worked during that entire evening back in April 1951 to stage a scene in which Craft would be found dead in Rob Lee's bar. Otherwise, there was something highly improbable in Easterling's story that he and Hope had watched their friend shot and waited for him to die without calling a doctor. Again, Easterling disagreed, saying that they had not waited for anything but instead had fled the scene, a story that is credible, even if it does not shed the best light on Easterling and Hope. "You mean to tell the jury," continued Mounger, "that you left a friend with blood spurting from his mouth and it never occurred to you to call a doctor to him?" Easterling replied, "I am afraid so, yes, sir." Mounger insisted that this story was a fiction, one that Easterling, and probably Hope as well, were telling at the behest of someone else. In fact, he said, Easterling had gone to the police because that is where "they were told to go," a suggestion that Easterling again denied.[17]

Also questionable, said Mounger, were Easterling's shifting accounts of why the men had returned to Lee's bar. Easterling countered that the return trip was "to see Hattie Lee Barnes" and "that has always been my story." Mounger disagreed, saying that Easterling once told him, Edd Craft, and others that he had no idea for the reason for the return to the bar, unless it was "to get merchandise," probably whiskey. Here, Mounger refers to his 1951 investigations into the shooting, if not specifically to the meeting in his Tylertown office. "It has been so long I don't remember," admitted Easterling. Reminded that he had once testified that he knew no purpose for the return trip, Easterling agreed that had once been his story. Mounger remained suspicious of why that story had changed.[18]

Easterling now said that prior to this trial, he had not revealed the true reason for the return visit—not at the 1951 Pike County inquest, hearing, or trial of Barnes. Why, asked Mounger? "After Lamar was killed," replied Easterling, "I wasn't going to tell it why he went back." Craft had returned to Lee's place "to see Hattie Lee Barnes." He knew that because Craft told him so. Again, Mounger pressed him, explaining to the jury that Easterling's statements about the return to the bar and the shooting had changed over time and in the presence of different people; that they were flatly contradictory; and that these obfuscations attempted to conceal the real story. In fact, maintained Mounger, Lamar Craft was not shot at Lee's place by Barnes at all. He had been shot dead elsewhere and his body brought to Lee's place to shield the actual killer's identity.[19]

Easterling stood his ground. Whatever he might have said previously, the men had not returned to Lee's place to steal alcohol, gambling equipment, or anything else. Lamar Craft climbed through that window because he intended to have Hattie Lee Barnes. Mounger stayed on Easterling, returning to the 1951 interrogation that Mounger conducted in his law office. There, said Mounger, Easterling told those men that "Lamar Craft was not killed at Rob Lee's place."

Easterling said he had not said that. Mounger pressed him: "I will ask you if you were not asked by me, 'Easterling, for God's sake tell the truth about this thing,' and then you looked at Mr. Craft and said, 'Mr. Edd, I can tell you this, he wasn't killed at Rob Lee's place.'" Again, Easterling insisted that he had never said such a thing.[20]

Undeterred, Mounger said that Easterling, after that conversation with Mounger and the Crafts, came up with a different story, and "that is the story you have gotten by with" or "part of the story after Lamar Craft was killed." Easterling's real aim, Mounger suggested, was to conceal the role of Rob Lee in the killing. "It is funny," said Mounger, "that you are assuming the same condition told by Rob Lee." Joe Pigott objected, noting that no one knew exactly what Rob Lee had to say, for Rob Lee had refused to testify about anything, even at his own trial for shooting Hattie Lee Barnes. While Mounger and the Crafts did not have Rob Lee on the stand, they maintained that Easterling had shaped a story to serve Lee's interests.[21]

Joe Pigott continued to build a story of his own, one about the reason the Crafts wished to avoid the truth. Pigott asked Easterling to elaborate upon a point. For what purpose had Craft wished to "see" Barnes? Easterling replied, "He said he was going in there to have sexual intercourse with her," a sanitized but believable statement. In response, Mounger continued to pick at Easterling's story, suggesting that he had helped clean up the bloody mess at Lee's place; that he had a share in some unidentified sum of six hundred dollars, seemingly taken from Craft's body; that the entire story now had been "rehearsed"; and that he and Hope had left a bleeding Craft at Lee's place, whether he had actually been shot there or not, summoning a cab rather than a doctor because they wanted to ensure that Craft died of his injuries before help arrived. Asked to explain his failure to tell McCalip, at whose house he and Hope asked to use the telephone, that someone had been shot and why he would not have used that telephone to call a doctor instead of a taxi, Easterling replied: "I don't know. Like I said, I was scared."[22]

Easterling's entire testimony, asserted Mounger, was bought and paid for. Again, Easterling disagreed; he was testifying only because he had been summoned. What he said, he insisted, was the truth. Why, then, continued Mounger, had Easterling offered varying statements about the men's return trip to Lee's place? What precisely had Craft said to him as he prepared to enter the building? Easterling repeated that he had warned Craft not to enter the building but that Craft said, "I am going to screw the Negro girl," a statement that seems closer to the mark than the one Easterling gave to Pigott. An exasperated Mounger replied: "Now are you finally fixed? Is that what you are going to say? Is that the end of it?" Replied Easterling, "That is all he ever said to me." Easterling concluded: "Mr. Mounger, I wasn't coming out in plain words and say it until I was forced to." But you lied several times, rejoined Mounger. "No, sir," replied Easterling. "I tell you the reason why I didn't tell it. The truth is after the boy was killed I didn't want to tell the reason he went back . . . He had a good name, that is the reason I didn't tell exactly why he went back there." Mounger said, "And that is it, is it?" Said Easterling, "That is all I can tell you."[23]

Testimony concluded, Joe Pigott again moved for a directed verdict on behalf of American National. Lamar Craft had met his death while "forcibly breaking and entering" Lee's place, "with the intent to commit a crime therein," thus negating the required payment of the double death benefit. Unlike his successful appeal to Judge Brady in 1951 for a directed verdict in Hattie Lee Barnes's trial, this time Brady disagreed. Judge Brady explained that no one knew—so far as the evidence presented here had shown—who shot Craft but that he had died of a bullet to the chest, "accidental means." As to Pigott's assertion that Craft had been killed under conditions that negated the double indemnity clause, even if he were attempting to have "unlawful intercourse" with Barnes, that itself did not constitute a felony "under our law." Of Easterling's statements, Brady noted that "there is considerable evidence that this witness's statements with reference to what transpired [at Lee's place] are conflicting." It was not, however, the duty of plaintiff Edd Craft to prove that his son had not been engaged in illegal activities but rather the duty of the insurance company to prove that he had been. So far as the court was concerned, the insurance company had not made that case. Lamar Craft had not, speaking strictly, been engaged in a statutorily prohibited occupation, such as, for example, the illicit trade in intoxicating liquor. No one proved that Craft went into the building attempting to steal anything. "Though it is a close case," admitted Brady, still it remained "a question of fact for the jury."[24]

The jury of twelve white men considered the evidence and decided that whatever Lamar Craft may have done on that evening of April 16 and 17, 1951, there was no legitimate reason to deny his family the accidental death benefit. On August 12, 1953, the court ruled in favor of Edd Craft, ordering the payment of $2,000, as Craft requested. The jury also awarded Craft the costs of the suit. Two days later, Joe Pigott moved for a verdict in favor of his client "notwithstanding the jury's verdict" and moved also for a new trial. Both motions were denied. Pigott then filed notice that American National intended to appeal to the Mississippi Supreme Court.[25]

In 1955, the Mississippi Supreme Court overruled the lower court's decision, deciding for American National on the grounds that "the plaintiff [Edd Craft] had the burden of proving that the death was accidental; and presumptions must yield to the proof, if it is to the contrary." Why was Craft killed? "To prevent the commission of burglary, which is a felony." Further, they held that "Hattie Lee Barnes was the only person seen in the tavern at the time; and if she, under the circumstances, killed the deceased, his death was not accidental within the meaning of the accidental death clause in this policy. In addition, because of his criminal conduct, the benefit was expressly excluded. The imminent danger of a great personal injury to Barnes afforded justification for her to fire the fatal shot."[26] Despite Edd Craft's best efforts, then, the Mississippi Supreme Court seemed convinced that Hattie Lee Barnes had shot Lamar Craft. And now twice, in her own criminal trial in 1951 and in this Mississippi Supreme Court decision in 1955, Mississippi courts said that Barnes, an African American woman, had the right to defend herself with lethal force.

Edd Craft filed this lawsuit to show for the record that his son had not been killed while trying to sexually assault a Black woman. Instead, Easterling's testimony, including his explanations for his initial reluctance to tell the truth, accomplished just the opposite. Edd Craft wished to believe and Breed Mounger argued that Easterling's hesitations and shifting accounts were an attempt to protect someone, surely Rob Lee. Craft said that in 1951 in Breed Mounger's office, he directly asked Easterling what happened to his son. According to Craft, Easterling "wrinkled up his face and looked down. He wouldn't look at me."[27] Craft was convinced that Easterling was lying or ashamed or both. Craft was right. Easterling's hesitation then and later to tell the full story did stem from his desire to shield someone from public scrutiny. But that person was not Rob Lee or even himself but instead Easterling's friend, Lamar Craft, the boy with the "good name," as Easterling told Breed Mounger.

8

HATTIE LEE BARNES AND THE *McCOMB ENTERPRISE-JOURNAL*

BY AUGUST 1953, the main elements of this larger story were resolved, with Hattie Lee Barnes acquitted of murdering Lamar Craft; Rob Lee and Walter Watson convicted of attempting to murder Barnes; and Edd Craft's lawsuit against American National still on appeal but having failed in its larger purpose of clearing his son's name. Other fundamental matters were not settled. Barnes remained in jail, charged with no crime; the State of Mississippi might need her should Rob Lee be tried for Lamar Craft's murder, so there she waited. The Barnes case had long interested reporter Charles Gordon and the *Enterprise-Journal.* In the late summer of 1953, however, that work went beyond covering the story. For Gordon, and for his editor Oliver Emmerich, the matter became one about fairness and the rule of law. They advocated Barnes's cause in the strongest possible terms. Few Mississippi newspapers of that era did more to demonstrate that injustice was being done by area authorities to an African American, particularly one who said that she killed a white man. Without the work of Emmerich and Gordon, Barnes might have languished in jail indefinitely. But with their help, and that of a group of McComb citizens, she was eventually a free woman.

In September 1953, Oliver Emmerich took up Barnes's case in his daily sidebar column, "Highlights in the Headlines." Emmerich enjoyed a distinguished career in McComb, dating from the 1920s. He and his newspaper became institutions; by the 1970s he was a venerable figure in the city. But in earlier years, especially in the 1960s, some white McComb residents resented or even hated Emmerich for his coverage of local "racial troubles," as many termed the revolutions of that era.[1] As Ted Ownby notes, Emmerich became "one of a handful of white Mississippi editors who publicized and criticized the worst of his community's actions in opposition to the civil rights movement."[2] Emmerich did not earn the acclaim—or notoriety, depending on one's perspective at the time—that came to Greenville's Hodding Carter, Lexington's Hazel Brannon Smith, or Pascagoula's Ira Harkey. All three of those journalists won Pulitzer Prizes for their coverage of white Mississippi's resistance to the civil rights movement. But not without a cost. For his outspokenness, recalled Hodding Carter's son, the family "lived in a sporadic state of siege." Smith's denunciation of the Citizens' Council and the Sovereignty Commission cost her advertisers and subscribers. By the 1980s, she was bankrupt, and her newspaper folded. Ira Harkey held out for even less time. He left the state in the 1960s. But Emmerich endured, publishing five afternoons a week for decades.[3] While many McComb people might not have liked what Emmerich and his reporters, such as Charles Gordon and Charles Dunagin, had to say about the area's civil rights movement, they read the *Enterprise-Journal.* Few Mississippi editors ran a paper that provided such consistent service, service that in the 1960s helped white people in the community to understand and some perhaps even to accept what they could not change.

Still, over the decades, it was rare for the newspaper to editorialize about an ongoing criminal case. And in the 1950s, Emmerich was generally cautious about community feelings on race, as he had every reason to be. But at Gordon's urging, Emmerich wrote about the Barnes case, carefully at first, but then with extraordinary boldness. Initially, Emmerich said only that "Charles Gordon has developed a chronological report on the case of Hattie Lee Barnes." Continued Emmerich: "The case is an unusual one and there are some who feel that the Negro woman possibly is being denied constitutional rights."[4] Note that Barnes is called a "Negro woman." No Mississippi newspaper would have referred to Barnes as a lady. Many would have called her a girl, regardless of her age. Here, she is a "Negro woman," not a "Negress," another term in wide use in the era. "Negro" is capitalized, a practice not always followed in the *Enterprise-Journal,* although that newspaper was more neutral in its capitalization practice than, for instance, the *Jackson Clarion-Ledger,* for which the refusal of capitalization was very deliberate. But Mississippi habits died hard. In subsequent coverage of the case, even in Gordon's coverage of the story, the newspaper referred to Barnes as a "Negress" and a "negress," sometimes using both spellings in the same story. But just as significant, and more potentially inflammatory, Emmerich referred to Barnes's constitutional rights. Even so, he used indirection: "there are some who feel that," qualifying even that statement with "possibly." Still, for any white public figure in Mississippi to state that African Americans had constitutional rights was unusual, and to suggest that an action of a nearby county court violated a Black person's rights was rarer still.[5]

The "chronological report" by Charles Gordon, as Emmerich called it, appeared a few days later. Running multiple pages, considerably longer than most stories from the period, it put a human face on the case and insisted that readers reflect upon Barnes's treatment, not only at the hands of Rob Lee but also at those of area courts and the law. It also featured the first photograph of Barnes to run in the *Enterprise-Journal* in any account of any element of the case.[6] The photo is a head-and-shoulders shot of Barnes, who looks directly into the camera. Her head is tilted slightly to the right; she wears a determined expression. The story gives her full name by that time: Hattie Lee Barnes Gardner.

Gordon's report is more than a chronology. It is a full retelling, with the benefit of two years' reflection, of events set in motion by the April 1951 shooting of Craft. The story "has become just about unbelievably tangled," leaving anyone trying to sort out the matter "lost in the maze." But Gordon was well positioned to sort it out, "entirely confident he holds, or has access to about as much data on the case as anybody else in the world." Much of what Gordon wrote had appeared in earlier stories, but that coverage had been written under deadline pressure. Here was his chance to correct and flesh out matters that had not been available to him earlier. Nothing Gordon wrote here fundamentally changed either his or Barnes's earlier accounts. But this is by far the most detailed account of the story that would appear in this or any other newspaper.[7]

Of the night of Lamar Craft's shooting, Gordon added a significant detail: "The place is said to have been broken into and robbed a few nights before all this happened." Who had been that robber, or whether Barnes had been working that night, Gordon did not say. But the recent break-in does explain Barnes's use of a gun when she heard menacing noises. Gordon also told readers how newspaper reporting worked. On April 17, "This reporter was called to the Blue & White grill [a McComb café on Highway 51 South] at 5 a.m., meeting sheriffs Lee and Bullock there and being told the events of the preceding four hours." Following up, Gordon wrote his initial story on the Craft shooting. Over the following weekend, Gordon would learn, Barnes was bailed out of jail in Magnolia, taken to Tylertown and interrogated, all in an attempt to make her finger Rob Lee as Lamar Craft's killer. On the afternoon of Monday, April 23, said Gordon, someone called him and told him "to come to a certain place in McComb 'if he wanted a good story.'" "He went," wrote Gordon, "and got a tremendous story."[8]

Gordon's extended story emphasizes two fundamental points: first, Barnes had been moved, held, and interrogated under irregular conditions. Many other Black Mississippians faced similar quasi-legal detentions and interrogations, but few had a Charles Gordon to report that fact. Second, readers who had followed the story since 1951 might have known that Barnes's story about Craft's shooting had been inconsistent. Indeed, that was a factor in Chancery Judge Hewitt's decision in denying her habeas corpus petition. But Gordon demonstrated why, under fierce pressure, Barnes's story had changed. Readers would also have seen that Barnes spoke openly and at length to Gordon, and Gordon believed that Barnes told him the truth. Why, Gordon asked Barnes, had she said at various times, both in 1951 and again in 1953, that she had not shot Lamar Craft, instead implicating Rob Lee? Only because, she told Gordon, "she was 'literally scared to death.'"[9]

Barnes spoke with Gordon that summer of 1953 from the jail cell where she awaited being used as a witness in the possible trial of Rob Lee for Lamar Craft's murder. She told Gordon of her extradition from Arkansas and fresh attempts to pressure her into changing the story she told at her 1951 trial. As she had said in her habeas corpus hearing, she told Gordon that district attorney Barlow visited her in Brookhaven on June 18, producing a handwritten statement for her to sign. Barnes told Barlow that she could not read. He promised to read it to her before insisting that she sign it. All this occurred without her having recourse to any advice, including legal counsel. Barnes told Gordon that the statement read to her did not "say specifically who killed Lamar Craft," but she continued: "It says that they all left the way that has been told many times before. It then says that Mr. Rob Lee and Leroy Collins came back to the joint with the dead body of Mr. Lamar Craft. They put the body on the bed, the statement says, the way I heard Mr. Barlow read it, then had me to shoot through the window." Why had Barnes agreed to sign the statement? "Because I was tired, scared to death and wanting to go back home, as they said I could do if I signed the paper. I signed it." But, insisted Barnes to Gordon, even as she signed the paper, she told the district attorney that she would not testify under oath to such a story and that she would insist upon her original version of events. What Barlow made of such a bold assertion, Barnes does not say. But now he had a document that gave Mississippi authorities the tool that they needed to hold Barnes. To that date, in September, 1953, wrote Gordon, the statement "never has been made available to Hattie Lee's lawyer, nor has it been made public."[10]

In August, wrote Gordon, he and attorney Joe Pigott went to Brookhaven to speak with Barnes. There, both men learned that Barnes had been taken to Pike County. They visited the jail in Magnolia, where they found Barnes, eager to speak with them. She shared a cell with another prisoner, "Alberta (Stringbean) Woods, a Summit negress serving out justice court sentences on morals charges." Pigott asked Barnes why she had not alerted him to her location. Barnes replied that she was "scared to ask" anyone to allow her to speak with him. Barnes told the men that she had not been physically abused in custody and that one southern Mississippi jail was much like another, that of Pike County being no worse than that in Lincoln County, except that in Brookhaven, "I could look out the window, and here there's not any window I can look out of." Nothing that local authorities had promised her about being released was true. She was resigned to remaining where she was, but she hoped that in the next term of court, the case in which she was held might come up, be resolved, and thus lead to her release. She told the men, "Now is when they need me at home," a reference to the fall's cotton harvest in Arkansas. "Since I am not there when they need me, I guess I might as well be here as anywhere."[11]

Her responsibilities back in Arkansas, noted Gordon, did not involve children. She had none, "nor is she expecting any." Barnes said again that in none of her detentions in the case, stretching back to 1951, had she been physically mistreated—other than being held against her will, without clear charges, and without the ability to consult her attorney, one should add. But there had been some close calls. In Brookhaven, for instance, Barnes raised the ire of a deputy when she contradicted his statement to a white woman visiting the jail that Barnes was being held there "for murdering a white man." In retaliation, the deputy moved her to an upstairs cell where she "did not have a light at night."[12]

Gordon wished to ask her one more question. Unlike practically every other person to whom Barnes spoke, Gordon advised her that she did not have to answer him or anyone else "until she was in a lawful court." He asked, "Who killed Lamar Craft?" Barnes replied without hesitation, "I did." That was what happened, Barnes affirmed, and she would say so in any forum, whether "before a grand jury, in open court, or anywhere else, 'because it is the truth.'" And it remained the truth, said Barnes, no matter what statements she might have signed. Barnes gave this interview before five men: Gordon himself; Joe Pigott; the jailer; a deputy sheriff; and a white prisoner. The story she told them was consistent with what she said when not under duress: she alone had shot Lamar Craft. The next term of court did not open until October 5, 1953, when a grand jury would set to work. There was the strong possibility, then, that Barnes would continue to be held for at least another month. "What happens next," concluded Gordon, "is anybody's guess."[13]

By anyone's measure, the *Enterprise-Journal* then moved from straight reporting to advocacy of Barnes. Prompted by Gordon's "chronological account," editor Oliver Emmerich wrote two fierce editorials in the late summer of 1953, both setting the case in contexts that he was certain readers would appreciate. The headline of the first one: "An Invitation to Federal Civil Rights Legislation." Having grabbed the reader's attention, he explained: "Mississippians have many things of which they can be rightly proud. And a few things of which they can rightly be ashamed." One of those things, wrote Emmerich, was the jailing of Barnes. Emmerich did not use her name, instead referring to "a Negro woman." Still, Emmerich's position was clear: "June, July, August, September—a long time to be jailed without a crime charged against the confined."[14] He also twice noted the "obviously prohibitive" bond under which Barnes was held. He framed his complaint as a matter of ideals and practicality. "The constitutional rights of every citizen must be respected if law and order is to prevail in this nation." If Mississippi were not careful, this case could damage things that local people prized as much as they did their constitutional rights: the ability to maintain Jim Crow. "This is the kind of thing," wrote Emmerich, "that prompts men such as Senator Hubert Humphrey to go up and down the nation decrying the affairs of the South . . . Mississippi is playing into the hands of the radical element of American politics." Emmerich noted the reaction of one local man, no doubt a white man, who said, "I shudder when I read such a thing because I know that the same thing could happen to me." One may be allowed to doubt whether this precise thing might have happened to a white man in Pike County, but the point is effective. This breach of constitutional rights, explained Emmerich, had happened not in some "distant land, but right here in Pike County, Mississippi."[15]

A few days later, in an even stronger editorial, published on the newspaper's front page, Emmerich set Barnes's case against one that had in fact happened in a distant land. He recounted the story of an Associated Press reporter who had been "thrown into a jail cell without having committed a crime" in Czechoslovakia, "behind the Iron Curtain." "The Finger of Condemnation," the headline of the editorial thundered, "Is Pointed at You." Emmerich's editorial is a tour de force on the primacy of the law, the responsibility of the press, and the duties of citizens in a land where people like to say, "Glory be to the flag of our Nation, our Constitution and all for which the flag stands and which the Constitution upholds." But Pike County, said Emmerich, should be ashamed to congratulate itself on its difference from Communist countries while "keeping a Negro woman behind iron bars . . . the sunlight dimmed before her eyes because there is not as much as a window in her cell." Like the reporter held in Czechoslovakia, Barnes "lingers in a jail cell, not because she has committed a crime but because the state feels it expedient to keep her in confinement." Such action, insisted Emmerich, was both morally wrong and a betrayal of basic American values. Citing Scripture, a powerful argument in the eyes of his readers, Emmerich called Barnes's confinement the "beam" in our eye, compared with which the "mote" in the Communist eye was relatively insignificant.[16]

"Write this on your own conscience," concluded Emmerich. "Every citizen who permits a person to unjustly linger in a dungeon-like cell in this country without voicing objection is just as guilty as any man or woman who permits such injustices behind the Iron Curtain. Think this over when you utter your end of the day prayer to God tonight." Emmerich's setting of the Barnes case in the context of the Cold War was audacious. Few public issues, other than the defense of racial segregation, were as visceral as the opposition to Communism. For Emmerich to say that holding Barnes was equivalent to a Communist government's detention of a reporter was a striking rebuke of the legal system of the area. Of all the editorials that Emmerich wrote on local matters over decades, few were more overtly critical of a basic local ideal and institution. Few pointed out so directly the degree to which racial injustice depended on the participation of local white people. Within a few years, it would be a real risk for a Mississippi newspaper editor who wished to keep his paper operating to be so boldly critical of such a fundamental matter.[17]

The writing of Gordon and Emmerich supplies one of those instances in which the press pricked the conscience of a community and goaded its members to quick, positive action. On September 15, Charles Gordon reported that McComb citizens had formed a committee to raise the $2,500 bond set for Barnes. She had been jailed for well over three months as a potential "material witness," although it still was not clear if Rob Lee would stand trial in the next court session, scheduled for October. "A group of white citizens of McComb," wrote Gordon, "planned today to go into action in the case." They were "aroused," he said, "by the seeming injustice of the continued holding in jail under so large a bond a woman who was tried and swiftly cleared of the only serious charge ever made against her." First, the group planned to petition Chancery Judge Hewitt to reduce the bond. In the meantime, they would solicit pledges of small donations. When a sufficient amount had been promised, trustees of the pledged fund would sign the bond for Barnes. The trustees asked for pledges or donations of either five or ten dollars. Accompanying Gordon's story was a "Hattie Lee Barnes Trust Fund Coupon." The coupon listed Mrs. Frank Stickney and Mrs. T. D. Magruder as trustees, with a local post office box address to which pledges or donations should be sent. Both Gordon's story and the coupon advised readers that monies would be returned should the bond be satisfied, or insufficient funds raised.[18]

For local people to raise money on behalf of an African American woman was itself not rare. White McComb congratulated itself then and later for its benevolent acts toward "colored neighbors," as Christmastime notices of goodwill usually put it. But this was a different matter, and not a simple instance of paternalistic white charity. This act challenged the basic fairness of the court's holding Barnes under these circumstances. To organize as "white sympathizers" of Barnes, as Gordon's reporting put it, was thus at least an implicit criticism of the system of local justice. That coupon and solicitation ran in the McComb paper for three days, and by the third day a great deal had happened. On Wednesday, Joe Pigott filed a motion with Judge Hewitt to reduce Barnes's bond from $2,500 to $500, noting that she would still pursue her habeas corpus appeal to the Mississippi Supreme Court. Hewitt ruled favorably on the bond reduction motion that day. By Thursday, then, it appeared as if Barnes would soon be out of jail. The campaign had raised practically all the $500 for the newly reduced bond. That sum, reported Gordon, should be ready in cash to present to the sheriff by Friday morning.[19]

By Friday, Barnes was indeed out of jail. Thanks to Gordon's reporting and Emmerich's slashing editorials, the case had drawn attention outside the area. Even a Canadian newspaper ran a UP wire service report that on Friday, Barnes, "a former Negro barmaid," had thanked "100 prominent citizens" who contributed to her bond fund. That story included a detail that Gordon's previous stories had not: the drive had been headed by Tom Magruder, head of the local Chamber of Commerce. His wife, then, was the Mrs. T. D. Magruder to whom funds were to be sent.[20] The *Jackson Clarion-Ledger* covered Barnes's release as well, adding, as one might expect of that paper, that Barnes was "an illiterate Negro woman."[21]

That evening, Friday, September 18, 1953, Hattie Lee Barnes left McComb by bus, certainly from the Greyhound station in downtown McComb, later the scene of a visit by Freedom Riders in 1961. She was free, her reduced bond of $500 "arranged by white friends she probably never heard of before," wrote Gordon. The cause for which she had long been held, as a "material witness" in a potential trial of Rob Lee for the murder of Lamar Craft, was felt by "many observers," according to Charles Gordon, to have "little chance of ever amounting to much." Where precisely she intended to go, Gordon did not say, but one can presume that she wished to be back in Arkansas with her husband. Before leaving, Barnes promised that she would return for the October term of court should she be needed as a witness.[22]

By September, Gordon's coverage of the case had drawn even more attention. Russell Lord, editor of the Maryland-based quarterly *The Land*, wrote to the *Enterprise-Journal*, calling Gordon's reporting "one of the most amazing news pieces, and one of the most competently-handled, that I have read for years." Other Mississippi readers similarly wrote to the paper, congratulating it and the people of Pike County who had taken up Barnes's cause. A Biloxi physician called efforts to raise bond for Barnes "a splendid gesture of sympathetic feeling for an unfortunate human being." A Greenwood man praised Emmerich's advocacy of "Justice and Humanity," recommending it as a model for all white Mississippians: "If more of the decent law-abiding, justice loving white people would go to the aid and rescue of Negroes, in many cases the crime would be lessened and the white man's financial burden would be reduced," a peculiar lesson to have drawn from the Barnes case.[23]

On September 7, 1953, the Pike County Board of Supervisors tied up loose ends from that county's involvement in the custody of Barnes. They approved the payment of $26.40 to Sheriff W. E. Moore for transporting Barnes from Brookhaven to Magnolia, and $65.00 to the Lincoln County sheriff for feeding Barnes for sixty-five days.[24] In October 1953, the fall term of the Pike County Circuit Court came as scheduled, beginning with the work of the grand jury. That body returned thirty-two "true bills" on a variety of cases large and small. But the indictment of Rob Lee for the murder of Lamar Craft was not among them. However, "it was said on good authority that the grand jury did investigate the affidavit," which had been filed earlier in the summer by district attorney Barlow. With the failure of the grand jury to return an indictment, Lee's bond of $7,500, on which he had been free all summer, "was nullified." True to her word, Hattie Lee Barnes returned to Pike County once again to tell her story. With no one to pressure her, she gave precisely the same account that she long insisted was true. She herself had fired two shots at a figure in the window of Rob Lee's tavern; she herself had shot Lamar Craft. With the grand jury's decision not to return an indictment against Lee, Barnes's $500 bond, the cause of so much grief for her through the summer of 1953, "was destroyed."[25]

But Barnes was not entirely finished with the legal system of Mississippi, nor it with her. Her action against the Pike County sheriff on her habeas corpus appeal was proceeding, scheduled to be heard by the Mississippi Supreme Court on December 7, 1953.[26] By October 27, however, with Barnes freed from custody, her bond dismissed, and the case against Lee having failed to materialize, the habeas corpus appeal was a moot point. The state Supreme Court sustained a motion to dismiss Barnes's appeal.[27] In a final act of reckoning, strictly speaking, the next meeting of the Pike County Board of Supervisors approved a payment of ten dollars to Barnes, perhaps a per diem for her appearance before the grand jury.[28]

In early 1954, Charles Gordon, compiling a list of top area stories for 1953, ranked the Barnes saga as the year's third-most important, that low in part because it had been a continuing story since 1951. In a brief postmortem on the case, Gordon would not retell it: "it took me 15 14-inch pages of typing paper the last time." But his newspaper "can always point with pride to the leading part it played in helping out a negro girl who had few other friends when we began making public the facts of her outrageous incarceration." Still, continued Gordon, "If Hattie Lee Barnes were a white girl, and these things had happened to her, the whole Lamar Craft death story could be worked into a reporter's dream of a money-making yarn." But Gordon concluded, with considerable understatement: "On the other hand, it seems safe to say that if she were a white girl, these things—nearly all of them—wouldn't have happened to her."[29] Gordon is certainly correct on both of these points, especially the latter.

In the spring of 1954, Rob Lee's appeal to the Mississippi Supreme Court of his conviction and ten-year sentence for shooting Barnes was denied. Lee maintained that he had not received a fair trial because of "prejudice of the trial judge."[30] Justice J. G. Holmes, writing for the court, held that the proof in the case clearly established Lee's guilt and that the "statements of the trial judge were no part of the record and could not be considered."[31] In reporting the denial of Lee's appeal, Gordon once more bid farewell to the Barnes case, or nearly did so, for over the years he would occasionally return to it. Lee's unsuccessful appeal "may have written a close-to-last period in the long-continued story of Hattie Lee Barnes." As he had done in January, Gordon again spoke to the case as a matter of narrative. "I am frequently asked why I don't make an effort to sell the story," he wrote. "Laziness," said Gordon, and "lack of time." It is very likely that local people did ask Gordon about the commercial possibilities of the story. It is even more likely that Gordon, by no definition lazy and with a family to feed, thought of whether the Barnes story would sell. Gordon expanded upon what he had said earlier in the year: the best reason that the story seemed not to have commercial possibilities was that "Hattie Lee Barnes is a negro girl—and the magazines, radio syndicates, et cetera, do not seem to get steamed up when that's the case."[32]

The sheer complexity of what Gordon called the Barnes-Craft-Lee case was one factor that might have limited its commercial appeal. A reader of a "commercial story" might also have wished for a more dramatic conclusion, such as the death of Barnes, a plot that would have anticipated *To Kill a Mockingbird.* In other ways, though, Barnes was no Tom Robinson, the unfortunate African American character of Harper Lee's novel. Unlike Robinson, Barnes had no children, a useful detail for enlisting a reader's sympathies. Also unlike Robinson (despite his fathering children), Barnes was not sexually neutered. Accounts of April 17, 1951, made Lamar Craft's sexual interest in Barnes abundantly clear. Some readers of the era might have found a story founded upon the specter of interracial sex to have been thrilling; others would not. Perhaps unfortunate as well for Gordon's commercial possibilities was the lack of a *Mockingbird*-type Scout Finch character, a child who learned useful lessons about the changing of individual hearts from Barnes's story. Even if such a child had existed here, those lessons might not have been as easily drawn. This story contained perhaps a less edifying message about community, including the capacity of people with power and influence, such as the Crafts, to shape local justice. And perhaps another message as well, one about the ability of a man like Rob Lee, at the end of 1953 and into the spring of 1954 still free on bond and able to evade punishment for his violence against Hattie Lee Barnes.

9

WHEN THE TRIALS WERE OVER

AFTER HATTIE LEE BARNES testified before the Pike County grand jury in September 1953, and that grand jury chose not to indict Rob Lee for murdering Lamar Craft, she never again was compelled publicly to tell what happened to her at Lee's bar on April 17, 1951. In the following years, however, certain patterns and practices that had been evident throughout the Barnes saga continued to resonate through southwestern Mississippi. Among them were the influence of the Craft family, the work of Charles Gordon, the regular eruption of violence at county-line roadhouses and elsewhere in the area, and the determination of Rob Lee to escape punishment for his shooting of Hattie Lee Barnes. Despite Edd Craft's sustained efforts to identify Rob Lee as his son's killer, the State of Mississippi never again took up the matter. But neither did Lee retire meekly to the state penitentiary to serve his ten-year sentence. Following the Supreme Court's denial of Lee's appeal in early 1954, Marion County sheriff J. V. Polk was ordered to take Lee into custody.[1] But Polk could not find Lee, apparently again in hiding, just as he had been after Walter Watson's conviction for shooting Barnes back in 1951. Once again, Lee's bond was forfeit, his bondmen liable for $5,000 until Lee surfaced and was arrested.[2] As had also happened in 1951, Lee eventually turned up, again in a hospital, this time in Columbia, Mississippi. He was in critical condition due to "stomach hemorrhages," but the state nevertheless took no chances with the slippery Lee, placing him under armed guard.[3] Lee recovered, and in a few days was out of there and in the Marion County Jail. He had entered the hospital on a Thursday, remained over the weekend under guard, and was released on Tuesday into the custody of Sheriff Polk. In jail, he awaited "further court action or pickup by state penal authorities."[4]

Rob Lee did eventually go to Parchman. As inmate #22539, he was processed into state custody on May 1, 1954. But he did not remain there for the duration of his ten-year sentence; far from it. Mississippi governor Hugh White apparently concluded that while attempting to kill Hattie Lee Barnes might have been illegal, it was not the sort of thing that should ruin a man's life. In 1955, then, with a stroke of his pen, Governor White delighted Rob Lee and bewildered both district attorney Vernon Broom and Judge Sebe Dale, whose work had sent Lee to Parchman in the first place. On July 2, White gave Lee "a ninety-day suspension of sentence," the news of which came to both Broom and Dale when they read about it in the Jackson newspaper.[5] The *Jackson Clarion-Ledger* was correct, erring only in reporting that Governor White had granted a "9-day suspension" to Lee, clearly a misprint.[6]

On September 24, 1955, Rob Lee's sentence was indefinitely suspended. "The second leave was granted on the strength of his good behavior while free," generous treatment indeed for a man convicted of attempting to kill someone and with a habit of evading the law.[7] What had become of Lee's confederate, Watson? With no lengthy appeal or ability to skip bond and elude custody, he had been at Parchman since October 20, 1951. And with no effective access to the governor's ear, there he remained. But like Lee, he did not serve his full ten-year sentence. On February 25, 1956, Watson was paroled. One and a half years later, he was discharged. Having had a lengthy taste of Parchman, Watson, whatever he did for the rest of his life, never went back.[8]

Given the favorable treatment that he had received in 1955 from one Mississippi governor, Hugh White, a few years later Rob Lee tried his hand with another one, J. P. Coleman. Lee petitioned Coleman for a "full pardon so that my civil rights might be restored." In the petition, Lee maintained that he had been a "law-abiding citizen" during this period of the suspension of his sentence.[9] It appears that Lee never received that pardon. But in the ensuing years, Lee maintained a low profile, much lower than he had done in the early and mid-1950s. Out of Parchman and back home, Lee seems to have been finished with Mississippi law and courts, and also with the operation of county-line roadhouses.

After Lee and then Watson were formally released from custody, the Hattie Lee Barnes case as a matter for Mississippi courts and other state institutions was finally concluded. For a long while, it disappeared from newspaper coverage, as one would expect, but it also remained a matter of intermittent area discussion and debate. Charles Gordon always remembered. A decade later, Gordon had occasion once again to refer to Lee, Barnes, and the Craft shooting. Gordon's gusto for crime reporting had not diminished. If anything, his eye for vivid detail had waxed. In 1964, he wrote of Wiley T. Bagwell, "a gaunt dragline operator" with a "long, livid scar" that "extended from his solar plexus into the shorts he wore as his only garment in the hot Pike jail." Bagwell had allegedly murdered a companion of his with a "metal claw hammer" after they "quarreled behind the ruins of the old Rob Lee tavern." "Death repeats," noted Gordon, reminding readers what had happened there to Lamar Craft in 1951.[10] That 1964 coverage provided the only photograph that ever ran of the Lee tavern, albeit badly deteriorated, as Gordon noted. The building seems never to have operated again as a roadhouse; but another generation of similar establishments took its place.

True to his word to Governor Coleman, Lee lived the rest of his life apparently as a law-abiding citizen. At least nothing that he did would ever result in a trial or a conviction. If he ever again dealt in the sale or distribution of alcohol, it was extraordinarily low-key. Robert Edward Lee, one of many so-named southern boys, was born in the Buford community, a place now "defunct," in Marion County, Mississippi, on February 7, 1900. By the time he registered for the draft during World War I, he lived in the Foxworth community in Marion County, where he spent essentially the rest of his life, except for that year at Parchman. By 1930, he farmed, working his own land in Marion County's Beat Three. He and his wife were then the parents of a four-year-old son, Glenn. His first wife, Lela Leigh Johnson, died in 1942.[11] Rob Lee then married and was later divorced from Ruth Martin, his subsequent business partner in the two Pike-Walthall county-line roadhouses. In declining health the last few years of his life, Lee came and went from the local hospital and occasionally a Jackson hospital, and then in his last months entered an area nursing home.[12] Lee died in the Marion County Hospital on July 28, 1975. Robert E. "Rob" Lee was seventy-five years old. Lee, an area newspaper circumspectly noted, was "a retired businessman."[13] He left two surviving children, Glenn and Ruth, as well as several siblings. In later decades, an area just off Highway 98 was still locally known as "Rob Lee Crossing." It was still a place for commerce, although not in those years for beer and whiskey but instead for hot biscuits and sausage, and hamburgers and hot dogs.[14] Ruth Martin Lee, Rob Lee's once estranged and then ex-wife, remarried in 1954, to Richard C. Duggan. She lived the rest of her life in the small Walthall County community of Kokomo. She died in 1997.[15] Through all the elements of the Barnes case, she seems never to have been subpoenaed. It is not clear whether she attended any of the trials. Descendants of Rob and Ruth Lee continue to live in Walthall and Marion Counties into the twenty-first century.

Edd Tunison Craft, unlike his son Lamar, lived to a ripe old age. He died in 1989 in a New Orleans hospital. He was eighty-eight years old.[16] At the time of his death, all of Craft's surviving sons lived in Tylertown, except for Milo, who lived in South Carolina. His obituary noted that he was predeceased by one son, Lamar; it remembered Edd Craft as a "retired dairyman" and as a former sheriff. His experiences with the justice system of southwestern Mississippi in the early and mid-1950s had only whetted his appetite to join in, it appears. In 1959, he ran again for sheriff, having not been successful in 1951. In a crowded primary field of thirteen candidates, "the largest field in Walthall County history," Craft won a plurality in the August election.[17] He and Alvin Sullivan faced a runoff in late August.[18] Craft prevailed and took office in 1960. In a development that Craft no doubt did not anticipate and likely did not welcome, his term coincided with the emergence of the civil rights movement in Walthall County. Whereas earlier African American discontent with the racial status quo could have been dismissed by men like Craft, or handled in ways that did not reach outside the county, new developments in this period came via "outside agitators," as white Mississippians began to call them. These developments also took place in a period of greatly increased media scrutiny of Mississippi racial matters. Edd Craft was not the only white Mississippi sheriff to blame civil rights activism on outsiders. Such a presumption was perhaps easier than to face honestly the long-standing local Black discontent with Jim Crow.

In 1961, Walthall County, like other Mississippi counties, witnessed renewed efforts at Black voter registration, assisted by "Negro vote instructors" from New York and Memphis, among other places.[19] Sheriff Craft, along with Tylertown city attorney Breed Mounger and Walthall County circuit clerk

John Q. Wood, were named in a Justice Department complaint that accused them of "coercing or intimidating" Black would-be voters, a complaint that all three men vigorously denied. Specifically, the federal charge sought to restrain Walthall County authorities from prosecuting John Hardy, a Nashville-based worker for the Student Nonviolent Coordinating Committee. Hardy had been charged with "disturbing the peace," a tactic quickly becoming a favorite tool of Mississippi authorities in their attempts to block voter registration and other civil rights activities.

That Justice Department complaint was rejected by US District Judge Harold Cox, a jurist with a habit of viewing civil rights work and workers with great skepticism. Walthall County events followed a pattern that would become familiar over the next few years. Civil rights workers and local activists would attempt voter registration or other activities. They would be met by resistance, often violent and often in conjunction with local authorities. That resistance would sometimes be followed by court action such as the filing of a complaint against local authorities. Judge Cox would hear the case and decide in favor of local authorities. An appeal would then reach the US Fifth Circuit Court of Appeals in New Orleans, which would then, sometimes on a two-to-one vote, as in this case, reverse Judge Cox's ruling.[20] According to the suit, Sheriff Craft had told Hardy, "Don't give me none of your head, boy, or I will beat you within an inch of your life."[21]

Sheriff Craft, like many other public men of his era, was called upon by the state's Sovereignty Commission to provide assistance in their task of checking the civil rights movement in Mississippi. In 1961, a Commission investigator visited Walthall County, where he found Sheriff Craft away on business but also found a deputy who assured him that they were having little difficulty with the NAACP and that on the whole, "the Negroes were displaying themselves in a very orderly kind of way." The deputy assured the investigator that Sheriff Craft would lend his fullest cooperation to state officials in their efforts to keep things orderly in Walthall County.[22] Edd Craft's term as Walthall County sheriff was marked by occasional complaints of violence against African Americans; some of those complaints he attempted literally to laugh off.[23] Not all of Sheriff Craft's activities in those years, of course, involved resisting the civil rights movement. Like other Mississippi law enforcement officials, he continued to chase down bootleggers and attend to other crime and violence in the county.[24]

Edd Craft, like other Mississippi sheriffs in that era, could not serve successive terms. For many of them, that one term in office as sheriff as well as tax collector seemed to provide an opportunity they could not afford to let slip away. In the fall of 1962, a Walthall County grand jury turned its attention to Craft, as well as other area officials, for "laxity, irregularities, and unlawful practices." Specifically, the grand jury's report found that law enforcement officials and justices of the peace had taken bonds or fines without recording or otherwise officially accounting for them. Too, Walthall County was developing a notorious reputation as a "speed trap," with Black motorists and out-of-area visitors being particularly targeted. "We are anxious," the grand jury said, "to see the good name of Walthall County be restored and retained."[25] Despite these irritations, Edd Craft seemed to enjoy being sheriff. He ran again for the office in 1967, one of six candidates. The August primary placed two of those candidates in a runoff election. Craft was not one of them. He finished in fourth place of the six candidates, spelling an end to his law enforcement career in Walthall County.[26] But in Walthall County he remained, devoting himself to his family and to his cattle business until he died.

Over the years, various other members of the Craft family found themselves involved in legal proceedings. In 1962, Edd T. Craft Jr., or "Bill," was arrested in a bizarre extortion plot. Sheriff Craft posted his son's bond. The case contains mild echoes of the Barnes story, in part because of young Craft's use of an African American accomplice, Willie Brister. Bill Craft and Brister allegedly attempted to extort $125,000, a staggering amount in those days, from "a young Pike County farm couple." Craft had apparently written the couple a letter claiming that if the sum of money were not left "under the Bogue Chitto bridge between McComb and Tylertown," then Craft would make public "obscene photos of the young wife." The couple alerted postal authorities, a fake package was placed under the bridge, and Brister, working for Craft, was arrested when he attempted to pick up the package. Like Hattie Lee Barnes many years earlier, Willie Brister while in custody weighed what he knew to be the truth against what seemed his immediate best interests. Why was he at the bridge?, a reporter asked Brister. To retrieve "my little drink I put out the night before," he said. Why had he told the authorities a different story? "When the law's got you, miss, you'll say what you think they want you to say—so maybe they'll turn you loose." Some things, then, seemed little changed from ten years earlier.[27] This scandal did not dissuade Bill Craft from later seeking area elective office. He might have imagined that local people would know him well enough not to hold the matter against him. In 1979, 1983, and 1987, he ran for county tax assessor and collector, an office by then separated from that of sheriff, but he was not successful. He came closest in 1983, when he managed a runoff election.[28]

Charles Gordon would write three more times about the Barnes case, once in 1973, in a column just after the death of Mississippi Supreme Court Justice Tom Brady. Gordon referred to the "minor part" his coverage had played in bringing Barnes's cause to public attention, offering greater praise for Joe Pigott's "battle for what he believed to be the right." Added Gordon, "the case and his work probably did more to open the door [for Pigott] . . . than anything else the lawyer ever did."[29] Five years later, Gordon again mentioned the Barnes case, calling it one of the "landmarks" in his years of covering law and the courts in Pike County. Again, he praised the efforts of "fledgling lawyer" Joe Pigott. Gordon wrote that there still lingered in the area some questions about the shooting, despite Barnes's insistence that she shot Craft: "Many people will contend to the end of time not only that someone other than Barnes killed Craft but also that the fatal shooting took place elsewhere."[30] What Gordon does not specify is who continued to contend that the place of Craft's killing and the identity of his killer were other than Lee's place and Hattie Lee Barnes. Perhaps the Craft family continued to make such an argument. Certainly Edd Craft had done all that he could from 1951 to 1953 to persuade the public and the courts of that scenario. But other than as a face-saving gesture from the Crafts, no other likely scenario or killer has ever been persuasively argued.

In 1980, Gordon reflected for a final time on the Barnes story. He remembered the great amount of ink that the *Enterprise-Journal* had given to his coverage. Gordon said that he had written "millions of words" on the Barnes case, a slight exaggeration. But in all that coverage, in the 1950s and in subsequent mentions of the story, Gordon never said conclusively, for he likely never knew, what became of Hattie Lee Barnes after she took the bus out of Pike County in 1953.[31] Finally, Gordon mused again on the skepticism that still prevailed among some local people about the truth of the case. After his long "summary" of the case appeared, said Gordon, a friend approached him and asked: "I read your story on Hattie Lee Barnes and Lamar Craft and all that. Now, I want to ask you. What has really happened in this thing?"[32] Why precisely the case nagged some local people is unclear. The questions Gordon received over the years do not point to some underlying discontent with Barnes's treatment but instead suggest suspicions that a larger conspiracy must have been involved in the death of Lamar Craft. But at the heart of "this thing," as Gordon's unnamed interlocutor put it, is a matter that for all its twists and turns is not complex: an African American woman shot a white man that she had every reason to believe intended to rape her.

10

THE REPORTER AND THE LAWYER

CHARLES GORDON ROSE EARLY. By 5:00 a.m., having read the Jackson and New Orleans newspapers, and fortified by the first of many daily pots of coffee, he left home on White Street in McComb to begin a workday that stretched well into the evening. As downtown McComb opened for business, one could often find Gordon at the Broadway Cafe, drinking more coffee, visiting, and always listening for a story. Then, at city hall, he examined the police blotter for the night's tally. Arriving at the *Enterprise-Journal* office on North Broadway, he consulted with Oliver Emmerich about that afternoon's edition. After that, he was off again, perhaps to a city board meeting or down to Magnolia when court was in session. In the evening, Gordon might stop by the Blue & White Grill or another local café—for the companionship but also always as a reporter. At his elbow in those days of the 1950s and later was a glass of milk, not alcohol, which he had put aside years earlier.

A driven man, from the early 1940s through the early 1980s, Gordon wrote countless thousands of words about his native soil. He loved the place he came from, but he insisted on knowing it fully and writing about it frankly. Gordon, however, would have rejected the idea that he was a crusader; he was, he frequently said, simply a newspaperman. Even so, for years he told his readers the truth about their community, even when that truth was unflattering. From city elections to local sports to the civil rights movement of the 1960s, Gordon covered everything of note that unfolded in Pike County. But of all his reporting, the Hattie Lee Barnes case he always remembered as some of his most significant work. Like attorney Joe Pigott, who represented Barnes in 1951 and 1953, Gordon's efforts ensured not only that Barnes was heard but also that she was eventually freed from the grip of Mississippi law.[1]

Writing until the end of his life, Gordon's last column was published in the *Enterprise-Journal* on November 9, 1982, just six days before his death at age seventy-two. The subjects of his last few stories represent his broad interests: local history, state elections, literature, and fittingly, one's last will and testament. Buried in McComb's Hollywood Cemetery, on his marker under his name is the notation "newspaper reporter," a title he much preferred to "editor" or any of its variants.[2] Within a month of his death, friends worked to fund a journalism scholarship in his honor at the University of Mississippi.[3] In 1983, Southwest Mississippi Junior College in Summit hosted a memorial dinner for Gordon. The featured speaker was beloved Mississippi writer Willie Morris, whose skills in journalism and storytelling made a fine complement to those of Gordon.[4] In 1992, Gordon was inducted into the Mississippi Press Association's Hall of Fame.[5]

Charles Butler Gordon, born in Amite County in 1909, was one of nine children. His parents, Charles Tucker Gordon and Lucile Margaret Butler Gordon, were longtime Amite County residents. Both are buried in the cemetery there at Liberty. It took Charles Gordon some time to find his calling: "He worked for a bank, a telephone company, a St. Louis shoe company, a Jackson tire service and a Memphis biscuit company before returning home in 1933 because of the Depression and ill health."[6] Back in Liberty, his hometown, he took a job with the New Deal's Works Progress Administration. There, he also began to write regularly for the local weekly, the *Southern Herald*, producing a column, "Taking the Liberty." But his newspaper work had begun even earlier. As a teenager, he covered high school baseball for that newspaper.[7] Now, having returned to Liberty and to journalism, Gordon finally settled into the career that he would pursue.

With the coming of World War II, Gordon moved to the *McComb Daily Journal*, an association with that city that would last, with some interruptions, through the end of his life four decades later. One of his first stories for editor H. Rey Bonney's *Daily Journal* told of the death of a local man, a McComb High School graduate, in the Japanese attack on Pearl Harbor. "Eighteen nations, at the latest count," wrote Gordon with his usual precision, "are at war with Japan." Notes of the decency that would characterize later Gordon's work are evident even in this straight news coverage. He told readers, for instance, that the coming of war would hold up the naturalization process of nearly a half million Italians and Germans living in the United States, among them very many who were "thoroughly American in every detail save name and consequently their luck is very bad."[8] With war tempers running high, journalists of longer standing would exhibit less sympathy.

Gordon's early work also displays the humor and eye for quirky local stories that would be evident through his last column in 1982. But his *Daily Journal* writing in the early 1940s consisted mainly of a daily front-page column, with observations on the war, other items of national interest, and local news commentary. What does not appear is the kind of detailed daily front-page coverage of politics, crime, and other local stories that would mark Gordon's work in the 1950s and 1960s. Still, Gordon's interest in the underdog is evident. In 1942, for instance, he noted horrific conditions on a Florida chain gang.[9] Gordon capped off a professionally significant year of 1941 with equally significant personal news. On November 7, he married Jonnie McDowell, the daughter of Mr. and Mrs. R. D. McDowell of the Smithdale community in Amite County. She had attended the McComb Business College and then worked in Liberty at the local office of the Agricultural Adjustment Administration, a New Deal agency. The couple would have three children: Nancy, Carolyn, and Mac.[10]

Gordon wrote for the *Daily Journal* until 1945, when it merged with the *McComb Enterprise.* Even with a newspaper audience reaching beyond the city itself, a small community like McComb, with a population of fewer than 10,000, could no longer support two daily papers. By 1950, notes Gordon's son Mac, the circulation of the now-combined newspapers was 5,200, not a robust figure, although numbers would improve through the decade.[11] By the time he began covering the Hattie Lee Barnes case in 1951, Gordon was forty-one years old, no longer a young man. He had lived and worked in many places, including Liberty, Jackson, McComb, Memphis, and St. Louis. Never a man with robust health, Gordon had also spent nearly two years in Sanitorium, Mississippi, being treated for tuberculosis. There, he read voraciously, a habit he retained for the rest of his life. Because of the low pay offered by the *Enterprise-*

Journal, which was common among small-town newspapers, to support his family Gordon took on additional work, including freelance pieces for a variety of publications. In Jackson, he had kept the books for various businesses, a practice he continued in McComb. "He could have been a CPA," says his son Mac. Readers of the *Enterprise-Journal* for years could find among the early year's classified advertisements a notice that Charles B. Gordon could prepare one's income tax returns, "evenings and weekends by appointment."[12]

In the 1950s and 1960s, the offices of the *Enterprise-Journal* were located on Broad Street in downtown McComb, close to city hall, the police department, and other sources of news and information. McComb in the period was vibrant, filled with cafés, department and specialty shops, movie theaters, a train depot and rail yards, and churches of many denominations. If a reporter needed to consult a banker, attorney, or automobile dealer, those were all close to downtown as well.[13] Most McComb residents in the 1950s found a good deal to be thankful for, as a generation that had grown up in economic hard times and war was in this period able to enjoy stability and the relative plenty of a robust American economy. Caricatures of the Deep South notwithstanding, most white residents did not think constantly of matters of race. Unlike their Black neighbors, they had the luxury of not having to do so. Social class distinctions were noted in McComb, even if not always a matter of direct conversation. A bridge and railroad tracks separated downtown McComb from "East McComb," a working-class district. But the fierce railroad strike of the early twentieth century was a distant memory. All white children went together to one high school. Like matters of race, social class distinctions in the 1950s were ones that many people in the town could go long without thinking about.

Oliver Emmerich's *Enterprise-Journal* was a town booster; signs of economic growth were an unalloyed good. The paper was also an evening fixture—in white homes, at least—and delivering it became a fondly remembered boyhood employment for a couple of generations. People in Amite County to the west and Walthall County to the east also subscribed. Its reporters went into those counties for stories, and the paper regularly ran columns of news from correspondents there. The newspaper appeared five days a week, with Saturday and Sunday as days of rest, for publication if not for the reporters. A typical issue contained eight pages. Emmerich's "Highlights in the Headlines" ran for decades on the front page's left column. But that material was generally light and chatty. There were also wire-service stories, syndicated columns, editorial cartoons, and a half dozen or so comic strips. Unsigned editorials on the paper's second page provided commentary on local, state, and national issues. Local readers looked to the paper for news about themselves too, of course, and the *Enterprise-Journal* provided it, far more fully than one finds in most dailies today, with story after story on local government, courts, and general community events. One also read of engagements and weddings, of hospital admittances and discharges, of births and deaths, and meetings of local clubs and organizations. Sports coverage was extensive, including McComb High's teams and the area's successful Little League baseball teams. African American readers would have found less in the paper about their schools and themselves, unless they had been charged with a crime.

From 1945 through roughly 1960, when the paper's staff expanded, Charles Gordon covered crime, sports, board meetings, and other matters of city and county government. He essentially decided layout as well as content of the newspaper. He also took many of the photographs that ran in its pages; others were taken by freelancers, including teenagers. Gordon's job was not finished when the day's paper went to press. In the evenings, he checked the office's AP teletype machine to make sure it held plenty of the yellow paper on which the national and international news would arrive, as that content would be needed first thing the next morning. Also at night, the telephone rang at Gordon's house, often as late as midnight. Those tips generated many stories. But Gordon also made regular rounds to hunt for news. For years he sported a haircut that was short even by contemporary standards. Every week he had his hair cut at the Five Points Barber Shop on Broadway near the *Enterprise-Journal* office. The shop was not only a companionable place but also one that supplied news and gossip, so Gordon could often be found at the Five Points even when he did not need a haircut.

John Emmerich, son of publisher Oliver Emmerich, was about twenty years younger than Gordon. At Gordon's death, he recalled the "workhorse" with whom he labored "side by side, typewriter by typewriter." "It was incredible," Emmerich wrote, "how much he knew about everything."[14] Like many reporters, Gordon occasionally presented a crusty exterior. "He was kind of a grouch," remembered Emmerich. "I'm not sure he enjoyed life nearly as much as he should have. He was cynical. He never took any exercise. He abused his body much of his life. But what a brain Charley had in his head."[15] A long-time friend and colleague also remembered him as "an old-time, self-taught country intellectual-journalist."[16] His son recalled his range of activities: "city selectman, school board member, library board member, Lions Club member, and active churchman." But it was in his work as a reporter that Gordon not only made a living but found profound satisfaction. "Being a reporter," he told his son, "was my only ambition in life. It's all I ever wanted to be." Gordon despised pretense in the newspaper as he did in other areas of life. When the *Enterprise-Journal* attempted to give Gordon the title of "news editor" or "city editor," he resisted. "There is only one title I will use . . . 'reporter' . . . There is no finer title, in my opinion."[17]

In the 1950s, Oliver Emmerich gave Gordon a great deal of latitude, because Gordon would have it no other way, and also because Emmerich trusted Gordon's judgment. Despite his heavy load, Mac Gordon recalls, his father never felt overworked. The judicial and political arenas fascinated Gordon. He came by his interest in crime naturally. His father was an attorney in Liberty; two of his brothers were attorneys as well. He also enjoyed covering chancery court, which heard cases of divorce, guardianship, and sanity hearings, among other matters. As he wrote, his son Mac remembers, year after year, and story after story, "he banged away and pecked at [his typewriters] viciously with two fingers . . . [H]e probably typed 60–70 words per minute."[18] Gordon was a keen observer of state politics, and for years offered prognostications not only of winners and losers but also of approximate vote tallies. His predictions were generally close to the mark. But always for Gordon there was the human element behind the news. A colleague remembered: "He knew the actual stories of the incests, hangings, suicides and sordid doings of the real South. He knew the backwoods stories of bootlegging and what a man will do to get a drink."[19]

Gordon's knowledge of what a man would do to get a drink, and what that drink might do to a man, came from hard, firsthand knowledge. Early in his time at the *Enterprise-Journal*, Gordon struggled with heavy drinking and was nearly fired because of it. Emmerich "hadn't fired me precisely," wrote Gordon. "He simply served notice that he was trying to find someone to take my place, and urged me to seek another location."[20] So in 1947, Gordon realized that he needed help. Few resources were available in Mississippi for alcohol treatment. Gordon availed himself of one of those few, entering the state mental hospital at Whitfield. Of that harrowing experience, he wrote a frank, not-for-publication account, "Nine Days in a Nuthouse." With little more than daily insulin injections to check withdrawal symptoms, Gordon and fellow patients received abundant tough talk from the doctor supervising their care. After Whitfield, Gordon simply returned unannounced one morning to work at the *Enterprise-Journal.* Despite his early occasional unsteadiness, in Gordon, Emmerich saw a man with the potential to put himself into harness and produce a five-day-per-week newspaper.

In 1967, to celebrate the thirtieth anniversary of his sobriety, Gordon wrote a column, "The First Drink's the Culprit," which was reprinted in 1972 and again in 1977. Back in 1947, he recalled, "I was a complete and thoroughgoing, if smallbore, alcoholic."[21] After his release from Whitfield, he made his way to Jackson, where he could have, he said, "bought a pint of whiskey in the odiferous men's room of one of the downtown Jackson hotels. But I didn't buy it. I was determined to get home sober, and I did." Gordon's sobriety and good reporting endured for the rest of his life. He followed a profession that seems often to bring hard drinking as an occupational hazard. But his resolve in the matter was firm.

Gordon stood about six feet tall. He was always slender because of his bout with tuberculosis. Gordon's daughter Nancy adds: "He always wore a button-down collared shirt and tie, and usually had a sport coat on, too. And a hat. Daddy would not have worn a ball cap or a knit shirt if his life had depended upon it."[22] Beyond his work, what did Gordon enjoy? "Only reading," his son recalls. "There's no way to even guess how many books he read in his lifetime, but thousands. When he wasn't at work or doing yard work, he was reading. The houses he lived in were always full of books and at times he'd have to haul some to the library to make room for others. He read a lot of fiction but loved long works of history, too. He listened to classical music on the radio from New Orleans. He detested rock and roll and country. He was not an athlete whatsoever—he tried golf when he was in his 50s and was miserable at it." Did he talk with his family about the stories he covered? His son Mac remembers: "He rarely did that at all. I'm sure he and my mother talked about some of the big stories but not to us. He took me to a world of college football games that other kids would die for. At Ole Miss and State, they'd let me sit in the press box with him. I cherish those daylong trips with him to dozens of games."[23]

Charles Dunagin was Gordon's colleague on the *Enterprise-Journal* through much of the 1960s, and again from Gordon's return to the paper in 1978 until his death in 1982. Gordon was "a good reporter," said Dunagin, himself a fine reporter. "We always got along well. He could really churn out copy."[24] The two men covered some of the most eventful years of the town's history. Gordon, Dunagin, and the *Enterprise-Journal* provided full, honest accounts of the civil rights movement and the violent backlash against it in McComb in 1961 and again in 1964. That spring, they reported the bombing of NAACP leader C. C. Bryant's barbershop in the Baertown section of town, an opening salvo in a summer's worth of terroristic activity, facts that some area white readers wished not to face.[25] However, Gordon recoiled from the idea that he was a do-gooder. In a letter to Oliver Emmerich, he wrote: "I am not a Negro hater in the sense that many of your and my friends in this section are. Neither am I a crusader for the 'Negro cause.' I have no intention of becoming either."[26] The contrast that Gordon establishes here reflects his sense of what a reporter ought to do: avoid extremes and advocacy, strive for a middle position, and report the news. Especially in such correspondence with his editor, he would have shied away from any suggestion that he was not an objective reporter.

Throughout his career, Gordon was objective in the sense that he gathered facts and wrote about matters honestly. But sometimes he did practice advocacy on behalf of people such as Hattie Lee Barnes who were treated unfairly, as he saw it, by powerful people and institutions. His work never aimed at a systematic critique of racial segregation in Pike County. As a busy daily reporter, he would not have seen that task as his responsibility. What did Gordon really feel about segregation itself? Again, he would not have seen the pages of the *Enterprise-Journal* as the forum in which to air his own convictions. Nevertheless, his coverage of crime and the emerging civil rights movement in McComb in the 1950s and 1960s explored contemporary institutions and local practices in ways that compare favorably with that of any other small-town Mississippi reporter of the era. At a time when some newspapers downplayed or even attempted to ignore the civil rights movement, Gordon and his longtime editor, Oliver Emmerich, told their readers the truth, even when it did not please them, as was often the case.

In the early 1960s, tensions developed between Gordon and Emmerich, as Emmerich hired his son John to help run the paper and then brought in

Charles Dunagin for further assistance. Gordon worked well enough with these men but seems to have resented anyone, especially younger men, who told him how to do his job. On more than one occasion, he threw what he had in his office into his car and left. In May 1968, readers of the *Enterprise-Journal* might have noted Gordon's departure, announced without fanfare. Oliver Emmerich, writing of three recent departures from the newspaper, one for marriage, one for retirement, and the third, Gordon's, because of "personal choice": "Charles Gordon, a reporter of the *Enterprise-Journal* since 1945, has resigned to become associated with the *Picayune Item*."[27] Gordon worked only briefly in Picayune, and then he was on to Jackson, where he covered state politics for the *Jackson Daily News*. By 1978, however, he returned to McComb, the *Enterprise-Journal*, and regular columns. There, Charles Gordon died in November 1982 of pancreatic cancer.

Of the major characters in this story, Gordon might not have been the easiest to know. But of all of them, he exhibited perhaps the most unalloyed record of accomplishment, presented nearly daily to the reading public for decades. In the 1960s and 1970s, Gordon produced columns at a prodigious rate, generally two or three a week. Reading them, one is struck by Gordon's humanistic sensibility, a description at which Gordon would no doubt have scoffed. He shared with many historians an awareness of the ironies of the writer's enterprise. A former colleague remembered: "It was as though Gordon . . . began to see writing, the pinning down of a fact or feeling, as an increasingly impossible task, something that could not be accomplished in anything so limited as sentences or paragraphs . . . But there was to Gordon still that core which sought and groped to pull itself to the bosom of the past—a past that always kept itself one step away."[28] Gordon indeed had a sense of the significance of the area's past, even as he saw living memories of the area die off. Those people's memories, he was aware, were irreplaceable. But Gordon was not simply a nostalgist or celebrator of the common man. Another colleague remembered: "He did not dote on history, or sentimentalize it or worship it. History was just something that was there for him all the time." Yet his writings carried "the veritable soul of the South as distilled in, say, Liberty, Mississippi. For Gordon carried Liberty around with him like an extra heart."[29] At his funeral in the Centenary United Methodist Church in McComb, Rev. N. A. Dickson, who officiated, said of Gordon: "He despised sham. He had no time for phoniness. He had a true sense of modesty." All of this may sound like conventional funeral rhetoric, but in Gordon's case, it seems also to have been fact.[30]

ATTORNEY JOE PIGOTT, like Charles Gordon, put down roots in McComb, raised a family there, and invested his energies in the city's life and institutions. Initially an attorney in private practice, Pigott spent the great bulk of his career as a public official, first as county attorney, then later as district attorney, school board attorney, and finally as a circuit court judge. Also like Gordon, Pigott was a man of conviction, especially during the challenging years of the 1960s. Throughout that decade, a grassroots civil rights movement and changes in federal law forced McComb authorities and institutions, like those in other places in Mississippi, to deal with voter registration, school integration, and the end of racial segregation in places of public accommodation. In public office, Pigott faced demands that consistently seemed difficult to reconcile. Some local people reacted to these developments with calls for law and order; others saw the maintenance of order as requiring a fierce, often violent, defense of Jim Crow; still others insisted on nothing less than full constitutional rights for all local people. When Pigott determined that community beliefs and pressures were on the wrong side of an issue, he risked at least unpopularity, if not his career and his family's livelihood, in saying so. From the mid-1950s through the mid-1990s, his positions were laid out as a matter of public record. Pigott never wrote an autobiography or memoir, but his career can be traced through Charles Gordon's *Enterprise-Journal,* as well as page upon page of the docket books in the Pike County Courthouse.

Unlike Gordon, however, Pigott's career had essentially only begun in 1951, when the twenty-five-year-old attorney was appointed by Judge Tom Brady to defend Hattie Lee Barnes in the Pike County Circuit Court. He took his stand as a young man, then, not much older than either Barnes herself or Lamar Craft. But as a World War II veteran, Pigott, like other men of his generation, had already experienced challenges and shouldered responsibilities greater than those known by many people his age. Adversity, they say, does something to character, either shaping or revealing it. Over the years, many Pike County people, despite their often-spirited disagreements with Pigott on specific matters, grew to respect him. They certainly voted for him. One still senses the legacy of Joe Pigott in Pike County. Attorneys of a certain age, all of whom at one time or another appeared before Judge Pigott, recall him as a firm, authoritative voice on the bench. Walking into the Pike County Courthouse today, one is still in the presence of Judge Joe Pigott. That language is not figurative, however, or even a consequence of the often-repeated stories of Pigott's words and deeds still told there. For in 2017, two years after his death, friends and admirers gathered in Magnolia to unveil a portrait of Pigott, attired in his judge's robes, in the courthouse in which he practiced law for more than forty years.[31]

Joe Ned Pigott was born on October 13, 1925, not in McComb or even in Pike County, but rather in the small community of Cybur in Pearl River County, some seventy miles southwest of McComb. His father, John Douglas Pigott, was a native of Dexter in Walthall County but was born there when it was still part of Pike County. J. D. Pigott, as he was often called, became a longtime area businessman, with interests in Walthall and Amite Counties before settling in McComb. Joe's mother, Patty Lou Williams Pigott, a Leake County native, was J. D. Pigott's second wife; his first wife, Oudia, had died in 1920. Joe Pigott had brothers, Arthur, Charles, Glen, and Jack, and a sister, Francis Jean.[32] Pigott grew up in a stable family of steadily increasingly prosperity and good reputation. A Boy Scout, he was a member of Troop 38, organized in Tylertown in Walthall County. Like generations of Mississippi Scouts, he attended Camp Kickapoo near Jackson. By the mid-1930s, the Pigotts had moved to McComb, buying a house in the Edgewood section of town. There, like his siblings, Pigott would go to school and make friends. In future years, city residents pointed to Pigott as a McComb boy; he felt his interests and identity bound up with theirs. By the fall of 1938, Pigott attended McComb High School. He continued his Boy Scout activities as a member of Troop 129, which met at the First Baptist Church, a church that Pigott and his family would attend for years and the church in which his funeral would be held in 2015. In an early indication of his determination and drive, Pigott earned the rank of Eagle Scout in 1940.[33]

A fine student, Pigott graduated from McComb High in 1942 at the age of sixteen, the same year that his mother died at age forty-two.[34] He had the good fortune in these still hard times to come from a family that could provide for college. Pigott continued his education, first briefly at Southwest Mississippi Junior College and then at the University of Mississippi. At Ole Miss in 1943, he joined Sigma Nu, a social fraternity, an important affiliation at the small school where these fraternities dominated campus social and political life.[35] As was common in those years, his higher education was interrupted by service in World War II. In August 1943, he was one of nineteen young Mississippi men (one of two from McComb) sent to North Carolina State University in Raleigh as part of the Enlisted Reserve Corps—the US Army A-12 Training Station—for officer training.[36] The program was designed for those who would turn eighteen years old during the following year. Pigott was then a sophomore at the University of Mississippi. In November, he returned home for a few days. By the following spring, Pigott was not an officer, however, but was instead an enlisted man. Private Joe Pigott had completed training at Georgia's Fort Benning and had been transferred to Camp Joseph P. Robinson in Arkansas. At Camp Robinson, Pigott received instruction as "an air force demolition engineer" and was "the first to receive wings at Stuttgart Air Field, Little Rock," an indication of parachute, not pilot, training. In the fall of 1944, still stationed in Arkansas, he returned to McComb to serve as an usher at the wedding of his brother Jack, also a private in the US Army.[37]

By November 1944, Pigott had been promoted to corporal. He had also been sent to England in anticipation of European service. Much desperate fighting lay ahead for Allied forces, who did not share our knowledge that German resistance would collapse by the following spring. If Pigott felt anxious about the war or his potential fate, his letters home do not reflect that fact. Describing conditions in England, he wrote: "The people here are right friendly." Like most American servicemen there, he found certain matters confusing, especially their "very complicated monetary system, which is so jumbled full of crowns, pence, and pounds." Among other things, the weather, too, was a change for this Mississippian: "I like it here very well but it is cold and damp." Again like most American soldiers, he was struck by the shortages in wartime Britain: "there is not an abundance of anything over here . . . The little kids hang around us begging for chewing gum, fruit, and candy, of which they seem to think that all Americans have an endless supply."[38]

Arriving in France on the last day of 1944, Pigott's unit, the 289th Engineer Combat Battalion, saw significant action in these last months of the war. They supported infantry through a variety of work, often conducted under fire, including bridge construction or demolition, road construction and mine placement or removal, and the movement of ammunition and other supplies that troops needed as they pressed the Germans toward the East. Along with other American forces, they pursued the German armies across the Saar, the Rhine, and the Neckar Rivers. Because of the fluid, quick movement of American fighting men in those months, members of the 289th also served as infantry themselves when needed; they carried light and heavy machine guns and other weapons. Within a month of their arrival, machine gun crews of the 289th had been sent to support other parts of the American Seventh Army as Gen. George Patton worked to control consequences of the German offensive, the Battle of the Bulge. Because of their action under fire, members of Pigott's unit received multiple commendations, including several Bronze Stars. By the late spring of 1945, various elements of the 289th had seen action not only in Germany but also in Austria and Italy.[39]

With Germany defeated, Pigott's unit, along with many other American troops, prepared for the invasion of Japan. Members of the 289th were in fact on troop ships in August 1945, when news of the Japanese surrender reached them. Then those men, including Sgt. Joe Pigott, came home. Pigott was scheduled to sail into New York in late August 1945.[40] By September, he was back in McComb, where he and the rest of the community took stock of the opportunities of the postwar world. He and several other servicemen were guests at a meeting of the Lions Club, a men's service organization, where they heard speakers address the possibilities of economic development in the McComb area. Pigott addressed the group as well. Described as a "Combat Engineer" who served "with Generals Patch and Patton," Pigott "told of his experiences in France, Germany, Austria, and other European sectors."[41] At that point, Pigott was not yet discharged but was instead on a thirty-day furlough. But soon he, along with millions of other men, was out of uniform and facing the challenges of readjustment to civilian life. For Pigott, that meant continuing his education and laying other foundations for a career.

In the late 1940s and 1950s, Joe Pigott, like many veterans, did not talk much about his World War II experiences. His attention was focused on making a future. By early 1946, he returned to the University of Mississippi as an undergraduate, determined to work toward a law degree as well.[42] The Ole Miss campus in Oxford, like others across the United States, swelled with returning veterans, whose numbers would soon increase still further under the generous provisions of the GI Bill. In 1945, enrollment at Ole Miss stood at just over 2,000 students; by 1947, enrollment exceeded 3,500. Many others were turned away because the university had no way to house or feed them.[43] Like many of these student-veterans, Pigott enthusiastically joined in a variety of campus activities. He was tapped for a business honorary fraternity and ran for student body vice president. That race was competitive, with Pigott making it into a two-man runoff; Pigott won. In the summer session that year, Pigott was named acting student council president, as the current president, in a preview of the rising generation's eagerness to shape Mississippi politics, had resigned that office to run for a seat in the Mississippi House of Representatives. Pigott even spent part of the summer of 1948 away from the Mississippi heat, working at Glacier National Park in Montana.[44] Pigott's interests and activities, as well as his decision to pursue a law degree, suggest a desire to throw himself back into plans that had been put on hold by the war and perhaps also indicate a young man whose focus had been sharpened by his time in uniform.

His years at Ole Miss set Pigott's career on its course, not only through the earning of a degree but also through the friendships made and the practical political experience he gained there. Compared with other state universities, Ole Miss was and would remain for a long time a small school, at which it was possible and indeed necessary to be broadly known, if one wished to achieve campus office or to lay the foundations for business or political success in the state. At Ole Miss, he completed both his undergraduate degree and a law degree; both degrees were awarded in 1949. Along with the Sigma Nu social fraternity, he was a member of the honorary fraternity Delta Sigma Pi; he served also as YMCA vice president.[45] Through the rest of his life, Pigott would display this pattern of settling into a place, making connections, joining service organizations, and working toward what he defined as his and his community's interests. To this point, one could have characterized Pigott as a young man with a habit of getting along, both personally and professionally. No one would have seen him as a reformer, or someone whose tastes were out of line with the bulk of his fellow white Mississippians, including the Ole Miss student body.

After the war and after his college education, Joe Pigott returned home, hoping to make good on his early promise. Despite his Pearl River County birth, Pigott thought of McComb as his hometown, which it had become through ties of residence, church, and schooling. People in the community embraced

Pigott, pegging him as a talented young man and eligible bachelor, well-liked and with a broadening array of civic interests. Before his involvement in the Hattie Lee Barnes case, however, nothing in Pigott's record reflected any special interest in questions of race. Nor was there any indication that he would be willing to stand against community prejudices. When McComb's civic and political leaders, one of whom Pigott may well have aspired to become by the late 1940s, considered local needs, few would have thought that any matter of race or race relations needed special attention. Economic development instead seemed the issue of real importance. But the Barnes case would become a defining moment in Pigott's life, especially in what it said about his character. For in that work, he demonstrated something that would separate him from other contemporary McComb men. Pigott would show that to him the law and leadership amounted to more than a reflection of community interests or a desire to get along for the sake of career aspirations.

In 1949, Pigott joined the McComb firm of Cassidy, McLain, and Alford.[46] By 1953, he had become a partner in the firm, now renamed Cassidy, McLain, and Pigott.[47] Pigott's early legal work, quite limited in 1951 when he defended Barnes, featured none of the drama of that case. In early 1950, for example, he represented the City of McComb in a suit brought to prevent the city from constructing more public housing units. Through the docket books of the Pike County Circuit Court in 1949, 1950, and into 1951, one sees in Joe Pigott a young attorney without a great deal of experience in significant cases, especially ones of criminal law. In those years, however, he had settled into the civic involvement that would characterize his years in the city. He took up Red Cross activities, serving as chairman of the local 1950 fundraising campaign. Pigott also began to explore business ventures as one of two incorporators of the Pike Amusement Company, potentially a movie theater operation. Like many small-town men with an eye on advancement, Pigott was a joiner, by 1950 a member of the Lions Club, soon followed by participation in other church and community activities. A young attorney, and certainly the junior member of his firm, Pigott handled no cases in his first year or so in practice in McComb that drew much public attention. He did, however, showcase his skills on another stage, joining an area Little Theater production, an interest that the Pigott family would pursue for decades to come. In his first area performance, he played a bailiff.[48]

After his work on the Barnes case was over, Pigott married and began to raise a family, all the while solidifying his reputation as a rising young man. On November 22, 1953, Pigott wed Alice Lorraine Holleman at McComb's Centenary Methodist Church, where she had served for three years as choir director. The marriage lasted until her death in 2015. Holleman was the daughter of W. C. Holleman of Hattiesburg and Ruth Holleman of Jackson. She was a graduate of Wiggins High School. A graduate as well of the St. Louis Institute of Music, Holleman had also attended that city's Washington University. In 1953, she taught at McComb High School as head of the voice department.[49] Their wedding received a full page of newspaper coverage, with meticulous description of the music, bride's dress, and of course listings of guests and family members. Neither Pigott nor Holleman came from old McComb families. But the attention to the wedding suggests that his handling of the Hattie Lee Barnes case, whatever else it may have brought him, did nothing to compromise his advancement in McComb or the regard in which city people held him.[50]

But the 1950s also brought less welcome news to the broader Pigott family. Joe's father, J. D. Pigott, and Joe's brother Arthur both had contracted tuberculosis, for which they were treated at the Mississippi Sanatorium. By 1954 both J. D. and Arthur seemed to be recovering, but the father's time there would stretch into a period of several years. J. D. Pigott, the local paper observed, was the father of six children, and despite his extended time away from his family, he had been "a thrifty man all of his life and he was able to provide adequately for his family when he had to give up his job. He had managed to send all of his children to college as they came along," a noteworthy achievement in Mississippi of that era. The four sons who had graduated were "a doctor, a lawyer, an engineer, and a musician." Daughter Jean was then a college student, with the youngest son expected to go as well.[51] J. D. Pigott lived to see his children embark on successful lives and careers, but he did not live long enough to see those lives unfold. He died in 1957 at age sixty-four, still being treated in the sanatorium for the tuberculosis that he could not shake. He had been active in McComb and earned respect in the community. A member of First Baptist Church and the Lions Club, he had also served for several terms as a member and president of the McComb School Board.[52]

By the mid-1950s, Joe Pigott himself was beginning to win election to area offices and organizations. In 1954, he was chosen president of the local post of the American Legion, a position that his father had held in 1941. A year later he was elected to the board of directors of the First Federal Savings and Loan Association. His wife, Lorraine, also joined in the variety of church and women's organizations that marked a family's standing in communities of the era.[53] By 1955, Pigott had added a bit of weight to his frame; he would remain a stout man until the end of his life. He had also begun to wear eyeglasses. He looked every inch a serious, though still youngish, man when he announced his first candidacy for public office, running for Pike County prosecuting attorney, as a Democrat, of course. Memberships in the American Legion, the Masons, the Shriners, the Lions, the Veterans of Foreign Wars, the First Baptist Church, and the Chamber of Commerce attested to Pigott's range of interests. The first of his children, a son, had been born. He had been active in community health drives for the Red Cross, and in campaigns against polio and, naturally enough, tuberculosis. Pigott reminded people of his Pike County roots, noting that he had attended the public schools in Magnolia and McComb, and said succinctly that he had "served with a combat group in Europe."[54] Pigott, then, had produced in less than a half dozen years a résumé that checked just about every box a potential voter might wish to see.

Pigott ran in an open field in 1955, with the incumbent, J. Gordon Roach, having chosen not to seek a fourth term. Pigott's opponent was another young McComb attorney, W. Vaught Lenoir Jr. Lenoir was a former city police court judge. But neither man had previously run for countywide office. In the campaign, Pigott stressed to voters his "mature judgment, honest convictions, and courtroom experience." In the August primary, which amounted to election to the office, as no Republican ran in the fall's general election, Pigott won with just over 53 percent of the vote. That spring had brought other public recognition to the Pigott family, with his mother chosen as area "Mother of the Year," with that citation noting her ability to handle her family's bouts of polio and tuberculosis, as she also helped manage their business interests.[55] Joe and Lorraine Pigott capped off an eventful year of 1955 with the birth of their second child, a daughter, Linda.[56]

As the county prosecuting attorney, Pigott assisted the district attorney in handling a steady load of criminal cases. He would serve in that office until 1963, when he was appointed district attorney after the incumbent resigned that office following his election as a chancery judge.[57] For much of his time as prosecuting attorney, Pigott saw the typical slate of work for the time and place: liquor violations, assault, burglary, robbery, and murder. These years laid the groundwork for Pigott's later career in significant ways. Over time, his work in the Pike County Circuit Court gave him a greater familiarity with the people of McComb, and they with him. His reputation as a steady, reliable man grew. His approach to public life was framed through the lens of the law. His job, as he saw it, was to maintain order by seeing that the law was administered fairly, although in this era that meant accommodation with the fundamental fact of racial segregation. What did Pigott think of the Jim Crow order in which he lived and worked? Unlike some public men of the time and place, he never felt the need to speak—in public, at least—in defense of racial segregation. Nor did he speak out against it. No man who held office in Pike County in the period did. If the justice administered in the Pike County Circuit Court was not racially equitable—and it was not—Joe Pigott nevertheless left a record there as even-handed as one could expect to find from the time.

Then came the civil rights movement of the 1960s. The efforts of local Black people and "outside agitators," as most white people called them, would challenge not only racial segregation but also Joe Pigott's efforts to balance public order, the demands of the law, and his conscience. In the summer of 1961, Pigott was county prosecuting attorney when activist Robert Moses attempted to assist in a voter registration campaign in the area. That campaign was rebuffed through a combination of violence and intimidation by private citizens, as well as various agencies of the law, efforts in which Pigott played no direct role. But Pigott, like most other McComb officials, seemed "caught off guard" when "black McComb began to stir," as historian John Dittmer wrote. Years later, Pigott said, "At that time I thought the black leaders were all ministers." He and others would soon learn otherwise. That same summer, McComb experienced its first café sit-in. Two young Black men, Hollis Watkins and Curtis Hayes, were arrested and charged with failing to "disperse and move on" and also with "conduct calculated to provoke a breach of the peace." Joe Pigott filed the affidavits under which the pair were charged. In October, Pigott was once again in court dealing with civil rights activities. Some one hundred students walked out of the local Black high school and, joined by a score of other protesters, marched on city hall. They were arrested, again on charges of disturbing the peace. And at the end of 1961, Freedom Riders successfully integrated the local bus station, much to the frustration of a large white mob gathered outside.[58]

Through 1962 and 1963, Pigott, as county prosecuting attorney and then as district attorney, might have believed that the civil rights movement had lost momentum, leaving McComb's institutions basically as they were. But the year 1964 would change all that. That summer, civil rights workers again chose McComb for voter registration efforts. And again, some local white people responded with violence. But that summer's wave of organized resistance—terrorism is perhaps the more accurate term—was noteworthy even by contemporary standards. In 1965 hearings in Jackson, the US Commission on Civil Rights noted some thirty-nine episodes from McComb in 1964 of cross burnings, beatings, assaults, bombings, arson, and attempted arson. The city's civic leaders reacted initially with caution or timidity. "Almost everybody," wrote McComb newspaper editor Oliver Emmerich, "was hysterically afraid." By late summer, Klansmen operated night after night with dynamite. Some Black residents prepared for self-defense. No one could pretend that the civil rights movement or the white violence would simply go away.[59]

The bombing campaign of 1964 eventually moved community leaders and area law enforcement to act against local Klansmen; and they acted from a variety of motives. Many, including Pigott, understood that as a basic matter of public safety, the vigilante action must be stopped. Others were also concerned about the damage being done to the city's reputation and business prospects. Many believed as well that if matters were not brought under control, McComb might face federal intervention, a prospect essentially every white resident wished to avoid. By September, Mississippi governor Paul Johnson suggested to Pike County officials that if they did not break the wave of bombings, he was prepared to send in the National Guard. Pigott, working with other area law enforcement agencies, pressed the investigations. People began to offer tips about what they had seen. Eleven men were arrested. The bombings stopped. Almost all the arrested men received suspended sentences, perhaps the best that could have been obtained under the circumstances. As reporter Charles Dunagin noted: "there would have been a good chance a jury would have found the defendants not guilty or mistrials would have resulted." For many years, however, Black area residents insisted that more could have been done and done sooner to stop the violence.[60]

Neither Joe Pigott nor any other white elected leader supported the civil rights movement, at least if that meant immediate, fundamental changes to local institutions. To one degree or another, in the 1950s and through most of the 1960s, they accepted the segregated society in which they had been raised as a fact of life. When evidence of Black discontent with that system became unavoidably obvious in the 1960s, their instinct was to see it as disruptive rather than as a legitimate movement for the redress of long-standing grievances. Along with most other Mississippi public officials in the era, Joe Pigott received questions from the state's Sovereignty Commission asking him for information about local residents who might be involved with the NAACP or other "subversive organizations." In 1961, Pigott answered several of these queries, assuring Jackson that the people in question were "reliable" and not part of any organized civil rights activities in the county.[61] Again like many officials, his reflexive response in the early 1960s was to see his area as sound and basically free of trouble. Once it became clear that there was organized activity in the county, Pigott, like other district attorneys, filed injunctions against protestors.[62] Later still, once civil rights groups had settled into longer-term operations in Pike County, Pigott, like other local people, still tended to think of civil rights leaders in terms of the "trouble" they seemed determined to make.[63] Old ways of thinking died slowly. But through the 1960s and into the 1970s, Joe Pigott saw that change had come to Pike County, whether one liked it or not. And the law was the law, whether it was made in Jackson or in Washington. Unlike some local people, Pigott counseled, demonstrated, and insisted upon obedience to that law.

Reflecting on his work in the 1960s, Pigott said of popular opinion: "You can go along with it, but you can't sleep good at night if you do."[64] Other McComb attorneys in 1950s and 1960s enjoyed a more lucrative legal practice than Joe Pigott. For Pigott, with a growing family, money was always a concern. But in these years, he chose a different path, one that led to hard public responsibilities during difficult times. In the 1960s, he represented the McComb school board as the city faced down the coming reality of public school integration, a development that many local white people simply refused to accept. In that era, the school board attorney's position was an unpaid one, but Pigott viewed it as work that simply had to be done if public education in the city were to survive. Pigott served as district attorney until 1972, choosing not to run for reelection in 1971. After a brief return to private practice, he seems to have missed public service. In 1974 he ran successfully for circuit court judge, Tom Brady's old position, from which Pigott retired in 1992. In the longer term, certainly by the 1980s and 1990s, when he had become a fixture on the bench in the Pike County Courthouse, Pigott had earned from many McComb people something of more enduring value than money: their respect. Upon his retirement, Pigott reflected: "I don't fish, hunt, or play golf. Never had time. All I've ever done is work."[65] That work in the 1960s and early 1970s entailed more risks and more courage than Pigott revealed here. It also displayed his continuing determination to see the law administered through a period of social change that neither Black nor white McComb would have imagined possible when Pigott's career began.

To the end of his life, Pigott remained proud of his representation of Hattie Lee Barnes. "It wasn't a very popular thing," he recalled in 2006. But it was the right thing to do, he maintained. In any case, he said, "I was a single man and I didn't have a whole lot to lose. I could have packed up everything in one suitcase and taken everything I had and skipped town." Pigott's wife, Lorraine, remained proud as well of her husband's determination to go against the grain of popular opinion. Of all his cases, she said, the one in which he represented Barnes "most illustrates his commitment to stick up for what's right in the face of adversity."[66] The Barnes case was pivotal for Pigott, and fortunate as well. Like the work of the fictional lawyer Atticus Finch, Pigott's representation of Barnes brought certain risks. He had no way to know just how inflamed public opinion against her might grow. In the Mississippi in which he had grown up, crowds had killed African Americans for less than Barnes had done. One can imagine scenarios in which his advocacy of Barnes could have ruined him, but it did not. From it, he seems to have learned that he could follow his basic sense of right and wrong and survive professionally. Had Barnes's case resulted in her conviction and execution, Pigott's path through the rest of the 1950s and 1960s might well have been much different. In those circumstances, had she or he been unsuccessful, to put it mildly, some men might have become bitter or cynical. But this of course did not happen, thanks to Pigott's successful resolution in 1951 to see justice done to Barnes.

Joe Pigott's career in law, especially in the public offices to which he dedicated himself, reflects a consistent ability to stand against the pressures he might have faced to do what was expedient for the reputation of the community or for particular members of it. It is not an exaggeration but a matter of fact to say that Hattie Lee Barnes owed her freedom and perhaps her life to Joe Pigott. In the end, what is most remarkable about Pigott's work for Barnes is not a matter of words spoken in a courtroom but rather the truth that he had the clarity of vision and courage to see through contemporary prejudices. He understood that regardless of race, at the heart of the matter was a woman defending herself against a man who intended to rape her. Pigott asserted that if the law meant anything, in Pike County or anywhere else, it had to apply to Hattie Lee Barnes.

11

A RAPE, A STABBING, AND A MORALS CHARGE

THE HATTIE LEE BARNES case shows how race, gender, and social status shaped not only the Mississippi justice system but also the broader structure of life in that time and place. While these categories of identity constituted fundamental social forces, they were not disembodied. Events of those years also establish the significance of individual character, will, and action—of people's decisions made within these contexts and constraints. Other legal cases that unfolded in the area in ensuing years, some of them involving the same actors who figured in the Barnes story, demonstrate the critical window in which that case occurred, and what changed and did not change between the 1950s and the 1960s in Mississippi and the nation. As one of the cases examined in this chapter demonstrates, national attention increasingly fell on Mississippi's Jim Crow system of life and justice, and local authorities knew it. But the operation of law and the courts also display the continuing significance of family, personal influence, and other kinds of power. Even as the civil rights movement began to challenge regional and American institutions, abiding forces, both personal and structural, could continue to compromise the attainment of justice in southwestern Mississippi.

On Sunday, May 13, 1956, four white men, ranging in age from their early twenties to their mid-forties, were arrested for the kidnapping and rape of a sixteen-year-old African American woman near the Pike-Walthall county line, the setting of much of the Barnes story. As he had done then, Charles Gordon reported this story in detail. A significant difference between the Barnes case and this story of race and violence is that from his initial report, Gordon showed local readers that the nation would watch how they handled this one. He noted that the *Chicago Tribune*, learning of the crime, contacted the McComb paper for information. The *Tribune* was concerned that when their story of the incident "hit the streets," "we will experience trouble here." Asked by Gordon to elaborate, the *Tribune* said that there "will be demonstrations among the Negroes and it is likely that some white girls here will be grabbed and assaulted in retaliation."[1]

Significant developments had occurred in the state, the region, and the nation since the 1951 arrest of Hattie Lee Barnes: the *Brown* decision, the formation of the Citizens' Councils, the murder of Emmett Till, an increased national scrutiny of southern racial segregation, and rumblings that Congress might take up civil rights legislation for the first time since Reconstruction. Many white Mississippians resented and increasingly resisted potential threats to the state's Jim Crow order. Most Black Mississippians hoped for change, but they would have seen little indication at the state and local levels to suggest that significant transformation would come soon. But Mississippians became increasingly aware that matters of race and justice no longer occurred under the relative darkness of earlier years. Still, the kidnapping and rape case that occurred in Pike and Walthall Counties in 1956 would also demonstrate that scrutiny by itself was no guarantor of justice. Local courts and other institutions retained considerable power to operate as they had done for as long as anyone could remember.

Charles Gordon told his readers a story that began, like the Barnes story, with white men and alcohol. The four arrested men had been on "a tour" of Pike County "amusement spots and taverns." Driving into McComb, they enjoyed a late-night chicken dinner at a café. According to later testimony, the men "were drinking, but not necessarily drunk." Then they armed themselves with a shotgun and went looking for sexual gratification. Stopping at the house of a Black man, they insisted that he accompany them to a nearby house where a Black woman and her teenage daughter lived. They attempted to persuade the Black man to force his way into that house and bring out one of the women; he refused. Then one of the white men broke into the house, emerged with the sixteen-year-old girl, and forced her into their car. Taking her to a nearby area, several of them, perhaps three of them, raped her.[2]

Alerted of the crime while it was still in progress, Walthall and Pike County sheriffs' departments hurried to the scene. Before deputies could make their way into the swampy area to hunt for the men and the teenager, the victim herself emerged from the woods, "accompanied by four men of her own race." She had "escaped from the white assailant by managing to get the gun and hitting him across the head with its butt," explained Charles Gordon. She came upon four Black men fishing. They accompanied her to the highway to seek help. Two brothers, Ernest and Ollie Dillon, and two cousins, Olen and Duroa Duncan, were quickly taken into custody. As much as any other area case within memory, the kidnapping and rape of the sixteen-year-old drew not only state but also national attention.[3] Local authorities, semi-official and official, reacted. The Board of Directors of the Pike County Citizens' Council met in McComb. Spokesman Gordon Burt Jr., later city mayor, said that the Council condemned "the atrocious incident" and that it "violated every principle for which the Citizens Council stands." He offered the county the assistance of the Council's "legal and judiciary committee."[4] District Attorney Mike Carr of Brookhaven received queries from news agencies throughout the country asking if he planned to seek the death penalty. He cited the relevant statute, which did allow it. All four men were charged with kidnapping; three of them were also charged with rape. Adding that the crime occurred the day before the victim planned to be married, Carr declared: "I intend to prosecute this case vigorously." Carr refused to set bond for the four men, held in jail in the county seat of Magnolia.

The kidnapping had taken place in Walthall County; the sexual assault occurred in Pike County. Responsibility for prosecuting this case would fall in part to Joe Pigott, now Pike County attorney. Both counties were part of the Fourteenth Circuit Court District, still presided over by Judge Tom P. Brady, who had heard the Hattie Lee Barnes trial in 1951. An attorney and judge of authority and standing in 1951, by 1956 Brady was a figure of wider reputation. Just before the kidnapping and assault, Brady prepared to travel to Birmingham, Alabama, to speak to a Citizens' Council meeting on the second anniversary of the *Brown* decision. That trip was prompted by some white southerners' concerns that Black Americans planned to spend the anniversary "in prayer and fasting."[5] In previewing the fall's court term, and especially this case, one that "will carry tremendous significance," the *Enterprise-Journal* described Brady as "author of the well known booklet 'Black Monday,' about many aspects of the current issues between the black and white races, ardent segregationist, and foe of any tendency that might lead toward 'mongrelization.'"[6]

At a Monday, May 28, preliminary hearing in the Pike County Circuit Court, Ernest Dillon explained that he was "too drunk and intoxicated" to know what he was doing, but that he would "take my punishment like a natural man." His brother Ollie, he claimed, had nothing to do with the crimes.[7] Testimony at that hearing echoed the Barnes case and underscored well-established Mississippi patterns of thought. To these white men, African Americans were for their use and pleasure. Neither a Black person's body nor home had a sanctity they felt bound to respect. A "young Negro," Stennis Gatlin, testified that Ernest Dillon came to his house and demanded that he leave with the men. Refusing Dillon's command to break into the victim's house, Gatlin was "sent packing" by Dillon. Another Black man, eighteen-year-old Marvin Williams, said that he was in the house when the white men forced entry. Ernest Dillon asked him where he lived. "In Magnolia," he replied. Dillon instructed Williams to point in that direction, then advised him to "see how fast you can get there." Williams left "on the double." Sheriff A. E. "Bill" Andrews of Pike County testified about his initial encounter with the victim; she was "wearing only a brassiere and had a ripped and tattered housecoat wrapped around her midsection." Ernest Dillon doubled down on his efforts to shoulder the blame, saying that "my brother tried to talk me out of it and had nothing to do with what happened. The Duncan boys didn't have anything to do with it."[8]

Charles Gordon noted that the crime "drew immediate nationwide attention to this locality and high praise to local officers for the dispatch and manner in which they moved to handle the case." The Associated Press filed continuing stories on the case, which were carried in Missouri, Maryland, Montana, Nebraska, Florida, Tennessee, Virginia, California, New York, North Carolina, and Indiana. The *Chicago Tribune* conducted their own reporting. Some of these reports named the sixteen-year-old victim, Annette Butler. News outlets' policies on naming of victims of sexual assault, even minors, were not well defined in the mid-1950s but were far looser than they would become in later years. Gordon explained the use of the victim's name in the *Enterprise-Journal* by noting that Butler's name and photograph had first run in *Jet*, the African American news weekly; that coverage itself stands as further indication of national interest in the case.[9]

On Tuesday, October 2, the grand jury returned fifteen indictments, including four against the men charged with rape and kidnapping.[10] Judge Brady appointed attorneys to defend them. The state's case was handled by district attorney Mike Carr and Pike County attorney Joe Pigott. "The faces of the men," reported Charles Gordon, "were dead white after a Summer of confinement in the Pike jail. Ernest Dillon, in particular, had changed greatly in appearance . . . [H]e had lost considerable weight and seemed almost without animation." In his jail cell in September, Ernest Dillon had cut himself with a razor blade, then decided he was "unable to go through with it," fashioning a tourniquet with a handkerchief. His self-inflicted injuries were not severe. Still, attorneys for Dillon filed a "suggestion of insanity" and asked to have their client's mental health assessed, as he had been "acting queerly" lately; he was sent to the state mental hospital at Whitfield for examination. The other three men's attorneys moved for a continuance until the spring term, partly on grounds that press coverage might prejudice the current jury pool.[11] By early November, doctors at Whitfield pronounced Dillon fit to stand trial, which would likely occur in the next term of court in March 1957.

The *Enterprise-Journal* had been outspoken in its advocacy of justice for Hattie Lee Barnes. In this matter, the newspaper never shied away from coverage of the case. But that coverage displays an awareness, even a defensiveness, about the broader racial narrative of which the story was a part. In Charles Gordon's preview of the spring court session, for instance, the case is placed into a certain context about the racialized nature of crime in Pike County. In the last three months, wrote Gordon, there had been a "large number of killings of negroes by other negroes that have taken place in Pike County . . . In the same length of time, there have been no major criminal events involving members of both white and colored races, and none in which only white persons were connected."[12] Editor Oliver Emmerich, so bold in 1953 in calling Barnes's detention a communist-style policy, was literally on the defensive about matters of southern race in these days. He appeared on a six-man panel in Chicago to discuss southern race relations. His task was to present "the Southern viewpoint." Emmerich's conclusions: "enlightened public opinion in South is not opposed to justice and progress for our Negro people" and the "campaigns of hate [against the South] now being waged in the United States are not conducive to the development of better understanding." That spring his newspaper, like many other southern papers of the day, was studded with stories of Black murderers, the failure of integrated schools in Washington, DC, and the determination of the South to manage its own affairs, so far as race went. Similarly, from its first coverage of this 1956 kidnapping and rape, the *Enterprise-Journal* seemed always concerned with what this case would say about Mississippi's ability to manage white-on-Black crime, especially one involving the rape of a minor. But a consequence of that defensiveness is that the victim here seems less of a human being in her own right than a character in a story about the national appearance of southern institutions.[13]

Separate trials were slated for the four men; they would also be tried separately on the rape and kidnapping charges. Once the trials began, even Judge Brady seemed conscious of appearances. The rape trials, Brady announced, would not be conducted in open court; spectators would be cleared from the courtroom. But such had always been his policy in rape cases, he explained, whether the victim was "white woman or Negro woman." However, the trial of Ernest Dillon did not go off as anyone had anticipated. It certainly did not offer, either to a local or a national audience, a reassuring story of a Mississippi jury handing down the right verdict. In a deal with prosecutors, Dillon pled guilty to a lesser charge of "committing assault with intended rape." Initial charges had carried a possible death penalty. The reduced charges carried a maximum sentence of life imprisonment. "We were ready to go to trial," insisted district attorney Mike Carr. But when the defense offered the plea deal, Carr advised Judge Brady that the state would not object. Carr elaborated, "Our purpose is to see that these men are punished," adding that "when you submit a case to a jury, there is always a jury question involved." The "jury question" is this case was whether twelve Pike County white men would convict another white man of a capital crime against an African American woman. At that time, and probably for a good deal longer, that was a question for a prosecutor in Mississippi seriously to consider. Judge Brady explained: "A man has a right to plead guilty if he wants to plead guilty to a lesser charge, if the state does not object."

Here, the state did not. Ernest Dillon seems to have been the ringleader of the kidnapping and rape. He was also, as it turns out, the only one of the four men to do time in prison. He would probably have been better advised to have taken his chances with the jury.[14]

Attorneys for Ollie Dillon, the brother of Ernest Dillon, filed a "suggestion of insanity" motion on his behalf, the same strategy that Ernest Dillon's attorneys had followed. In this instance, the move produced better results—or at least results that kept him out of Parchman penitentiary. Ollie Dillon, ruled a "schizophrenic," was confined for an indefinite term at the state mental hospital at Whitfield.[15] Olen Duncan was the first of the men to stand trial. The victim testified to her serial rape by three of the men, with Olen Duncan threatening to "cut her neck off" if she did not comply. When Ernest Dillon had initially forced his way into her house, she said, he told them that he was a law officer who was there to arrest her "for sacking up." District attorney Mike Carr's concerns about Pike County juries apparently were well-founded. Olen Duncan was acquitted of the rape charge. An unofficial report of the first ballot said that ten were for acquittal and two for a guilty verdict. After supper and another hour's deliberation, those two men changed their votes to not guilty.[16]

Both Olen and Duroa Duncan faced trial for kidnapping. Both men changed their pleas on that charge from not guilty to no contest. Each one received from Judge Tom Brady a two-year prison sentence, suspended, with five years of probation. Both men had also been charged with rape, with Olen Duncan having already been acquitted of that charge. Duroa Duncan's trial for rape resulted in a hung jury and a mistrial. Duroa Duncan was not retried. Instead, he was allowed to enter a plea of guilty on a lesser charge, "unlawful fornication with a member of another race." For that admitted crime, he received a two-year sentence, suspended.[17] That "unlawful fornication" charge was possible under a 1956 change to Mississippi statute, which made it a crime to have sexual intercourse "with a member of a race to whom marriage would be illegal." Both trials were handicapped by the absence of Marvin Williams, the victim's fiancé, who apparently had fled the state, perhaps to New Orleans, and could not be located. Those pleas and the sentences, wrote Charles Gordon, "brought an end to one of Pike County's most sensational and widely-publicized criminal cases of recent years."[18]

Observers considered how the Pike County quest for justice was playing on a state and a national stage. "What has happened so far," wrote the *Jackson Clarion-Ledger*, "is grist for the mills of the South's critics." Black Mississippians had been quick to draw their own conclusions. At a "meeting of Negroes" of Jackson, one man, a war veteran, said: "When we commit a crime against white society, the trial is speeded while the fever is high, and the sentence is severe. When a white man commits a crime against a Negro, there are delays and the trial isn't held until feelings have died down. The sentences are not severe."[19] However, neither district attorney Mike Carr nor county attorney Joe Pigott attempted to sweep this crime under the rug. Four men were arrested practically as soon as the crime was committed. None of the men were from families, like the Crafts, able to exert much influence over the process. Area white men of standing understood how bad the crime looked. Everyone realized how matters might have played out had the victim been white and the assailants Black. But those local men of power and influence, as district attorney Mike Carr knew, did not decide the fate of the Duncans and the Dillons. A jury did. And to a degree, Judge Tom Brady did.

Circuit court juries represented fairly well an area's white, male population. Their tastes and judgments shaped how they heard evidence and arrived at verdicts. Most—but not all—of them would have denied that they were overtly using the judicial system to deprive African Americans of their rights or to protect white men against punishment for crimes against Black people. But jurors brought to their work assumptions about the meaning of jury service. They understood its tie to voting rights; jurors were drawn from lists of registered voters. District judges explained to them the connection between citizenship and jury service. That service cut across lines of education and social class. It marked them as members of a white community. To the degree that they shared the community's prejudices, they shaped justice in the courts toward that end. The same might be said of a district court judge. In these cases, neither Judge Brady nor the Pike County jury seem to have done anything improper, speaking only in the strict legal sense of the term. But one can be allowed to imagine that the fact would have been of little comfort to the sixteen-year-old victim, her family, or other Black Pike County residents.

At the end of the year, Charles Gordon regretted that this case had brought "a most distasteful—and undeserved notoriety" to "a community, an area, and a state."[20] Matters came to final resolution in April 1957, as Judge Tom Brady pronounced sentence on Ernest Dillon. Dillon received twenty years "at hard labor" at Parchman. In a reflection of how much racial segregation occupied Brady's thinking in these days, he observed that Dillon's crime reflected "a belief in integration, since no action could be more in contrast with the beliefs of the segregationist." Further, said Brady, Dillon's actions "had brought bitter condemnation on the state of Mississippi," and Mississippi would "come in for a whole lot more of vitriolic abuse from people who hate the South."[21] The real shame, he seemed to say, was not the damage to the victim but rather to the state's reputation—and possibly its ability to defend Jim Crow. Brady and other men of influence recognized that national opinion mattered to an increasing degree. White Mississippians would have to manage their affairs under a level of scrutiny they had not received in earlier years. Brady's concerns also reveal an incipient tension in the region between working-class white people and their better-positioned neighbors. Increasingly, white people of property and standing worried that working-class white people might spoil matters for everyone, and that the management of race relations in these increasingly perilous years would involve keeping more careful check on both Black and working-class white people.

THROUGH THE 1950S, Charles Gordon continued to cover crime in southwestern Mississippi. He also continued to advocate the cause of people he believed were receiving unfair treatment at the hands of the law. As he had done in 1951 with Hattie Lee Barnes, in 1957 Gordon took up the case of a young African American woman, Nellie Grace White. She was, Gordon later wrote, "a friendless, not too worthy, Negro woman who killed another human being." Still, wrote Gordon, a number of area people felt that given White's circumstances, this was an instance in which "something should be done."[22] White, twenty-four years old and pregnant, stabbed to death a Black man, Rufus S. Lampton, who had "molested" her at the Moonlight Inn, "a Negro beer joint" on McComb's Summit Street.[23] Lampton, thirty-eight years old, had recently been paroled from Parchman penitentiary, where he had served ten years for murdering his wife and her father in Walthall County. According to White, she was attempting to eat dinner with her friends when Lampton "began meddling with me and wouldn't quit." Despite her repeated warnings to Lampton to leave her alone, he persisted in touching her and using "cuss words" to address her. Producing a concealed knife, White stabbed Lampton in the chest.[24]

Like Barnes, White did not deny the killing. Also much like Barnes, White was a woman in an unenviable position. She had recently moved to McComb from nearby Brookhaven, where she had left a husband "too mean to live with," a previous husband having deserted her. Of her five children, three were dead. She was "far advanced in pregnancy" with her sixth child. White's pregnancy, wrote Gordon, as well as the felonious background of her victim, might mean, he hoped, that White could be free on bond while she awaited the birth of her child. What might have happened with White's bond, no one had the chance to see. After White spent only two days in the Pike County jail, a surprised jailer, Fleet O'Quin, took White to the local hospital, where she gave birth to a son.[25]

In another parallel to the Barnes case, there was some confusion about the victim's death. Lampton, he wrote, "came to the McComb vicinity last weekend to attend the funeral of a brother in Tylertown and, instead, met death on the concrete floor of an ice house that had been made into a beer parlor."[26] That much was certain. But who precisely was legally at fault in Lampton's death? Pike County authorities arrested a second woman, a minor, and charged her as an accessory to the murder. Reports suggested that this second person had supplied White with the knife she used to stab Lampton to death. The trials of White and Mamie Lee Floyd, the minor charged as an accessory, were set for March 1957. With no Joe Pigott to offer a vigorous defense, both women accepted a deal to plead guilty to reduced charges of manslaughter. Neither the circumstances of the killing nor White's recent motherhood seemed to carry much weight with Judge Tom Brady. White was sentenced to twenty years "at hard labor" in the state penitentiary; Floyd received five years.[27] As in the Barnes case, Gordon felt that justice was not being done. He kept the story of White on the newspaper's front page, in part through detail designed to draw sympathy for her. Shortly after White was sent to the penitentiary, her son, in the care of a friend since her arrest, nearly drowned but was revived by McComb firemen.[28]

Gordon argued that if Judge Brady had been fully aware of the facts of the case, he would have been more lenient in his sentence. Some of those facts would have been not only White's hard-luck background but also the character of the man she stabbed and a more detailed version of the events in the bar that night. Gordon began writing on White's behalf: to the judge, the prosecutor, the district attorney, and the state senator. Other local people began to weigh in as well. In 1962, the case reached the ear of Governor Ross Barnett, who suspended White's sentence.[29] Even more than in the Barnes case, then, Gordon here acted as an advocate. It is not clear how much or even if White knew of Gordon's efforts on her behalf. If he was not a crusader on behalf of the "Negro cause," as he had written to Oliver Emmerich several years earlier, he most certainly was a crusader on behalf of Nellie Grace White.

Gordon revisited Nellie Grace White's story in a lengthy 1962 article. Although the White case is much less complicated than that of Hattie Lee Barnes, one common feature stressed in Gordon's reporting is the role of local paternalism. Of White, Gordon told "how a group of white persons of Pike County—sparked perhaps by this reporter's interest in the case—went to work a year ago and got her released from Parchman."[30] Typical of Gordon, he downplayed his own efforts on White's behalf. This episode, like McComb's bond-fundraising campaign for Hattie Lee Barnes in 1953, says something about white paternalism and the operation of justice in the Deep South. Gordon's coverage of White's parole effort and the Barnes bond-fundraising campaign stressed the readiness of white people of goodwill to aid "friendless" African Americans. One supposes that neither Barnes nor White were literally friendless. Strictly speaking, the common element in both stories is the usefulness of well-placed white friends for Black women like Barnes and White. In both cases, the person to whom white McComb extended goodwill was a woman. Fewer African American men in Parchman might have expected or received such assistance. A cynic might also note that double murderer Rufus Lampton, whom White stabbed, was perhaps the kind of man whose death would not have excited a good deal of outrage. In reviewing the White petition for parole, Governor Ross Barnett might well have thought that his killing did not amount to that much of a crime after all, a statement of sorts about the value placed on Black lives in Mississippi of the era.

The Mississippi justice system throughout the Jim Crow era showed African Americans the advantages of having friends like these. However problematic racialized paternalism may seem, one might also recognize that such assistance could be offered by someone like Gordon in a time when direct attacks on the judicial system might not have been productive. Then and later, small-town justice and other matters of power and authority in the Deep South operated on wheels greased by personal connections. We have little access to what people like Barnes and White thought of white efforts on their behalf. There is little doubt of two things, however. They knew that they were ensnared in a system in which they were fundamentally disadvantaged. And they would have been profoundly relieved, however it was accomplished, to be freed from a Mississippi jail or prison.

WELL INTO THE 1960S and beyond, personal connections and family power continued to matter in the administration of southwestern Mississippi justice. After the Barnes cases were over, Edd Craft and his family exercised such power. Having influence could literally mark the difference between escape and prosperity or ignominy and the grave. Wendell Craft, the son of Edd and brother of Lamar, ran for mayor of Tylertown in 1957 in a three-man contest. All candidates were of course Democrats. Unsuccessful in that first attempt for the office, Wendell Craft then pursued a variety of community social and business interests, serving as a member of the board of directors of the town's chamber of commerce.[31] He was also a military veteran and a member of the American Legion. Not everything in Mississippi was explicitly tied to race in those days, but many things were. Craft's Legion duties involved hearing a case against the Jackson-area "Negro American Legion post" that charged members with using their position to advance the work of the NAACP. The Legion was apparently concerned to keep its members from "dabbling in politics," with at least one white Legion officer resigning to concentrate on the business of the Citizens' Council. Craft clearly enjoyed his American Legion work, winning election in 1958 as vice commander of the South Mississippi District. In 1959, fellow legionnaires elected him state commander.[32]

His year as commander, 1959–60, was an eventful one, as he spoke throughout the state and anticipated that Mississippi would play a leading role in the organization's annual convention. Mississippians were proud that year, as another of their daughters had been chosen Miss America and would participate in the state's contingent at the Legion's national parade. But Mississippians were by that time sensitive to national slights and snubs, and the national Legion magazine's failure to provide coverage of Mississippi events prompted calls from the Vicksburg Legion post for the magazine's editor to resign. Craft, pouring oil on troubled waters, assured Mississippians that the slight was unintentional. In the year after his state presidency, Craft enjoyed the afterglow of his time in office, literally and figuratively passing along the gavel, speaking throughout the state, and basking in thanks and congratulations for his service.[33]

Events of 1964 would prove less happy. On November 9, Craft, forty-two years old, was arrested in the restroom of a Hattiesburg hotel and charged with "unnatural intercourse." Arrested with him was fifty-nine-year-old Emmett Lamar Kincaid of Jackson. Kincaid was a travelling auditor for Mississippi's State Auditing Department. As a Forrest County grand jury considered charges against the men, Kincaid "took his life with a gun." The *Jackson Clarion-Ledger,* a newspaper capable of remarkably petty acts, ran Kincaid's obituary along with a story about his arrest. The items were placed in a continuing column so that a reader of the obituary could not avoid the story. Kincaid had resigned from the auditor's office on the Saturday immediately following his arrest. His body was found near his automobile behind the state fairgrounds. He was a graduate of the University of Mississippi and a World War II veteran of the United States Navy. As he contemplated suicide, he likely felt "friendless and alone," as Charles Gordon said of Hattie Lee Barnes and Nellie Grace White. He would certainly have understood that his career had been ruined. In Mississippi in that era, a man who enjoyed sex with men, exposed before the law and in the pages of the state's newspapers, in many ways was without friends and advocates.[34]

But Wendell Craft had the advantage of having both friends and effective advocates. Attorneys for Craft requested a continuance; the judge granted it. Craft's attorneys argued that "in the light of psychiatric examination," Craft too might commit suicide if he were forced to testify. "Kincaid's death, as well as other circumstances," said the Hattiesburg newspaper, "had contributed to Craft's mental condition at that time." As was common in a "morals case," the paper identified both men by full name, noting that James Wendell Craft Jr. of Tylertown was a former state commander of the American Legion.[35]

On January 6, 1965, after fifty minutes of deliberation, a jury in the Forrest

County Circuit Court found Craft guilty. Craft maintained his innocence, saying that his arrest was "a matter of mistaken identity." However, Hattiesburg police detective Dempsey Lawler insisted that "there could be no mistake in identity." Hattiesburg police had targeted the hotel restroom. Three other men had been arrested there and tried in November 1964; each received a five-year sentence. Of the three additional November arrests, one was Craft's; another was the deceased Kincaid's; a third had not yet come to trial.[36] At Craft's two-day trial, his defense offered multiple character witnesses, including "his wife, two physicians, two ministers, a state senator, a sheriff, and a circuit clerk." The state offered as witnesses two police officers.[37] While the list of defense witnesses is impressive, the verdict says something about the limits of the Craft family's power; despite their respectability and influence in Marion County, two counties to the west of Forrest County, they were unable to sweep away Wendell Craft's arrest. Local newspapers, however, did not cover the incident. Like the other men convicted of the same charge in that court, Craft received a five-year sentence. He promptly posted bond, remaining free while his attorney appealed the conviction.[38]

While the Craft family could not prevent the Forrest County conviction, they had better luck in Jackson. In December 1965, the Mississippi Supreme Court ruled favorably on the appeal, granting Craft a new trial. Noting errors in the circuit court trial, the supreme court held that testimony about Kincaid's suicide should not have been admitted, nor should the court have allowed Craft's character witnesses to have been cross-examined "on matters related to the case."[39] One of the justices who heard the appeal was Tom P. Brady. Craft's co-counsel was the old friend and attorney for various Craft family interests, Breed Mounger of Tylertown.[40] While the court's opinion noted that the "facts" of the case were "not appropriate for the printed page," the *Craft* decision became a frequently cited case, one that set precedent on matters of the cross-examination of witnesses and also on expectations of privacy in the use of public toilets.[41] There is no evidence that the district attorney for Forrest County decided to pursue a new trial of Wendell Craft. So there the matter ended. By 1966, Craft reassumed public duties, including some with the American Legion, serving as a delegate to that year's national convention in Washington, DC. In 1969, as a member of the three-man Mississippi Athletic Commission, Craft helped to deny Cassius Clay a permit to fight in the state.[42]

People in his hometown of Tylertown knew of Wendell Craft's legal troubles, but they were forgiving. In 1980, they elected him mayor. In 1981, another hometown boy, Jon Hinson, a US representative, was arrested in Washington, DC, on charges of "committing oral sodomy." Mayor Wendell Craft "would not comment on the arrest." He said: "We don't know what to talk about. We don't know the situation." One local man did say of Hinson, "When a boy gets grown, goes off, you know—things can happen."[43] By 1981, Tylertown, a city of 2,000 people, was still one of those places, as people say of most small communities, where everybody knows everybody else. People understood that whatever Wendell Craft might have done back in 1964, he still came from a good family. In 1989, Craft was defeated in the Democratic primary in his bid for reelection as Tylertown's mayor.[44] Still, he had served two terms, from 1981 to 1989. He tried once more for the mayor's office, in 1997, but was decisively defeated, ending his political career in Walthall County.[45]

The restroom sex case against Craft is admittedly a coda to the larger Barnes story. But it is one that reflects themes that ran through the Barnes saga of 1951 to 1955. It shows the significance not solely of race in Mississippi but also of money, standing, and access to the levers of power. Lamar Craft's brother Wendell weathered this potentially devastating incident, which could have landed him a five-year term in state prison, because of his family's confidence in navigating the law and courts in Mississippi. He also clearly had the support of family in other ways, something that other actors in this episode, specifically Emmett Kincaid, presumably did not. With that support, one might enjoy a full life in a community that would, as in Wendell Craft's case, forgive and forget, or at least not speak of such matters.

James Wendell Craft Sr. died on December 6, 2009. He was eighty-seven years old. An electrical engineer with a degree from Louisiana Tech University, he had owned Simmons Department Store in Tylertown. He was remembered as an active member of his church, Tylertown United Methodist, having served for years as a delegate to the state's annual conference of Methodists. Former mayor of Tylertown, Rotarian, military veteran, longtime member of the American Legion and the Army National Guard, past president of both the Mississippi Municipal Association and the Mississippi Retail Association, Craft's obituary gives evidence of his deep roots and long service in Walthall County and the state. Unlike the obituary of Emmett Kincaid, the man with whom he was arrested in 1964, Craft's obituary is silent on the morals case in which he was enmeshed in his earlier days.[46] Craft, like his wife, his parents, and most of his siblings, is buried in the Tylertown Cemetery. Emmett Kincaid, like Craft, is buried in his hometown. There, in Rankin County in the Pelahatchie Cemetery, he rests in a solitary grave.[47]

12

FAME AND NOTORIETY AFTER THE BARNES CASE

WHEN THE TRIALS OF Hattie Lee Barnes and all the others were over, some of them left the area entirely. Others remained in Pike, Walthall, or Marion Counties, seeing quietly to their affairs, living out their lives without ever again becoming a party to matters that led to court or prison. A few achieved a degree of fame or, in some cases, a species of notoriety. One of those people whose life did not unfold over the years, in southwestern Mississippi or anywhere else, was of course Lamar Craft. Before his death at the age of twenty-two, Richard Lamar Craft left few traces in the public record, not uncommon for a midcentury southern rural boy. Born in 1928, Craft was a shade too young to have served in World War II. In 1943, as a fifteen-year-old, he showed beef cattle at livestock shows, a testimony to his father's successful work in that field. In high school, he played end for the Tylertown High School football team. After high school and Air Force service, he went to Mississippi Southern College in Hattiesburg, where he pledged a social fraternity, Pi Kappa Alpha.[1] His life was structured around work, family, and friendships, one can presume, until his death on April 17, 1951. Of his character and habits, one can recover little. Public statements about those matters, much to his father Edd Craft's chagrin, were offered through testimony by his drinking companions James Easterling and Oscar Hope, and by Hattie Lee Barnes, who might have been the first to say that she scarcely knew him. Craft was survived by one sister and five brothers. Between 1998 and 2016, all of them died, severing the last direct living ties between this story and the Craft family.[2] Had Lamar Craft not made what even he might have allowed to have been a poor decision on that April evening in 1951, one cannot say what his fate might have been. But it likely would not have been to serve as the catalyst for a complex set of legal cases.

On the other hand, Breed O. Mounger, attorney for the Craft family in the 1950s and 1960s, had happier experiences with courtrooms, the law, and posterity. He enjoyed an immensely successful career of more than fifty years. A powerful courtroom litigator, he earned a reputation as the attorney one would want were one facing serious criminal charges in southern Mississippi. His name stretches across the dockets of many counties, primarily but not exclusively as a defense attorney; he had a hand in nearly every matter of legal consequence. By the time of the Barnes case, Mounger had practiced in Tylertown since the early 1930s. He knew the area well, developing friendships or working relationships with practically every man of power and influence in a several-county area. He also sought elected office early, announcing in 1931 his candidacy for Marion County prosecuting attorney.[3] He held a series of county offices through the years as he retained and built his private practice. Lines between the two areas were not always strictly drawn. No scandal attached to the custom; it was simply the way that business was done.

While still in his twenties, Mounger began building the organizational and professional ties that laid the foundation for his career. In Tylertown, he organized a chapter of the Rotary Club, a men's service organization; in 1936, he became its first president. Over the years he also joined the Masons and the Shriners. In 1937, attorneys of Walthall, Pike, and Amite (immediately to the west of Pike) Counties formed a tri-county bar association. Previously, Amite and Walthall Counties had no bar association. The formation of that organization, otherwise seemingly inconsequential, points to another fact about legal life in southwestern Mississippi in that era. It was a small world. Attorneys, especially ones who had been in practice since the 1930s, such as Breed Mounger and Thomas Brady, knew each other well. They argued against each other numerous times, and sometimes served as co-counsel on other cases. Some spent years as a circuit or local judge. These men, and men they all were, had long-established working arrangements, always informed by the knowledge that they would see each other again.[4]

Attorneys like Breed Mounger settled matters not only in the courtroom but also over hands of cards or drinks or during after-church strolls. Off-the-record discussions of pending cases—common then and later—not only helped to settle cases but also built understandings of how things were expected to work. Younger attorneys were thus socialized into local legal etiquette and practice. In these conversations and visits, considerable business was transacted, but there was no court reporter to take it down; that record, so significant, so shaping, is unrecoverable. A recommendation, a remark that a particular young man was "all right," an invitation to speak at a local club or church group; all were markers of arrival and likely guarantors of future success. One 1938 area social committee, for example, included Mounger, B. D. Statham, Robert B. Reeves, and J. Gordon Roach, men who served in coming decades as circuit judge, county prosecutor, and private practice attorneys of great influence.[5] Their wives too were sociable, running a great range of women's organizations and committees. All these ties mattered, making an already homogeneous legal community even more of an insider's club.

During World War II, Breed Mounger participated in community organizing and fundraising efforts; he chaired the Navy Relief Fund drive in Tylertown.[6] Then he joined the Navy in 1942, serving as a communications officer and navigator aboard the USS *Pathfinder.* Discharged in 1946 as a lieutenant commander, Mounger earned two Purple Hearts.[7] After the war, he retained an interest in sailing and in flying as well, maintaining a pilot's license for years. By the time of the Hattie Lee Barnes case, Mounger was a man with a broad legal and civic reputation, and also one with a demonstrated investment in the community. His reputation extended well beyond Walthall County. From 1958 to 1959, he served as president of the state bar association. In that capacity, he testified in 1959 before a US House Judiciary subcommittee. Pending civil rights bills were unconstitutional, he said. And no one should erroneously presume that the Supreme Court's *Brown* decision was the law of the land.[8] Such was the position that most white attorneys in Mississippi would have taken, at least in public.

Mounger spoke, a colleague remembered, "with an air of extreme confidence, an almost arrogant tone of authority." As well he might. Through the 1950s and 1960s, he honed his reputation as a defense attorney, one of the very best in the area. In 1960, when Mounger defended a Pike County teenager charged with shooting his school superintendent, Judge Tom Brady referred to Mounger as "one of the ablest attorneys in Mississippi."[9] That was standard professional courtesy, but in Mounger's case, it happened also to be true. Because Mounger was not a district attorney or a district judge, the civil rights movement of the 1960s fell relatively lightly upon his professional shoulders. When it did cross his desk, it would have seemed more a nuisance than a fundamental challenge. In 1961, as Tylertown city attorney, he was co-defendant, along with his old acquaintance and client Edd Craft (now sheriff), in a lawsuit filed by area Black residents charging violations of their voting rights.[10]

Breed Mounger made his living—and a good living it was—as a defense attorney. But he also did the public's work in lesser-paying capacities. For thirty-eight years, he was Tylertown's city attorney. He also served as Walthall County attorney, attorney for the local school board, and for the county's board of supervisors. As a civic-minded man, Mounger likely saw this work partly as a matter of duty. But those offices all paid other dividends, not the least of which was that they put Mounger in a position to know as much about pending legal matters of all sorts as anyone in the county. And as the board of supervisors' attorney, he had a direct hand in the selection of jury pools, a very useful thing indeed.[11]

Mounger spent the great majority of his seventy-one years in Walthall County. There he is buried beneath a modest marker in the Tylertown Cemetery.[12] From it, one would hardly guess the figure that he cut for two generations of area residents who needed effective legal counsel. On his death in 1982, a fellow attorney remembered Mounger as "a superb advocate, a tireless adversary, and probably the most effective all-around lawyer I have yet to meet." One of his pallbearers was Tylertown's mayor, Wendell Craft, the son of Edd Craft and the brother of the slain Lamar Craft, and a man who, thanks to Mounger's services, avoided five years at Parchman penitentiary in the 1960s.[13]

Other figures who played some role in the Barnes case had less lengthy, less distinguished careers. One of these was Robert Eugene Lee, sheriff of Pike County from 1948 until 1952. At Rob Lee's bar on April 17, 1951, he found Hattie Lee Barnes and the body of Lamar Craft. Lee clearly enjoyed being sheriff. He ran unsuccessfully for the office again on several occasions. Like other Mississippi lawmen of his era, he served during a period when there was, practically speaking, white law and Black law. An element of Black law included the forceful interrogation of African American prisoners, a tradition for which Lee found himself in court in the 1950s, when attitudes about the practice, both in the state and beyond, were beginning to change. Sheriff Lee and four other Pike County law enforcement officers were indicted by a federal grand jury on charges of conspiring to deprive a Black man, Murray Gray, of his constitutional rights by attempting to flog a confession out of Gray.[14] It is no excuse for Sheriff Lee to say that in this practice he did little more than other Mississippi sheriffs of the era, but that is a fact. After he left the sheriff's office, Lee later worked, as did many area men, for the Illinois Central Railroad. Lee died in 1989 at the age of seventy-six, after falling some twelve feet from an oak tree as he attempted to climb into his deer stand. Unlike some of the attorneys or judges who figured in the Barnes story, he no longer held a public position of authority when the civil rights movement came in full force to southwestern Mississippi.[15]

One of those men who did have to navigate those changing times while still in public office was Judge Sebe Dale, the circuit judge who heard the Marion County trials of Walter Watson and Rob Lee for the shooting of Hattie Lee Barnes. Dale remained on the bench into the 1960s. One finds traces of Dale in the files of the Sovereignty Commission, the state agency charged with defending racial segregation. Dale was guarded in his dealings with the Sovereignty Commission, but cooperative, as very many public men were in that period when the Commission wielded considerable power. In 1961, a Commission investigator reported that Dale told him that as a judge, he was not well-positioned to offer detailed reports to the Commission on civil rights activities in his area. But Dale reported that he had not experienced "any trouble" with the NAACP, a statement that one may take in a variety of ways. Few district judges or county attorneys might have wished to suggest that local Black people were causing any "trouble" that local authorities could not manage. Dale explained to the Sovereignty Commission investigator that he was not a member of the Citizens' Council, of which the Commission was essentially a state arm. "He might be involved in a case," explained Dale, "where the NAACP was involved and he did not want to take the chance of being disqualified." Such an explanation stands to reason, of course, but that situation did not prevent other judges, law enforcement officials, and elected officials from embracing the Council, whether from support of its goals or a calculation of the number of votes it could command in that period. Still, Dale assured the investigator that he was a "States Righter and would stay one as long as he lived." "The judge was very nice," the investigator concluded.[16]

One judge who took a much more forceful public position on the emerging civil rights movement was Thomas P. Brady. As a district judge, he heard the trial of Hattie Lee Barnes as well as Edd Craft's suit against American National. As a state supreme court justice, he heard the appeal of Wendell Craft's conviction on a morals charge. Brady died in 1973 in Houston, Texas, after open heart surgery; he was sixty-nine years old. Brady had been in declining health for the previous year or so, having been granted a leave of absence from the Mississippi Supreme Court, where he had served since 1963. He is buried, unlike most of his extended family, in the Rose Hill Cemetery in Brookhaven. His tombstone tells the observer that Brady was a "Jurist—Author—Statesman." Of these claims, most certainly the first two are not subject to doubt.[17]

From the mid-1950s, Brady's reputation was inseparable from his role in the founding and intellectual support of the Citizens' Council movement. As did many members of the Citizens' Council, Brady saw his efforts as a middle way: a means of preventing the chaos that would ensue should segregation fall but also avoiding violent means of preserving Jim Crow. "We were the deterrent, the one deterrent," he later said, "that [checked] the organization of mobs and the operation of lynch laws in Mississippi." So some of them seem to have believed; so some of them claimed for decades after the 1950s. Brady traveled the country explaining the Citizens' Council stand: "I made 692 speeches and I spoke from California to Washington [DC]." That position, he maintained, amounted to more than a defense of Jim Crow. The Citizens' Councils, he hoped, would be "the nucleus for a conservative party in the United States, irrespective of locale and irrespective of creed or color." Brady was not the only white southern figure or American figure in that era who imagined the restructuring of American politics into a new conservative coalition.[18]

An avowed segregationist, Brady also insisted that his intellectual creed amounted to more than that. Thus, he offered a qualified defense of the publication of the Pentagon Papers: "a public that is in the dark and knows nothing about what is going on is helpless to protect itself." Closer to home, he ruled in a case against the City of Greenville that an African American man had the right to use a public park. He also reversed the conviction of a Black man because African Americans had been excluded from the jury that indicted him.[19]

But one should not read too much into those decisions; Brady was essentially a consistent man. In later years, he recognized that many things had changed in Mississippi since he wrote *Black Monday,* his denunciation of the *Brown* decision, but "basic issues are pretty much the same."[20]

Brady never offered an apology for his work or writings from the 1950s or 1960s. He likely felt that he had nothing for which to apologize. As a practical matter, his 1973 death meant that he did not have to explain anything while seeking reelection from a newly broadened state electorate. In the same words that appeared on Brady's tombstone, Governor Bill Waller, a man who represented a new direction in Mississippi politics, remembered Brady as a "great jurist, author, and statesman." In a judgment with which no Mississippian might take issue, provided one looks at it the right way, Waller added: "Justice Tom Brady was a man of rare dedication and devotion." National coverage of his death drew only a brief paragraph or so, all of which note in the first sentence that he was "the intellectual godfather of the segregationist Citizens Council movement."[21]

The *Jackson Clarion-Ledger,* long a strong admirer of Brady's work, remembered him as one of the state's "most literate sons." "The jurist's strong views," it noted, "had both critics and defenders, but his integrity was not attacked nor his workmanship on the bench and in chambers challenged. He never let his personal view interfere with his administration of the law," a view that we may understand might not have been shared by all Mississippians.[22] Perhaps the most neutral thing that one can say about Brady is that he stands as one of those Mississippians who lived into an era in which some of the fundamental things that he took for granted had changed. But it is also true that Brady's views—and those of men who shared them, many of whom sat on judges' benches in Mississippi in the 1950s and 1960s—shaped an uneven system of Mississippi justice, one that spurred the civil rights movement into action.

In Brady's career, one might note a certain irony. Turning his energies against the civil rights cause, he became more than a Mississippi district judge. He became for a brief period a man whose name resonated throughout the region and beyond. That career was capped with a seat on the Mississippi Supreme Court. But now, nearly fifty years after his death, Brady is not remembered, especially by historians, with the respect that he might have wished.

Had Brady lived a generation earlier, he might have had a comfortable but more obscure career. Perhaps a career like that of his father, Thomas J. Brady Jr. The elder Brady, like his son, was an attorney. He practiced in Brookhaven for nearly a half century. Not nearly so well-known a figure as his son, he was nevertheless a man of standing in Lincoln County. His obituary remembers him as "a man of integrity, keen business judgment and the possessor of a brilliant mind . . . He was a member of the Baptist Church, and a former Sunday school teacher and had confided to members of the family that he was ready for the final summons, whenever it came his time to pass on." Like his son's, Brady's tombstone also carries a message, but this one seems somewhat at odds with the obituary's statement of Brady's preparation for his "final summons." It tells us: "I have no hope of reward, or fear of punishment."[23]

With their rewards and occasional punishments, roadhouses on the Pike-Walthall county line, similar to the one in which Lamar Craft was shot dead, also endured. They remained places of companionship and conviviality, but they also figured occasionally as the settings of violence and death. Those places and the stories they generated continued to say significant things about social class and race in southwestern Mississippi. Area law enforcement authorities, however, likely thought of the bars not in those broad terms, but instead as objects of perennial concern, if not constant nuisance.

One of those bars, operated for several decades by Ab Travis, stands as a figurative if not literal successor to Rob Lee's places. Travis's business was located along old Highway 24, near Walker's Bridge, a swimming hole familiar to generations of area young people. The area near Walker's Bridge was also the site of another watering hole, a bar operated by a man with the Faulknerian surname of McEwen. In March 1969, five Pike County young men, four of them minors and "all . . . Negroes" went on a "berserk spree" of "arson, attempted arson, and burglary" that targeted bars, two country stores, and several farms. The trouble started when the young men failed to "obtain service" at McEwen's bar. County-line roadhouses were not always scrupulously observant of the legal drinking age. And one of the would-be patrons, a Vietnam veteran, was of age. Whatever the reason for the refusal of service, whether it was their age or race or something said or done by them or by another patron, the young men were "thrown out, maybe roughed up a little," said Pike County sheriff Robert "Tot" Lawson.[24]

They retaliated by gathering makeshift "Molotov cocktails" and attempting to set fire to several places in the area, though not, perhaps surprisingly, to McEwen's bar. Starting with Ab Travis's place, they went on to a nearby country store. Both fires, set by throwing gasoline-filled bottles from moving vehicles, were quickly discovered and extinguished. They were more successful in their attacks on area farmers, igniting four houses, barns, or farm structures, with an attempt on another one failing only because they had run out of gasoline. Capping the evening with a burglary of another country store, this one in Walthall County, they took oil, cigarettes, milk, ice cream, and sandwiches.

The men were recognized at various points throughout the evening. When they returned to their homes the next morning, law enforcement officers were waiting. If these things had happened in earlier years, and even if the four arsonists had been white, the incidents would still have been alarming enough, particularly to those people who lost hay, barns, or other property to the fires. By 1969, however, and with the arsonists being Black, the crime spree suggested to some area white people matters beyond the significance of the property damage. For one thing, local people, like many other Americans in those years, were convinced that law and order was breaking down. Further, the race of the four arrested men would have seemed to them evidence that a particular kind of law and order—the policing of Black people by white ones, and an apparent Black acceptance of that policing—was another one of those things that had in recent years changed for the worse. However, this arson binge was no general insurrection. At least it did not lead to any immediate further incidents. But everything had begun with young Black men being refused service at a bar. Then there was the matter of the men being "roughed up," as Sheriff Lawson put it. Earlier generations of Black Pike County men might have seen those facts as something they would have to take, whether they liked it or not; these men did not. Some things in Pike County had changed.

Not all roadhouse incidents involved matters of race. The year 1976 was a bloody one at Ab Travis's place, with two murders on the premises. There in July, Cue Jefferson, a timber buyer and former Walthall County sheriff's deputy, sat with his wife. Sam Lewis and his brother approached the couple and "made remarks." Travis threw out the Lewises, but they returned. Both Sam Lewis and Cue Jefferson were armed with .38 caliber pistols, the seeming weapon of choice for close-quarter shootings in southwestern Mississippi.

About 8:30 p.m., the men exchanged fire. Jefferson was wounded in the hip; Lewis, hit in the leg and stomach, was dead on arrival at the McComb hospital. Jefferson was charged with murder. Sheriff Lawson observed that the altercation stemmed from "an old grudge."[25] In November, Travis's bar was the site of another killing, this one during a 9:00 p.m. fight outside the tavern. Nineteen-year-old Edward Quinn fatally stabbed twenty-four-year-old Willie Ray Magee in the throat; the fight again stemmed from "an old grudge," said Sheriff Lawson.[26]

Again in 1983, Travis's place figured in a local murder, although the killing appears not to have occurred on-site, no doubt to the relief of Travis. A forty-four-year-old Tylertown woman, Laura Bell Magee, was charged with killing forty-seven-year-old Larkin Walker, her boyfriend of twelve years. He was discovered lying in a pool of blood beside his pickup truck in a wooded area near old Highway 24 near the Pike-Walthall line. Local authorities first suspected that Walker died of natural causes. Subsequent X-rays ordered by the Pike County coroner revealed that a hole near his eye had not been produced by natural causes but instead by a bullet, which remained lodged in his skull. He and Magee had last been seen together Sunday night, as they left Travis's place. This time, Sheriff Lawson did not attribute the killing to an old grudge.[27]

Area roadhouses drew a various clientele, ranging from the area's rural and working people to middle-class area teenagers looking for companionship, thrills, and, of course, access to beer. They also remained, in the 1950s and for some time to come, one of those Mississippi institutions that were segregated by race, but that fact would have seemed too self-evident for white patrons to have noted. Most of the violence that unfolded in them was recorded, if it was recorded at all, in the arrest records and court dockets of Pike or Walthall County. Because these incidents occurred with regularity, the specifics of most of them are long forgotten, except by people directly touched one way or another. To the bulk of the area population, roadhouse violence seemed just part of the pattern of life, almost a southern cliché: beer joints, Saturday night, and a fight, a stabbing, or a shooting.

Events of the Hattie Lee Barnes story, like many of these other roadhouse killings, gradually receded from memory in Pike and Walthall Counties. Charles Gordon stopped writing about it; some people involved with the various cases and trials moved away; essentially everyone who figured in any direct way with it is now dead. The cemetery in Tylertown contains two graves with markers that read "Richard Lamar Craft." One is that of Edd Craft's son, shot dead in 1951. The other is that of a son of Lamar Craft's brother, Jay L. Craft. An Air Force veteran who served in Korea, J. L. Craft did not reside in southwest Mississippi at the time of his brother's killing, and thus played much less of a role in its aftermath than did some of his other brothers. But he named a son after his brother. That Richard Lamar Craft was born in 1955. He died in 2015, having lived and worked with Walthall County Crafts, among whom he is laid to rest.[28]

In the Tylertown City Cemetery, along with many members of the Craft family, one may also find the graves of attorney Breed Mounger and former sheriff Marshall Bullock, who in 1951 responded to the report of a shooting at Rob Lee's place.[29] But one grave not to be found there is that of Hattie Lee Barnes. After 1953, with her testimony before the grand jury that chose not to indict Rob Lee for killing Lamar Craft, the State of Mississippi was officially finished with her. Then she returned to Arkansas and to her husband, Leon Gardner. In 1954, Charles Gordon noted that "at last account," there she remained, working as a tenant farmer on former Governor Laney's land.[30] No doubt she felt herself well rid of the Mississippi justice system. Perhaps she returned to the Tylertown area to see her mother. If she did, she was quiet about the matter, certainly wishing to draw as little attention to herself as possible. It is just as likely that she did not return to Mississippi, for a time, at least. She had no obligation, official or otherwise, to inform any white Mississippian of her comings and goings. There is no evidence that Barnes kept in touch with Joe Pigott, Charles Gordon, or any other white Mississippian with whom she had been associated in that chapter of her life. Had any of them thought to write her, she likely could not have read the letter. There is also no reason to believe that she would have felt the need to leave a forwarding address with any of them. She knew all too well that the State of Mississippi seemed able to find her, should authorities there decide that they needed her again.

EPILOGUE

Challenges, Questions, and Some Conclusions

THE BROADER STORY OF Hattie Lee Barnes demonstrates certain facts. Imperatives of Jim Crow, as systemic practices, meant that from birth, Barnes lived in a place in which she was undereducated, disenfranchised, and in which her opportunities were circumscribed because she was an African American woman. Mississippi in that era represented perhaps the worst of what America had to offer its Black citizens. Gender also shaped Barnes's world. Essentially everyone in a position of authority whom Barnes encountered—judges, sheriffs, deputies, attorneys, and employers—was not only white, but a man as well. Most white Mississippi women of the era might not have said that they were second-class citizens, but in significant ways they were. They could not serve on juries, for instance, and in common with other American women, their employment opportunities were limited by law and custom. Many white men and some white women might have pointed to an alleviating attitude of chivalry or some gestures of paternalism—a lip service, at least, to the sanctity of white womanhood. Barnes would have enjoyed none of this protection, such as it was.

This story also illustrates the operation of democracy and public institutions, both formally and as a matter of tradition. These sheriffs, judges, prosecutors, coroners, and other local, county, and state officials were elected officials, ones who had to be attentive to the voters' beliefs and convictions, should they wish to remain in office. Many of the beliefs of these voters had to do with race, and what ought to be done to protect the segregated social order they insisted on having or at least supported to one degree or another. Since its admission as a state in 1817, Mississippi had a passion for local control and democracy, or so they frequently said. But that enthusiasm for democratic participation existed side by side with an equal passion for racial control. A recent study of Mississippi's legal system concludes that the state's "legal history features two overarching but conflicting themes: a steadfast quest for a purified democracy, coupled with an equally steadfast quest to create a diametrically opposite legal system for its black half."[1]

But this is not solely a story about the operation of deep social forces or the formal work of government or other institutions. Nothing in the events recounted here would have unfolded the way that they did without the will and action of strong individual personality. The most significant of these actors is Barnes herself. She was unusually bold and resilient. Despite numerous attempts to silence her in one way or another, she was determined to tell the truth as she knew it to be. Similarly, Joe Pigott and Charles Gordon worked against the grain of popular opinion, and without exaggeration, risked popularity if not personal safety in a society that was increasingly becoming less tolerant of dissent, especially on matters of race. Without the unusual will of Barnes, Pigott, and Gordon, it is unlikely that there would be very much of a recoverable story about Hattie Lee Barnes, Lamar Craft, and the roadhouse shooting. Under other, quite common Mississippi circumstances, a woman like Barnes might have shot a man like Craft and been sent, without a great deal of fanfare, to Parchman penitentiary.

However, because the story of Hattie Lee Barnes was not typical, it was remembered in certain quarters, especially by Joe Pigott and Charles Gordon. It has also attracted recent attention. In 2019, a seventeen-minute film, *Mississippi Justice,* told of Barnes's shooting of Lamar Craft, the work of Pigott and Gordon on her behalf, and her acquittal. The filmmaker, Dr. Wilma Mosley Clopton, is a longtime chronicler of African American life in Mississippi. Clopton recalled that when she learned of the Barnes story, she "immediately wanted to see something happen."[2] The story, said Clopton, was on the one hand about the injustices done to Barnes because she was an African American woman, but also a story of Pigott and Gordon, white men who swam against the current of popular opinion to do what was right. "There's a void of information," she said, "not just about people of African descent in Mississippi, but about the good people of Mississippi who are doing things and have always done things and have gone unrecognized." Brad Pigott, Joe Pigott's son, and like his father an attorney, appears in the film. Like Clopton, Brad Pigott sees in the Barnes saga examples of principled conduct. Of Charles Gordon, Pigott said: "He was a force of nature . . . He was passionate about this young woman and what was happening to her and the injustice of it."[3]

Like anyone attempting to reconstruct this story, Clopton is aware of what time and other factors have done to evidence one might wish to have. "Because the story is almost 65 years old, Clopton said there will be holes in the film." She observed, "One of the hardest things in doing a film of this intricacy is trying to stay focused on the target."[4] A press release for the film contains errors, one trivial. Joe Pigott is described as the area's "newest, youngest public defender." Pigott was young; he was Barnes's defender. But the State of Mississippi had no system of public defenders in the 1950s, nor would it for decades to come. Another error is more significant: "They wanted her to change her story and say that it wasn't she who shot Craft, but that it was . . . Rob Lee the bar owner who shot Craft. After all, Rob Lee was a Black man and convicting him would be easy. No one wants to hear about a white man trying to rape a black woman." Rob Lee was, of course, a white man.[5]

McComb attorney Ronald Whittington serves as narrator of *Mississippi Justice.* He explains that he learned of the Barnes case only a few years before this film was made, certainly some time before 2015, the year both Joe and Lorraine Pigott died. At the end of a visit to the Pigotts' home, said Whittington, Mrs. Pigott presented him with a copy of Joe Pigott's statement to Judge Brady in 1951, explaining that it represented a significant case in her husband's career. That statement, which Whittington here refers to as a "transcript" of Pigott's words, serves as the narrative and dramatic heart of *Mississippi Justice.* The re-creation of those words, both moving and effective as storytelling, is also somewhat problematic. In the film, Pigott's motion to Judge Brady is depicted as a speech delivered before a jury, which was surely not the case in 1951. Some of the words of that statement one can believe to be very close to what Pigott argued in that courtroom. Using *Weathersby v. Mississippi,* a 1933 Mississippi Supreme Court decision, Pigott said that in the absence of contradiction by "material particulars," the court must accept a defendant's version of events, such as the one Barnes told about Craft climbing uninvited into what amounted to her home. Clearly, Judge Tom Brady found that argument to be relevant and persuasive.

But the film also says that in arguing his motion, Pigott spoke these words to Brady:

> Judge, I realize that you are a popular speaker at meetings of the Citizens Council, expressing expectations that the social circumstances will not change and sharing hope that members of the white race and black race can harmoniously live in separate neighborhoods, attend separate schools and enjoy separate facilities.
>
> What you say is well received and because you are a well-educated, articulate speaker and represent the judicial system: your followers believe in the legality and constitutionality of their cause. But, we both know, that the law should be applied equally, and that the rights to enjoy all of the constitutional guarantees belong to us equally regardless of race.
>
> We are a patriotic people—proud of our past and to deny this Defendant the full measure of her rights and the complete protection of our constitution would bring dishonor to our flag, disrespect for the law and desecration to the grave of every fighting man who has paid the supreme sacrifice to guarantee such rights even to this Defendant.
>
> Your Honor, this is your moment to decide whether to grow old stooped trying to stay on the level of people who want you to be one of them—one of the "Good Ole Boys"—or you can stand erect and have them look up to you with respect for having known and followed the high road. I have confidence that you will make the decision that will let you sleep at night and look proudly into the faces of your own grandchildren and know that you have done your duty and kept your oath.[6]

The words here are striking, even moving. They are also prescient. In the 1960s and later, their assertion of equality before the law and a respect for constitutional guarantees of that equality would become a broadly shared understanding of what the civil rights movement was fundamentally about. But such a position about the rights of African Americans was not commonly heard in Mississippi courtrooms in the early 1950s. One can hardly imagine a young Mississippi attorney with the daring to stand before a segregationist judge and address him not only on constitutional law but also on the need to think about his reputation as he aged. All strong stuff, every bit worthy of an Atticus Finch.[7]

However, given the absence of a trial transcript, there is no definitive contemporary evidence that Joe Pigott spoke these precise words in court in 1951.[8] The language itself invites some skepticism. A motion for a directed verdict is often not couched in such rhetoric. Many are appeals to specific elements of the law or other defined procedure and precedent, not to a judge's thoughts about his conscience as he ages, the regard in which his grandchildren might hold him, the graves of fighting men, or the honor of the flag. Reporter Charles Gordon, who wrote many thousands of words on the Barnes case, said nothing specific then or later about Pigott's words to Brady. Gordon quoted and paraphrased Brady's words to the jury, but nothing of the motion by Pigott. Such language, if it had accompanied the motion, would have been newsworthy. Many Mississippi circuit judges, then and later, might have been offended by the presumption of a twenty-five-year-old attorney admonishing them to remember their oath and their duty. But still, as we have seen, Joe Pigott was capable of bold action.

Could Pigott have said something to this effect to Judge Brady, perhaps in his chambers? Nothing indicates that the judge and attorneys retired to Brady's chambers to consider the motion. Could Pigott have discussed the matter with Brady in some other way before the trial or during a recess? Such a discussion would have been unrecorded. Finally, some of these words literally could not have been spoken in 1951. In 1951, Joe Pigott would not have referred to Judge Brady's speeches to the Citizens' Councils, because the Citizens' Councils did not then exist.[9] In short, the words later ascribed to Pigott cannot be considered a definitive representation of what he said to Brady in 1951. It cannot be proven that he said nothing of this sort to Brady. But no contemporary source or witness, other than Pigott himself, ever said that he did. The document, read in the film by Ronald Whittington, likely represents Joe Pigott's efforts, years after the fact, to record what had happened in the courtroom in 1951. But that itself is not a reason to discount the words of this reconstruction. While many motions for a directed verdict would have been less dramatic, it is just as likely that this one was not. Joe Pigott knew that this was his only real chance to keep Barnes out of the hands of the jury. He would certainly have thought deliberately about what he would say to Judge Brady. A motion offered with emotion and rhetorical calculation, then, would not only not have been out of place but also must have seemed to Pigott a necessity.

The later version of Pigott's speech to Brady adds another element to the story that is not present in Gordon's reporting. In it, and in the courtroom scene in Clopton's *Mississippi Justice,* Brady ordered the courtroom cleared so that Barnes, accompanied by Pigott, could safely exit, the strong implication being that such caution was necessary because of potential mob action against Barnes.[10] While there is no doubt that some people in the courtroom would have been surprised or even outraged by this dismissal of charges, there is no evidence that a mob gathered. But there is also no doubt that Barnes would not have wished to remain on the scene any longer than she was required to do. These qualifications aside, filmmaker Wilma Mosely Clopton is correct on many central matters: the Barnes case demonstrates the dangers Barnes faced in shooting a white man; Barnes was freed because of the principled work of Joe Pigott and Charles Gordon; and the story has inherent drama.

Recent tellings of the Barnes story, including Clopton's film, the discussion of that film in the McComb newspaper and other media, and surely this book as well, demonstrate one of the chief hazards in the search for Hattie Lee Barnes. A common feature in narratives about Mississippi is the attempt to find heroes and villains. The Barnes story, to the degree that it is remembered, sometimes seems one about the bravery of Joe Pigott and Charles Gordon as much as it is about Barnes herself. "I never talked with my father about it much," said Brad Pigott. "But it's interesting what any of us will do when we're 28 years old." "You are," said Pigott, "a little ambitious to tell the world it's messed up and needs to change." But like Charles Gordon, it seems unlikely that Joe Pigott in the early 1950s would have described himself as a crusader. Instead, he probably would have construed his work here in much more personal and professional terms: on a fundamental point of law, the system of Mississippi justice was wrong and seemed headed toward an unjust conviction of an innocent woman. Nor would Hattie Lee Barnes likely have seen her case as having much to do with broader social issues. To both Barnes and Pigott, their energies were aimed at the more immediate goal of rescuing Barnes from the shadow of the state's electric chair.[11]

Still, both Pigott and Gordon did a good deal more than they had to do in the name of professional diligence or ethics. Few white men in that time and place would have done so much. Both men seem to have been driven by a sense that a profound wrong was being done. Joe Pigott could not have calculated that his representation of Barnes would do him much immediate professional good. Some people in the area would have understood the principle of an indigent woman's need for an attorney. Others would have resented Pigott's taking a Black woman's case when the victim was a white man. If anyone threatened Pigott for his representation of Barnes, he did not speak publicly of it; so much more the credit to him, then, if that happened. None of this is to discount any element of Pigott's representation of Barnes. It needs, however, no dramatic embellishment. For dramatic embellishment can overshadow another, equally valid way to look at the Barnes case. Individual bravery and resolution were by themselves no guarantors of success or survival, then or later in Mississippi. The Barnes story might just as well be told as one about the capriciousness of Jim Crow justice in Mississippi.

The way that the Barnes story can be told—by a historian, at least—is dependent upon evidence. Many details of the life of Hattie Lee Barnes are difficult to recover. Even Barnes's age is subject to frustrating variations in different accounts of the story. In a 2005 recounting of the case, Barnes is described as twenty-five. In a 2019 story, her age is given as twenty.[12] Barnes's marriages are not part of a clear public record—certainly not in the ways that the marriages of many white people were. No account of the case, either in the 1950s or more recently, tells what became of Hattie Lee Barnes after the cases were disposed of by the Mississippi legal system. They do not say where she went after the mid-1950s, whether she remained married to Leon Gardner or married someone else, if she had children, under what name she lived, where she spent the rest of her life, or even when she died or where she is buried.

To put it mildly, one would wish to know more about Hattie Lee Barnes. What were the details of her life before she shot Lamar Craft? After the trials were over, where did she go and how did the rest of her life unfold? Some of these facts, even if records are elusive or missing, are potentially recoverable. But other matters likely are not. What, for instance, did Barnes think of Pigott and Gordon? From her jail cell, she talked openly and apparently frankly with Gordon. But why? Gordon calculated that telling the truth about the injustices being done to Barnes would work favorable pressure upon white public opinion and even on the unfolding legal process. But would Barnes have dared to think so? Barnes, who could not read newspapers, likely had little direct impression of Gordon's work, other than perhaps a sense that he was a man of influence. It seems unlikely that she sought him out; Gordon, a man accustomed to pushing for sources, instead probably approached her.

What did she make of Pigott's advocacy? She had no choice but to accept her court-appointed attorney if she were to have legal representation. But how clearly did Pigott explain to Barnes what he would do on her behalf and why? The content of the conversations between the two of them, including the tone and other less tangible elements, are matters that cannot be recovered. If Joe Pigott made notes on the case, they either have not survived or have not surfaced. A work of fiction might imagine those encounters. But as tempting as it is to presume or guess in the name of storytelling, a work of history must resist, or else go beyond what the evidence supports.

Similarly, extant details of Lamar Craft's life do not offer a full portrait. To the degree that Craft's story is part of the public record, he is remembered as someone shot in a roadhouse window during the commission of a crime. We cannot say if this was an aberrant act or one that Craft's earlier actions had prefigured. What of the nature of the friendship between Craft, Easterling, and Hope? How did Craft's family remember and speak about him in future years? Outside the courtroom, did they ever again encounter Rob Lee, and what might they have said to him about the shooting? After the two Craft brothers' 1951 attempt to assassinate Lee, it does not appear that they ever again decided physically to exact revenge against him. Family conversations and potential chance encounters with Rob Lee over the years are further matters for which no documentation exists.

What documentation does exist? In writing a book on a later case prosecuted by district attorney Joe Pigott, I learned of his work for Barnes.[13] Pigott's legal records, especially the ones dealing with his private practice, cannot be found in archives. In the early 1990s, when he still served as judge, Pigott maintained a home office, recalls one writer. His garage held "stacks of documents on the desk and in every corner."[14] It is possible that in that collection, there were materials on his defense of Hattie Lee Barnes. Or perhaps not. By the 1990s, the matter was decades old and long settled.

In early 2020, I drove to Pike, Walthall, and Marion Counties for records stemming from the shootings of Craft and Barnes. In none of those county courthouses did the original case files still exist. That is not rare. Mississippi courthouses deal in new and recent business. Old files are lost, ruined, or sometimes discarded if storage is limited. Records of cases that are nearly seventy years old, involving people long dead and some of them long forgotten, have a tendency somehow to slip away. Those courthouses did still hold the folio-sized docket books in which business was entered. There, one finds entries from indictment through final disposition. While those are only the skeletons of the stories, they do provide documentation of how the county legal system dealt with each of these cases.

In Marion County, where Lee and Watson were tried for shooting Barnes, I received cordial assistance from several people, one of whom dug through many boxes in the old county jail, which serves as a courthouse annex and repository. But the Lee and Watson files were not to be found. Similarly, in Walthall County, where Edd Craft sued the American National Insurance Company, one can find records of the filing and disposition of the suit, but no file of the case itself. In Pike County, where Barnes was tried, I also learned that the case file could not be found. Perhaps it would turn up, I was told. Later, the circuit clerk emailed me that it had not. That file would have contained copies of subpoenas for witnesses and perhaps also various motions and instructions to the jury. The names of people subpoenaed can be gleaned from the docket book and can be inferred from press coverage of the trial. But the file would not have contained a copy of Joe Pigott's motion for a directed verdict, for it was presented orally, not in written form. That court file would not have contained a copy of the trial transcript. With Barnes's acquittal, there would have been no real need for one. This is not to say that a transcript of the Barnes trial was not made. Any attorney—perhaps even Breed Mounger—might have had his own purposes in ordering a copy. As a party much interested in the larger story of Barnes, it is possible that Joe Pigott might have wished to have one. But if a trial transcript exists, it remains in private hands.

However, the trials of Walter Watson and Rob Lee resulted in convictions and then appeals to the Mississippi Supreme Court. The insurance company suit filed by the Craft family also was appealed to the state supreme court. At the Mississippi Department of Archives and History in Jackson, then, one can find hundreds of pages of records from these cases, including copies of the original county court files and the trial transcripts that were prepared as part of the appeal process. Still extant as well is the file of the habeas corpus motion, ultimately unsuccessful, that Pigott filed on behalf of Barnes as she sat jailed in southwestern Mississippi awaiting her possible use by the state as a witness in the trial of Rob Lee that never occurred.

Along with Charles Gordon's writing, these documents represent the fullest existing source of the story from 1951 to 1955. But they do not include attorneys' notes, as such notes were not court records. Neither can one find any materials from sheriffs, deputies, or police officers. Further, what does not exist in any form is testimony from Barnes, Watson, or any other African American that is not mediated through the Mississippi legal system. All their statements must be read with the realization that they were reluctant participants in an unfriendly, if not outright adversarial system. This is not to say that their testimony is unreliable, but one cannot presume that it represents what they really thought, in distinction to what they believed it was in their best interest to reveal. Barnes's words—our only source of her voice—are mediated through legal documents. Even in Gordon's accounts of what Barnes told him, her words are inflected through the lens of a white person, albeit one who evidenced real sympathy for Barnes.

Transcripts of legal proceedings have other limits. They do not convey tone, attitude, nonverbal responses, or the ways in which people carried themselves in the courtroom: none of these are the business of a court reporter to take down. The eye of a reporter such as Charles Gordon can supply some of these details. There, we hear how various parties in the trials looked or how they reacted to certain testimony. Even so, a record of what happened in the courtrooms of southwestern Mississippi represents only a portion of the Barnes story. For many other matters, neither a court reporter nor a newspaper reporter was present.

Before leaving southwestern Mississippi in January, 2020, I met with Ronnie Whittington, the McComb attorney who served as narrator of Dr. Wilma Mosley Clopton's *Mississippi Justice*. After a brief telephone call, he invited me to his law office. On a conference table, we spread out our gathered documents, sharing what we knew of the case. Whittington told me that he had seen the Barnes case file in the Pike County Courthouse, but when he saw it, he did not say. He provided the only indication that I have received that Hattie Lee Barnes returned to or perhaps remained in the area after these matters were concluded. He told me of a conversation with a woman at Magnolia Electric, an area power cooperative, who had known Barnes. That person told Whittington that Barnes was buried "at Sunny Hill." In Walthall County are two Sunny Hill churches. I drove to them and walked their cemeteries but found no grave for Barnes. My letters to both of those churches, asking for their assistance in locating Barnes's grave, should she in fact be buried there, have so far gone unanswered.

WHAT FINALLY IS THE significance of the Hattie Lee Barnes story and its associated cases and trials? The matter held area people's attention for a time. It provides an example of a Black Mississippian's being acquitted of murdering a white person, and of a white person's being punished for attempting to kill a Black person, facts that might surprise some people with certain impressions of Mississippi in the 1950s. But the case did not usher in a new day in Mississippi justice. Because Rob Lee's efforts to kill Barnes were not successful, she does not figure as a martyr in a literal sense, either in the quest for civil rights or for anything else. She never asked for or received any compensation for her extended detention at the hands of the Mississippi legal system. She never in subsequent years seems to have made efforts to publicize her story, either for financial gain or any other reason.

What is officially remembered and commemorated in Mississippi, as in the rest of America, has always had something to do with questions of power. In this case, there is much less of an active memory or retelling than one finds in other cases of murder or interracial violence. Practically no one with a direct connection to this case is still alive. Unlike Monroeville, Alabama, the Macomb of Harper Lee's novel, no one in McComb or Magnolia seems to have proposed an annual reenactment of the trial of Barnes. To be fair to Pike County, however, no one has written a novel or made a full movie about the case, so the reenactment as a tourist attraction might have limited appeal. But one imagines that some of the same dynamics that currently play out in Alabama with *Mockingbird* reenactments might be seen in Pike County, should anyone wish to undertake such a project. For white fans of *To Kill a Mockingbird*, the story inspires warm, often self-congratulatory feelings. African American reactions to the story are somewhat less enthusiastic. For Black residents of Pike County, a memorialization of the Hattie Lee Barnes story might serve as something other than a tale about individual courage. It might say things about the persistence of racial injustice and the dangers the legal system posed and continues to pose to Black residents.[15]

These matters suggest reasons why it is important to remember the Barnes case. Many African Americans—as well as many white people of common means—found themselves enmeshed in the legal system of Mississippi without the resources, the luck, or perhaps the will evidenced by Hattie Lee Barnes. They appear in the docket books of southwestern Mississippi courthouses as people indicted and tried and upon whom sentence was passed. Their stories typically were not extensively treated in local newspapers, unless for cases of murder or some other lurid crime, except as tallies of a grand jury's work. They went to Parchman to serve their time; their survived their ordeal or perhaps did not, and they returned to the county where they had previously lived, or they did not. The Barnes case, then, opens a window onto a process that was often essentially unknown, except to the people who were in the hands of the law. It also sheds light upon the operation of rural and small-town Mississippi life of the era—of the operation of social relations and the importance of knowing the right people.

Through the Barnes case—and in later years—one sees the influence of the Craft family. Not enough influence ultimately to insist that the public record of Lamar Craft's death tell the story they wanted told. But they did have the power to conduct essentially a shadow investigation of the case from the beginning. One can hire attorneys and private detectives anywhere, of course. But not everywhere does the legal system cooperate so fully with them as it did in Walthall and Pike Counties, with the Crafts and Breed Mounger being given access to witnesses and the ability to interrogate them under circumstances that might not have made it clear to everyone that the Craft-Mounger investigation was not part of the formal legal process. They also, of course, persuaded a Walthall County jury to accept their version, or at least find for them, in the suit Edd Craft filed against American National Insurance. We cannot know why that jury ruled the way that it did. To what degree was their verdict shaped by their understanding of the legal issues at play and to what degree was it influenced by their judgment of the personalities and reputations of the family involved? Even though the Mississippi Supreme Court found that jury's decision an error, the initial verdict does say something about county-level Mississippi justice.

In 1950, Mississippi had a population of about 2.2 million people. Personal and familial ties mattered. Knowing someone was the social grease that enabled transactions of many kinds. People believed that their judgment of a person's character and reputation was the yardstick by which most interactions should be measured. Attorneys who tried cases such as these well knew that fact. Black Mississippians did have ties of family and friendship. But the influence of these ties rarely extended directly into a Mississippi courtroom. Still, defenders of the status quo liked to say—and some no doubt believed—that habits of paternalism prevailed in the state, ones in which Black people could look to their white neighbors for assistance with legal difficulties or other troubling matters. In a sense, perhaps, there was some truth to that assertion. White influence could intervene in the police or judicial process as men of influence and standing saw fit. But the process was capricious. "In Jim Crow Mississippi," notes Neil McMillen, "where justice was bound by caste and where full citizenship was a white prerogative, the tension between social justice and social control was nearly always resolved in the interests of the dominant race."[16] Black Mississippians would have preferred an equitable system of justice to one allegedly tempered by paternalism. But that of course is precisely what Hattie Lee Barnes did not face.

Some measure of paternalism might be said to have operated in Barnes's situation because of what her case did not feature. Joe Pigott and Charles Gordon were able to help Barnes, and Judge Tom Brady did listen to Pigott's motion on her behalf, and the white people of McComb did respond to the appeal to raise money for her bond, and Oliver Emmerich was willing to write a strong editorial decrying her treatment at the hands of the law, all for one reason: Hattie Lee Barnes posed no threat to the racial order of Mississippi in the early 1950s. She had killed a white man. But the circumstances of that killing had nothing to do with a dispute over wages or working conditions, for instance, let alone voting or access to a segregated place. Nor was Barnes a man, in which case Judge Brady's comparison of her with a white woman's defending herself almost certainly would not have come as readily to his mind. It is too much to say that a species of chivalry played into the thinking of Pigott or

Gordon. But the fact that Barnes was a woman certainly meant that defending her was a less risky proposition than defending a Black man might have been. Had this case involved an African American man breaking into a closed roadhouse seeking a white woman, that would have seemed a familiar southern horror story, one in which the villain had a certain expected end.

After 1955, as the records of Pike and Walthall and Marion Counties indicate, the courts continued to mete out justice in the customary fashion until changes in national law compelled them to cease doing so, if only in the most overt ways. At the time, white observers of the Barnes story probably did not conclude that the case demonstrated the need for systematic changes, either in Mississippi's legal system or in the broader patterns that shaped the lives of Black and white Mississippians. Little in the Barnes case or its handling might have suggested to them the need for radical change. If anything, a white person in the area in the mid-1950s could have concluded that the case showed the ability for decent human action to ensure justice. A white attorney ably took up Barnes's cause. A white journalist consistently pointed out the injustices being done to her. Area whites opened their pockets to contribute to a fund for Barnes herself. Nothing more, they probably thought, needed to be done. To most of them, what else could be done? Like most white southerners of the period, even if they questioned some of the specific acts of cruelty or discrimination against their Black neighbors, they might have believed that the system of Jim Crow itself was one of those matters about which one could do very little. It had been around forever, it seemed.

Black perspectives on the case are far more difficult to recover. Perhaps no Black person, including Barnes herself, would have seen the case as showing any broader point about Mississippi justice—certainly no point that would have reflected favorably on the system. If they did view this story as having a moral, it was one confirming what they already well knew. Mississippi justice was at best capricious. Practically all the cards that mattered were held in the hands of white people. The system of justice, politics, and the broader culture in Mississippi remained one in which personal connections and influence mattered very much. In such a system, the assistance of well-positioned white people could at times be a necessity. In such a system, the options available to Black Mississippians were constrained in fundamental ways. One might try to avoid entanglements; one might resist; one might pick up and leave. No

Black person in the area would have looked upon the Barnes case as one that changed anything fundamental. Hattie Lee Barnes had no apparent desire to act as an advocate for anyone's cause other than her own. In future years, she did not speak about what had happened to her, at least in public, or at least in ways that would become apparent to a white audience. Such was her right. Little that had happened to her suggested the point of anything other than seeking a way out of immediate troubles. In the end, with the help of Joe Pigott and Charles Gordon, Barnes boarded a Greyhound bus and left Pike County, Mississippi. Despite the great odds stacked against her by the place she was born and the workings of the legal system that had ensnared her, Hattie Lee Barnes survived.

NOTES

INTRODUCTION

1. The bar's formal or legal name is unclear. Nor did area people consistently refer to it as a bar. In trials, hearings, and newspaper coverage, then and later, it was termed a tavern, a roadhouse, a joint, "Rob Lee's Place," or simply "Lee's place." Clearly, though, Rob Lee's bar was open to the public, not simply a bootlegger's house where alcohol was sold. Further, everyone distinguished the bar in which Craft was shot from an adjacent "place," also owned by Lee and operated for African American patrons. Pike County business, or "privilege," licenses for the year 1951 no longer exist (Pike County tax collector Gwen Nunnery, email to author, 30 November 2020).

2. *Enterprise-Journal,* 17 April 1951; *Monroe (LA) News-Star,* 18 April 1951; *Jackson (MS) Clarion-Ledger,* 18 April 1951; *Tylertown Times,* 19 April 1951; State of Mississippi v. Hattie Lee Barnes, Pike County Circuit Court, Case #10,338. That court file apparently no longer exists, as I note in the epilogue. Other details of the evening of April 16–17, 1951, are explored in cases discussed in the pages below, including Edd Craft v. American National Insurance Company, Case #797, Walthall County Circuit Court, as well as in the appeal of that decision, American National Insurance Co. v. Edd Craft, Walthall County Circuit Court, Case #39,476, 7 Feb. 1955; 222 Miss. 847, Supreme Court of Mississippi.

3. As I note below, in a 1951 trial, Barnes gave her age as twenty-one (State of Mississippi vs. Walter Watson, Case #2066, Marion County Circuit Court, trial transcript, 18). In a 1953 trial, she said she was twenty-three. Throughout the coverage of this story from 1951 through 1953, however, and in subsequent accounts in later decades, Barnes's age in 1951 is generally but not consistently given as twenty-two. If we believe Barnes herself, however, she was twenty-one years old in 1951.

4. *Enterprise-Journal,* 18 April, 19 April 1951.

5. *Greenwood Commonwealth,* 17 April, 18 April 1951; *Shreveport (LA) Times,* 18 April 1951.

6. *Enterprise-Journal,* 17 April 1951; *Greenwood Commonwealth,* 17 April 1951; *Enterprise-Journal,* 19 April 1951.

7. *Enterprise-Journal,* 25 October 1951.

8. As historian Gene Dattel notes, "the relative cost of hand labor versus the mechanical cotton picker completely eliminated the human field hand" (Dattel, *Cotton and Race in the Making of America: The Human Costs of Economic Power* [Lanham, MD: Ivan R. Dee, 2009], 357).

9. For an insightful examination of the challenges, including ethical challenges, that arise when seeking a historical figure who may have wished for anonymity, see Françoise N. Hamlin, "Historians and Ethics: Finding Anne Moody," *American Historical Review* 125, no. 2 (April 2020): 487–97.

10. Danielle L. McGuire, *At the Dark End of the Street: Black Women, Rape, and Resistance—A New History of the Civil Rights Movement from Rosa Parks to the Rise of Black Power* (New York: Knopf, 2010), 232.

11. Telisha Dionne Bailey, "'Please Don't Forget about Me': African American Women, Mississippi, and the History of Crime and Punishment in Parchman Prison, 1890–1980" (Ph.D. diss., University of Mississippi, 2015), 12–13.

12. Two recent studies of perhaps the most notorious Mississippi murder of the 1950s are Devery S. Anderson, *Emmett Till: The Murder That Shocked the World and Propelled the Civil Rights Movement* (Jackson: University Press of Mississippi, 2015); and Timothy B. Tyson, *The Blood of Emmett Till* (New York: Simon and Schuster, 2017).

13. Pete Daniel, *Lost Revolutions: The South in the 1950s* (Chapel Hill: University of North Carolina Press, 1999).

1. A ROADHOUSE SHOOTING AND ITS CONTEXT

1. www.almanac.com/weather/history/zipcode/39648/1951-04-16; www.moonpage.com/index.html?go=T&auto_dst=T&m=4&d=16&y=1951&hour=22&min=50&sec=52.

2. *Enterprise-Journal,* 17 April, 18 April 1951. The American League featured the St. Louis Browns, a team followed by fewer southwestern Mississippians, and by fewer St. Louis residents as well, for that matter.

3. *Enterprise-Journal,* 16 April 1951.

4. *Enterprise-Journal,* 20 February 1951. On inflation, see www.usinflationcalculator.com/.

5. *Enterprise-Journal,* 16 April 1951.

6. *Enterprise-Journal,* 16 April 1951.

7. On the civil rights movement in Pike County, see Charles Payne, *I've Got the Light of Freedom: The Organizing Tradition and the Mississippi Freedom Struggle (Berkeley: University of California Press, 1995),* 111–31; and John Dittmer, *Local People: The Struggle for Civil Rights in Mississippi* (Urbana: University of Illinois Press, 1994), 99–115, 266–71, 303–14. On 1964, see also Bruce Watson, *Freedom Summer: The Savage Season That Made Mississippi Burn and Made America a Democracy* (New York: Viking, 2010), 86–87, 135–36, 263–64; and Joseph Crespino, *In Search of Another Country: Mississippi and the Conservative Counterrevolution* (Princeton, NJ: Princeton University Press, 2007), 112–13, 119–30, 155–56.

8. On the civil rights movement in various Mississippi towns and counties, see William Sturkey, *Hattiesburg: An American City in Black and White* (Cambridge, MA: Harvard University Press, 2019); Patricia Michelle Boyette, *Right to Revolt: The Crusade for Justice in Mississippi's*

Central Piney Woods (Jackson: University Press of Mississippi, 2015); Françoise N. Hamlin, *Crossroads at Clarksdale: The Black Freedom Struggle in the Mississippi Delta after World War II* (Chapel Hill: University of North Carolina Press, 2012); and Jason Morgan Ward, *Hanging Bridge: Racial Violence and America's Civil Rights Century* (New York: Oxford University Press, 2016).

9. For a collection of some of the best recent scholarship on the period, see Ted Ownby, ed., *The Civil Rights Movement in Mississippi* (Jackson: University Press of Mississippi, 2013). On the broader culture that informed the Barnes case, see Stephen A. Berrey, *The Jim Crow Routine: Everyday Performances of Race, Civil Rights, and Segregation in Mississippi* (Chapel Hill: University of North Carolina Press, 2015).

10. An early and influential essay on this topic is Jacquelyn Dowd Hall, "The Long Civil Rights Movement and the Political Uses of the Past," *American Historical Review* 91, no. 4 (March 2005): 1233–63.

11. Thomas D. Clark, *Pills, Petticoats, and Plows: The Southern Country Store* (Indianapolis: Bobbs-Merrill, 1944).

12. Ted Ownby, *American Dreams in Mississippi: Consumers, Poverty, and Culture, 1830–1998* (Chapel Hill: University of North Carolina Press, 1999).

13. James C. Cobb, *The Selling of the South: The Southern Crusade for Industrial Development, 1936–1990*, 2nd ed. (Urbana: University of Illinois Press, 1993); see esp. 5–34. McComb native and Mississippi governor Hugh L. White persuaded the Mississippi legislature in 1936 to pass his Balance Agriculture with Industry Program (see Ted Ownby and Charles Reagan Wilson, eds., *The Mississippi Encyclopedia [Jackson: University Press of Mississippi, 2017]*, 63).

14. For a brief overview, see "Judiciary," in *Mississippi Encyclopedia*, 672–73. For a full study, see Joseph A. Ranney, *A Legal History of Mississippi: Race, Class, and the Struggle for Opportunity* (Jackson: University Press of Mississippi, 2019).

15. *Enterprise-Journal*, 17 April 1951.

16. Dittmer, *Local People*, 52–53.

17. https://worldpopulationreview.com/us-counties/ms/walthall-county-population; https://www2.census.gov/library/publications/decennial/1950/population-volume-2/37779777v2p24ch2.pdf.

18. www2.census.gov/library/publications/decennial/1950/pc-02/pc-2-27.pdf.

19. https://mississippiencyclopedia.org/entries/walthall-county/.

20. https://mississippiencyclopedia.org/entries/walthall-county/.

21. On Pike County's early history, see Martin J. Hardeman, *The Structure of Time: Pike County, Mississippi, 1815–1912* (New York: Peter Lang, 1999). See also James L. McCorkle Jr., "The Illinois Central R.R. and the Mississippi Commercial Vegetable Industry," *Journal of Mississippi History* 29 (May 1977): 155–72. For population in 1950, see www2.census.gov/library/publications/decennial/1950/population-volume-2/37779777v2p24ch2.pdf.

22. www.co.walthall.ms.us/historical-info.html.

23. https://mississippiencyclopedia.org/entries/walthall-county/.

24. For population in 1950, see www2.census.gov/library/publications/decennial/1950/population-volume-2/37779777v2p24ch2.pdf; https://mississippiencyclopedia.org/entries/marion-county/.

25. In 1950, approximately 600,000 Mississippians lived in "urban territory" as defined by

the US Census, while more than 1.5 million Mississippians lived in "rural territory." Only fifteen cities in the state had a population of more than 10,000 people. McComb in Pike County was one of them (www2.census.gov/library/publications/decennial/1950/population-volume-2/37779777v2p24ch2.pdf).

26. *Enterprise-Journal,* 2 January 1951.

27. *Enterprise-Journal,* 9 January 1951.

28. *Enterprise-Journal,* 22 March 1951.

29. See Alex Heard, *The Eyes of Willie McGee: A Tragedy of Race, Sex, and Secrets in the Jim Crow South* (New York: Harper, 2010). McGee was executed in the state's portable electric chair.

30. John R. Skates Jr., "World War II as a Watershed in Mississippi History," *Journal of Mississippi History* 37 (1975): 131–42; Neil McMillen, ed., *Remaking Dixie: The Impact of World War II on the American South* (Jackson: University Press of Mississippi, 1997).

2. THE CASE AGAINST HATTIE LEE BARNES

1. *Enterprise-Journal,* 10 August 1951. In that August primary, Edd Craft ran second to Rufus Dillon, necessitating a runoff election, won by Dillon, who received 1,844 votes to Craft's 1,572 (*Enterprise-Journal,* 29 August 1951).

2. *Enterprise-Journal,* 22 May 1989; *Clarion-Ledger,* 10 April 1930.

3. *Enterprise-Journal,* 23 March, 8 August 1938.

4. www.ancestry.com/interactive/2442/M-T0627-02073-00203?pid=124255902&backurl=https://search.ancestry.com/cgi-bin/sse.dll?indiv%3D1%26dbid%3D2442%26h%3D124255902%26tid%3D%26pid%3D%26usePUB%3Dtrue%26_phsrc%3DOjJ156%26_phstart%3DsuccessSource&treeid=&personid=&hintid=&usePUB=true&_phsrc=OjJ156&_phstart=successSource&usePUBJs=true#?imageId=M-T0627-02073-00203.

5. *Enterprise-Journal,* 28 September 1950.

6. *Enterprise-Journal,* 17 April 1951.

7. *Greenwood Commonwealth,* 17 April 1951; *Monroe* (LA) *News-Star,* 18 April 1951.

8. *Clarion-Ledger,* 18 April 1951; *Enterprise-Journal,* 18 April 1951.

9. Mississippi's justices of the peace operated inferior courts (technically speaking) throughout the state. An elected magistrate, the justice of the peace operated his court sometimes in the back of a store or in his home. While they often heard matters involving small debts, they could also hear minor criminal complaints as well (https://mississippiencyclopedia.org/overviews/law/). A person committing a criminal offense in a Mississippi county might find himself before one of three courts. There was the justice of the peace court. Then there was a county court, which in this era heard only cases dealing with contested amounts of less than three thousand dollars. There was also the district court system, which had jurisdiction over a several-county area. On the county courts, see, for example, *Enterprise-Journal,* 14 May 1956. Within municipalities such as McComb, there was also a city or police court.

10. *Enterprise-Journal,* 19 April 1951; *Clarion-Ledger,* 20 April 1951.

11. www.findagrave.com/memorial/84263779/edd-tunison-craft.

12. *Tylertown Times,* 19 April 1951.

13. *Tylertown Times,* 19 April 1951.

14. *Tylertown Times,* 19 April 1951.

15. *Tylertown Times,* 19 April 1951.

16. *Hattiesburg American,* 5 July 1951.

17. *Enterprise-Journal,* 18 April 1951.

18. *Enterprise-Journal,* 17 April 1951.

19. The Supreme Court threw out the convictions in that case because of the state's frank admission of the beatings of the plaintiff (www.lexisnexis.com/community/casebrief/p/casebrief-brown-v-mississippi).

20. *Enterprise-Journal,* 19 April 1951.

21. *Enterprise-Journal,* 19 April 1951.

22. *Enterprise-Journal,* 19 April 1951. That article does not give Magee's name. It also misidentifies him as Barnes's father.

23. In this era, each county was served by a county prosecuting attorney, who assisted the county's district attorney in prosecutions. The district attorney served more than one county, generally two or three in the area.

24. *Clarion-Ledger,* 20 April 1951.

25. Clayton Sledge Allen, "The Repeal of Prohibition in Mississippi" (master's thesis, University of Mississippi, 1992); *Clarion-Ledger,* 20 April 1951.

26. *Enterprise-Journal,* 21 July 1939.

27. *Enterprise-Journal,* 10 July 1940.

28. On period elections dealing with alcohol, see Anne Ophelia Bailey, "A Statistical Analysis of the Liquor Referenda in Mississippi, 1934 and 1952" (master's thesis, Mississippi State College, 1953). On the earlier movement for Prohibition, see William Graham Davis, "Attacking 'The Matchless Evil': Temperance and Prohibition in Mississippi, 1817–1905" (Ph.D. diss., Mississippi State University, 1975).

29. *Enterprise-Journal,* 4 January 1949.

30. *Enterprise-Journal,* 12 April 1949.

31. *Enterprise-Journal,* 28 April 1949.

32. *Enterprise-Journal,* 27 April 1964.

33. *Enterprise-Journal,* 19 April 1951; *Clarion-Ledger,* 20 April 1951.

34. In 1949, however, two Pike County establishments operated by Ruth M. Lee, "one white and one for colored," were padlocked by order of the chancery court. It is likely that these were the two places still operated by the Lees in 1951 (*Enterprise-Journal,* 6 June 1949).

3. TWO ATTEMPTED MURDERS

1. *Enterprise-Journal,* 24 April 1951.

2. *Enterprise-Journal,* 24 April 1951.

3. At some point after February 1955, Joe Pigott created a timeline of the case, stretching from the April 17, 1951, shooting of Lamar Craft through the February 7, 1955, Mississippi Supreme Court ruling in favor of the American National Insurance Company, the subject of chapter 7

(copy of Pigott's timeline in author's possession, courtesy of Brad Pigott, "[Joe Pigott], State vs. Hattie Lee Barnes for Murder of Lamar Craft in Pike County, MS"). The timeline gives the man's name as "A. B. Hinson."

4. *Enterprise-Journal,* 24 April 1951.

5. *Enterprise-Journal,* 24 April 1951.

6. Donald A. Cabana, "The History of Capital Punishment in Mississippi: An Overview," available at http://mshistorynow.mdah.state.ms.us/articles/84/history-of.

7. *Enterprise-Journal,* 24 April 1951.

8. *Enterprise-Journal,* 24 April 1951. Those conflicting accounts would surface in testimony given in Edd Craft's suit against the American National Insurance Company.

9. *Enterprise-Journal,* 24 April 1951.

10. "[Joe Pigott], State vs. Hattie Lee Barnes for Murder of Lamar Craft in Pike County, MS."

11. *Tylertown Times,* 17 May 1951; *Enterprise-Journal,* 16 May 1951.

12. *Tylertown Times,* 17 May 1951. In a photograph, deputy sheriffs Jim Duckworth and Neville Patterson point out the damage to the vehicle *(Enterprise-Journal,* 18 June 1951).

13. *Enterprise-Journal,* 11 May 1951.

14. *Hattiesburg American,* 16 May 1951; *Enterprise-Journal,* 16 May 1951; *Monroe (LA) News-Star,* 17 May 1951; *Clarion-Ledger,* 17 May 1951; *Delta Democrat-Times,* 16 May 1951. The *Tylertown Times* reported that Lee was taken to and treated in the Marion County General Hospital, located in Columbia.

15. *Enterprise-Journal,* 15 June 1951.

16. *Hattiesburg American,* 15 June 1951. The newspaper described Lee as Barnes's "bootlegging employer," noting that he "is listed with the state tax collector as a retail liquor dealer."

17. *Clarion-Ledger,* 16 June 1951. In this account, Barnes said that Lee had shot her three times, and Watson twice.

18. *Tylertown Times,* 21 June 1951.

19. McLaren, however, was not district attorney for Marion County; R. G. Livingston was. But these cases were overlapping. Area law enforcement officers, including district and county attorneys, commonly cooperated on investigations, if not on prosecutions themselves, although occasionally they did that as well.

20. *Tylertown Times,* 21 June 1951; *Clarion-Ledger,* 16 June 1951. This story as well identified Lee as "a Marion County bootlegger."

21. *Tylertown Times,* 21 June 1951; Statement of Walter Watson, Hattiesburg, Mississippi, June 16, 1951, attached as exhibit in Marion County Circuit Court File, Case #2066.

22. Statement of Walter Watson, Hattiesburg, Mississippi, June 16, 1951, attached as exhibit in Marion County Circuit Court File, Case #2066.

23. Statement of Walter Watson, Hattiesburg, Mississippi, June 16, 1951, attached as exhibit in Marion County Circuit Court File, Case #2066.

24. Statement of Walter Watson, Hattiesburg, Mississippi, June 16, 1951, attached as exhibit in Marion County Circuit Court File, Case #2066.

25. Statement of Walter Watson, Hattiesburg, Mississippi, June 16, 1951, attached as exhibit in Marion County Circuit Court File, Case #2066.

26. Statement of Walter Watson, Hattiesburg, Mississippi, June 16, 1951, attached as exhibit in Marion County Circuit Court File, Case #2066.

27. Statement of Walter Watson, Hattiesburg, Mississippi, June 16, 1951, attached as exhibit in Marion County Circuit Court File, Case #2066.

28. *Enterprise-Journal,* 18 June 1951.

29. *Tylertown Times,* 21 June 1951.

30. *Tylertown Times,* 21 June 1951.

31. *Enterprise-Journal,* 21 June 1951.

32. *Enterprise-Journal,* 21 June 1951.

4. THE TRIAL OF WALTER WATSON

1. *Enterprise-Journal,* 25 June 1951.

2. *Clarion-Ledger,* 23 June 1951. Throughout the unfolding legal saga, the Jackson newspaper would describe Lee as "a retail liquor dealer in this dry state." An Alabama newspaper referred to Lee as a "white bootlegger and trigger man" (*Alabama Tribune [Montgomery],* 6 July 1951). Mississippi's circuit courts in that era operated only during limited, defined spring and fall terms. The term in which Lee and Watson were indicted opened on June 18, 1951 (Marion County Circuit Court Docket, June term, 1951, p. 121, Marion County Courthouse, Columbia, Mississippi). The case was State of Mississippi v. Walter Watson, Marion County Circuit Court, Case #2066.

3. Marion County Circuit Court Docket, June term, 1951, pp. 124–27, Marion County Courthouse, Columbia, Mississippi.

4. *Enterprise-Journal,* 25 June 1951.

5. "[Joe Pigott], State vs. Hattie Lee Barnes for Murder of Lamar Craft in Pike County, MS," copy of timeline in author's possession.

6. *Tylertown Times,* 28 June 1951. This photograph is one of only two of Barnes that were published during the years of the case.

7. State of Mississippi v. Walter Watson, Marion County Circuit Court, Case #2066.

8. *Enterprise-Journal,* 27 June 1951; State of Mississippi vs. Walter Watson, Case #2066, Marion County Circuit Court, trial transcript, 4–5, 20.

9. In 1956, Duncan would find himself in the Marion County Courthouse, charged with murdering another Walthall County farmer, William Packwood. The shooting, which occurred just inside the Marion County line, stemmed from a dispute over posted property signs (*Clarion-Ledger,* 24 September 1956; *Enterprise-Journal,* 25 September, 13 December 1956; *Columbian-Progress* [Columbia, MS], 27 September, 4 October 1956).

10. State of Mississippi vs. Walter Watson, Case #2066, Marion County Circuit Court, trial transcript, 9–10.

11. State of Mississippi vs. Walter Watson, Case #2066, Marion County Circuit Court, trial transcript, 11.

12. State of Mississippi vs. Walter Watson, Case #2066, Marion County Circuit Court, trial transcript, 13–14.

13. State of Mississippi vs. Walter Watson, Case #2066, Marion County Circuit Court, trial transcript, 15–16.

14. State of Mississippi vs. Walter Watson, Case #2066, Marion County Circuit Court, trial transcript, 18.

15. State of Mississippi vs. Walter Watson, Case #2066, Marion County Circuit Court, trial transcript, 18–19.

16. State of Mississippi vs. Walter Watson, Case #2066, Marion County Circuit Court, trial transcript, 22–23.

17. State of Mississippi vs. Walter Watson, Case #2066, Marion County Circuit Court, trial transcript, 22–24.

18. State of Mississippi vs. Walter Watson, Case #2066, Marion County Circuit Court, trial transcript, 30–31.

19. State of Mississippi vs. Walter Watson, Case #2066, Marion County Circuit Court, trial transcript, 31–32.

20. State of Mississippi vs. Walter Watson, Case #2066, Marion County Circuit Court, trial transcript, 33–34.

21. State of Mississippi vs. Walter Watson, Case #2066, Marion County Circuit Court, trial transcript, 49.

22. State of Mississippi vs. Walter Watson, Case #2066, Marion County Circuit Court, trial transcript, 50.

23. State of Mississippi vs. Walter Watson, Case #2066, Marion County Circuit Court, trial transcript, 51–52.

24. State of Mississippi vs. Walter Watson, Case #2066, Marion County Circuit Court, trial transcript, 54–55.

25. State of Mississippi vs. Walter Watson, Case #2066, Marion County Circuit Court, trial transcript, 59–61.

26. State of Mississippi vs. Walter Watson, Case #2066, Marion County Circuit Court, trial transcript, 70–77.

27. Instructions to the jury are in State of Mississippi vs. Walter Watson, Case #2066, Marion County Circuit Court.

28. *Tylertown Times,* 28 June 1951.

29. For the photograph of Duckworth and Watson, the only photo of Watson published during the Barnes saga, see *Tylertown Times,* 28 June 1951.

30. The appeal and its denial are included in the file of State of Mississippi vs. Walter Watson, Case #2066, Marion County Circuit Court. Watson furthered his appeal in Walter Watson vs. State of Mississippi, Mississippi Supreme Court Case #38,282.

31. https://mississippiencyclopedia.org/entries/parchman-prison/. See also William Banks Taylor, *Down on Parchman Farm: The Great Prison in the Mississippi Delta* (Columbus: Ohio State University Press, 1999); and David Oshinsky, *"Worse Than Slavery": Parchman Farm and the Ordeal of Jim Crow Justice* (New York: Free Press, 1996).

32. *Tylertown Times,* 28 June 1951.

33. *Enterprise-Journal,* 27 June 1951.

34. *Tylertown Times,* 28 June 1951.

35. *Enterprise-Journal*, 27 June 1951; *Clarion-Ledger*, 28 June 1951.

36. *Tylertown Times*, 28 June 1951.

37. *Clarion-Ledger*, 15 July 1951.

38. *Enterprise-Journal*, 16 July 1951.

39. *Enterprise-Journal*, 17 July 1951.

5. THE TRIAL OF HATTIE LEE BARNES

1. *Enterprise-Journal*, 3 October 1951.

2. *Enterprise-Journal*, 1 October 1951.

3. *Enterprise-Journal*, 13 December 2015; www.findagrave.com/memorial/155951183/george-winston-cutrer.

4. *Enterprise-Journal*, 5 October 1951; State of Mississippi v. Hattie Lee Barnes, Pike County Circuit Court, Criminal Docket, Case # 10338. The court's docket book contains entries from indictment through the dismissal of the case. The court file itself seems no longer to exist.

5. *Enterprise-Journal*, 5 October, 11 October 1951.

6. *Enterprise-Journal*, 24 October 1951.

7. *Enterprise-Journal*, 24 October 1951. This story gives Barnes's age as twenty-three. Earlier coverage had given her age as twenty-two. During the trial of Walter Watson, Barnes herself said—or at least the trial transcript says—that she was twenty-one. In Rob Lee's trial in 1953, Barnes said that she was twenty-three.

8. The jury that heard Barnes's trial consisted of the following men: V. T. Broomhall, L. L. Lewis, C. L. Roberts, E. B. Wilkinson, W. H. Farmer, Emil Cotten, O. C. Allen, Homer Godbold, Felix Bearden, Gordon Banister, Will Speed, and Ernest Hughes.

9. *Enterprise-Journal*, 24 October 1951.

10. *Enterprise-Journal*, 24 October 1951.

11. www.findagrave.com/memorial/72284014/oscar-hugh-hope.

12. *Enterprise-Journal*, 25 October 1951.

13. *Enterprise-Journal*, 25 October 1951.

14. *Enterprise-Journal*, 25 October 1951.

15. *Enterprise-Journal*, 25 October 1951.

16. *Enterprise-Journal*, 25 October 1951.

17. www.ancestry.com/interactive/2442/M-T0627-02073-00120?pid=124245785&backurl=https://search.ancestry.com/cgi-bin/sse.dll?indiv%3D1%26dbid%3D2442%26h%3D124245785%26tid%3D%26pid%3D%26usePUB%3Dtrue%26_phsrc%3DOjJ45%26_phstart%3DsuccessSource&treeid=&personid=&hintid=&usePUB=true&_phsrc=OjJ45&_phstart=successSource&usePUBJs=true.

18. *Enterprise-Journal*, 25 October 1951.

19. For a work critical of Mississippi's coroner system, see Radley Balko and Tucker Carrington, *The Cadaver King and the Country Dentist: A True Story of Injustice in the American South* (New York: Public Affairs, 2018), 59–60.

20. *Enterprise-Journal*, 25 October 1951.

21. *Enterprise-Journal,* 22 June 1934; 22 March, 19 April 1935; 31 March 1936.

22. A man with a sense of humor, Cain advertised his services just before the 1936 presidential election as "free to the Republicans." After Alf Landon's defeat, Cain announced that the "autopsy was completed at 11 o'clock last night, and the verdict was that Alf Landon died politically from being misled by selfish interests, particularly Al Smith, chronic bellyacher" (*Enterprise-Journal,* 3 November, 4 November 1936; 25 July 1939). Cain was reelected without opposition in 1939 and would serve as Pike County coroner, with one four-year interruption, until 1953 (*Enterprise-Journal,* 23 April 1946; 6 May 1953; 15 October 1956).

23. *Enterprise-Journal,* 25 October 1951.

24. *Enterprise-Journal,* 24 October 1951.

25. *Enterprise-Journal,* 25 October 1951.

26. *Enterprise-Journal,* 25 October 1951; *Hattiesburg American,* 25 October 1951; *Clarion-Ledger,* 25 October 1951; *Alabama Tribune* (Montgomery), 2 November 1951; State of Mississippi v. Hattie Lee Barnes, Pike County Circuit Court, Criminal Docket, Case #10338.

27. In some contemporary instances, such as a rape trial, a judge might not have allowed spectators in the courtroom at all. One such case was scheduled to be heard in the same term as Barnes's case. It involved a white man indicted for "alleged mistreatment" of his ten-year-old daughter (see *Enterprise-Journal,* 25 October 1951). We do have evidence of the exact procedure and wording of a later motion by Pigott for a preemptory verdict. There, the plaintiff rested. For the defense, Pigott said simply that he wanted "to make a motion." The jury was sent out. Pigott delivered a motion that contained no flourishes. It consisted of exactly 150 words (Edd Craft vs. American National Insurance Company, Walthall County Circuit Court File, Case #797, 79–80). That case is the subject of chapter 7.

28. *Enterprise-Journal,* 25 October 1951.

29. *Enterprise-Journal,* 25 October 1951.

30. *Enterprise-Journal,* 30 November 1951.

31. *Clarion-Ledger,* 25 October 1951.

32. *Hattiesburg American,* 25 October 1951.

33. *Alabama Tribune* (Montgomery), 2 November 1951. The story gives Brady's name as "Tom B. Grady" and also misspells the names of district attorney McLaren and Joe Pigott.

34. *Jet,* 8 November 1951, 23–24. The notice gives Brady's name incorrectly as "Tom P. Grady."

35. https://digitalcollections.usm.edu/uncategorized/digitalFile_5836a78a-6ff7-4fde-8a0a-9d1ae935de16/.

36. https://digitalcollections.usm.edu/uncategorized/digitalFile_5836a78a-6ff7-4fde-8a0a-9d1ae935de16/.

37. https://mississippiencyclopedia.org/entries/thomas-p-brady/; Daniel M. Hoehler, "Thomas P. Brady: A Passion for Order" (master's thesis, University of Mississippi, 1998).

38. Ranney, *A Legal History of Mississippi,* 6–7.

39. *Enterprise-Journal,* 25 October 1951.

6. THE TRIAL OF ROB LEE

1. *Enterprise-Journal,* 17 December 1951; Walter Watson v. State of Mississippi, Supreme Court Case #38,282.

2. *Clarion-Ledger,* 18 December 1951. The Jackson newspaper added a significant, previously unreported detail: it was Lee who arranged to bond Barnes out of jail before taking her to Leland back in the spring.

3. *Enterprise-Journal,* 17 December 1951.

4. *Enterprise-Journal,* 23 December 1952.

5. These two witnesses were Homer Regan and William Garner. Curiously, although they could not be located for testimony in the June 17 trial, they were able to appear the following day for the appeal (Rob Lee v. State of Mississippi, Supreme Court Case #39,082).

6. *Clarion-Ledger,* 18 June 1953; *Enterprise-Journal,* 17 June 1953.

7. *Enterprise-Journal,* 17 June 1953.

8. *Alabama Tribune (Montgomery),* 17 June 1953.

9. State of Mississippi v. Rob Lee, Marion County Court file #2065, trial transcript, 14.

10. State of Mississippi v. Rob Lee, Marion County Court file #2065, trial transcript, 16.

11. State of Mississippi v. Rob Lee, Marion County Court file #2065, trial transcript, 17–18.

12. State of Mississippi v. Rob Lee, Marion County Court file #2065, trial transcript, 18–19.

13. State of Mississippi v. Rob Lee, Marion County Court file #2065, trial transcript, 19–22.

14. State of Mississippi v. Rob Lee, Marion County Court file #2065, trial transcript, 22–26.

15. *Alabama Journal (Montgomery),* 18 June 1953; *Enterprise-Journal,* 18 June 1953; *Clarion-Ledger,* 18 June 1953.

16. State of Mississippi v. Rob Lee, Marion County Court file #2065, trial transcript, 30–32.

17. State of Mississippi v. Rob Lee, Marion County Court file #2065, trial transcript, 33–34.

18. State of Mississippi v. Rob Lee, Marion County Court file #2065, trial transcript, 35–36.

19. *Enterprise-Journal,* 18 June 1953.

20. *Alabama Journal (Montgomery),* 18 June 1953. In this account, the jury deliberated for eight minutes, not five, still extraordinarily quick work (*Columbian-Progress* [Columbia, MS], 18 June 1953).

21. *Jet,* 2 July 1953, 16.

22. *Enterprise-Journal,* 18 June 1953.

23. State of Mississippi v. Rob Lee, Marion County Court file #2065, trial transcript, 35–36.

24. State of Mississippi v. Rob Lee, Marion County Court file #2065, trial transcript, 46–47.

25. State of Mississippi v. Rob Lee, Marion County Court file #2065, trial transcript, 49–52.

26. Rob Lee v. State of Mississippi, Mississippi Supreme Court Case #39082.

27. *Enterprise-Journal,* 24 June 1953.

28. *Enterprise-Journal,* 7 July 1953.

29. *Enterprise-Journal,* 7 July 1953.

30. Caruthersville, Missouri, in Pemiscot County, is located deep in Missouri's bootheel, in a southeastern county bordering the Mississippi River. Caruthersville is well over 150 miles from Helena, Arkansas.

31. Nor was the marriage recorded (or any marriage for Leon Gardner between 1950 and 1956) in neighboring New Madrid County. Telephone call to New Madrid County Recorder of Deeds, 23 November 2020. No marriage was recorded in Dunklin County (Dunklin County recorder of deeds, email to author, 23 November 2020).

32. Helena is also the birthplace of the iconic country singer Conway Twitty.

33. *Northwest Arkansas Times* (Fayetteville), 15 March 1951.

34. *Enterprise-Journal,* 7 July 1953.

35. *Enterprise-Journal,* 7 July 1953.

36. *Enterprise-Journal,* 14 July 1953.

37. *Enterprise-Journal,* 15 July 1953.

38. *Enterprise-Journal,* 15 July 1953.

39. Hattie Lee Barnes Gardner v. Sheriff of Pike County and the State of Mississippi, Pike County Case #16,082.

40. Hattie Lee Barnes Gardner v. Sheriff of Pike County and the State of Mississippi, Pike County Case #16,082.

41. Hattie Lee Barnes Gardner v. Sheriff of Pike County and the State of Mississippi, Pike County Case #16,082.

42. Hattie Lee Barnes Gardner v. Sheriff of Pike County and the State of Mississippi, Pike County Case #16,082.

43. Hattie Lee Barnes Gardner v. Sheriff of Pike County and the State of Mississippi, Pike County Case #16,082.

44. Hattie Lee Barnes Gardner v. Sheriff of Pike County and the State of Mississippi, Pike County Case #16,082.

45. *Enterprise-Journal,* 15 July 1953.

46. *Enterprise-Journal,* 21 July 1953.

47. *Enterprise-Journal,* 21 July 1953.

48. *Enterprise-Journal,* 21 July 1953; *Clarion-Ledger,* 21 July 1953; *Columbian-Progress (Columbia, MS),* 23 July 1953; *Enterprise-Journal,* 23 July 1953.

49. *Clarion-Ledger,* 24 July 1953.

7. DOUBLE INDEMNITY

1. *Enterprise-Journal,* 15 July 1953; Edd Craft v. American National Insurance Company, Walthall County Case #797.

2. *Enterprise-Journal,* 13 August 1953.

3. Edd Craft vs. American National Insurance Company, Walthall County Circuit Court File, Case #797. *Enterprise-Journal,* 13 August 1953.

4. Edd Craft vs. American National Insurance Company, Walthall County Circuit Court File, Case #797, trial transcript, 62.

5. Edd Craft vs. American National Insurance Company, Walthall County Circuit Court File, Case #797, 16.

6. Edd Craft vs. American National Insurance Company, Walthall County Circuit Court File, Case #797, 72.

7. Edd Craft vs. American National Insurance Company, Walthall County Circuit Court File, Case #797, 62–63.

8. It is a testimony to court reporter Miss Tommye Thomas's virtue, if not her accuracy, that she was innocent of the spelling of Seagram's, which she gave as "Segram's."

9. Edd Craft vs. American National Insurance Company, Walthall County Circuit Court File, Case #797, 73–75.

10. Edd Craft vs. American National Insurance Company, Walthall County Circuit Court File, Case #797, 75–76.

11. Edd Craft vs. American National Insurance Company, Walthall County Circuit Court File, Case #797, 78.

12. *Enterprise-Journal,* 13 August 1953; Edd Craft vs. American National Insurance Company, Walthall County Circuit Court File, Case #797, 80.

13. Edd Craft vs. American National Insurance Company, Walthall County Circuit Court File, Case #797, 80–83.

14. Edd Craft vs. American National Insurance Company, Walthall County Circuit Court File, Case #797, 84.

15. Edd Craft vs. American National Insurance Company, Walthall County Circuit Court File, Case #797, 84–89.

16. Edd Craft vs. American National Insurance Company, Walthall County Circuit Court File, Case #797, 89–90.

17. Edd Craft vs. American National Insurance Company, Walthall County Circuit Court File, Case #797, 91–92.

18. Edd Craft vs. American National Insurance Company, Walthall County Circuit Court File, Case #797, 92–94.

19. Edd Craft vs. American National Insurance Company, Walthall County Circuit Court File, Case #797, 95–96.

20. Edd Craft vs. American National Insurance Company, Walthall County Circuit Court File, Case #797, 96.

21. Edd Craft vs. American National Insurance Company, Walthall County Circuit Court File, Case #797, 98.

22. Edd Craft vs. American National Insurance Company, Walthall County Circuit Court File, Case #797, 101–4.

23. Edd Craft vs. American National Insurance Company, Walthall County Circuit Court File, Case #797, 105–8.

24. Edd Craft vs. American National Insurance Company, Walthall County Circuit Court, Case #797, 116–22.

25. Edd Craft vs. American National Insurance Company, Walthall County Circuit Court, Case #797, 53–55.

26. American National Insurance Co. v. Edd Craft, No. 39476, 7 February 1955, 222 Miss. 847, Supreme Court of Mississippi.

27. Edd Craft v. American National Insurance Company, Case #797, Walthall County Circuit Court.

8. HATTIE LEE BARNES AND THE *McCOMB ENTERPRISE-JOURNAL*

1. J. Oliver Emmerich, *Two Faces of Janus: The Saga of Deep South Change* (Jackson: University Press of Mississippi, 1973). On Emmerich's broader career, see David R. Davies, "J. Oliver Emmerich and the McComb *Enterprise-Journal*," in *The Press and Race: Mississippi Journalists Confront the Movement, ed. Davies* (Jackson: University Press of Mississippi, 2001), 111–34. See also David R. Davies, "J. Oliver Emmerich and the McComb *Enterprise-Journal:* Slow Change in McComb, 1964," *Journal of Mississippi History* 57, no. 1 (March 1995): 1–23.

2. https://mississippiencyclopedia.org/entries/j-oliver-emmerich-sr/.

3. David R. Davies, ed., *The Press and Race: Mississippi Journalists Confront the Movement* (Jackson: University Press of Mississippi, 2001); on Carter, see 26–93; on Smith, see 233–62; on Harkey, see 173–207. See also Susan Weill, *In a Madhouse's Din: Civil Rights Coverage by Mississippi's Daily Press, 1948–1968* (Westport, CT: Praeger, 2002); https://mississippiencyclopedia.org/entries/hodding-carter-jr/.

4. *Enterprise-Journal,* 4 September 1953. The *Enterprise-Journal* was also an exception to typical Mississippi journalism in other ways: Emmerich began to use "Mr." and "Mrs." and other "courtesy titles" to refer to African Americans (https://mississippiencyclopedia.org/entries/j-oliver-emmerich-sr/).

5. *Enterprise-Journal,* 4 September 1953.

6. But neither had they run any photograph of any other party in the various cases.

7. *Enterprise-Journal,* 8 September 1953.

8. *Enterprise-Journal,* 8 September 1953.

9. *Enterprise-Journal,* 8 September 1953.

10. *Enterprise-Journal,* 4 September 1953.

11. *Enterprise-Journal,* 8 September 1953.

12. *Enterprise-Journal,* 8 September 1953.

13. *Enterprise-Journal,* 8 September 1953.

14. *Enterprise-Journal,* 10 September 1953.

15. *Enterprise-Journal,* 10 September 1953.

16. *Enterprise-Journal,* 14 September 1953.

17. *Enterprise-Journal,* 14 September 1953.

18. *Enterprise-Journal,* 15 September 1953.

19. *Enterprise-Journal,* 17 September 1953.

20. *Windsor Star* (Ontario, Canada), 18 September 1953.

21. *Clarion-Ledger,* 18 September 1953. The *Shreveport (LA) Times* ran much the same story on the same date but referred to Barnes as "an illiterate negro woman," without the capitalization of "Negro."

22. *Enterprise-Journal,* 21 September 1953. The *Columbian-Progress* (Columbia, MS) ran Gordon's story under his byline, 24 September 1953.

23. *Enterprise-Journal,* 22 September 1953.

24. *Enterprise-Journal,* 29 September 1953.

25. *Columbian-Progress* (Columbia, MS), 15 October 1953.

26. *Clarion-Ledger,* 20 October 1953.

27. *Clarion-Ledger,* 27 October 1953.

28. *Enterprise-Journal,* 2 November 1953.

29. *Enterprise-Journal,* 4 January 1954.

30. *Hattiesburg American,* 8 March 1954.

31. *Clarion-Ledger,* 9 March 1954.

32. *Enterprise-Journal,* 9 March 1954.

9. WHEN THE TRIALS WERE OVER

1. Polk himself would meet a violent death, assassinated by shotgun blast on the front porch of his home in 1960 (*Columbian-Progress* [Columbia, MS], 28 April 1960).

2. *Columbian-Progress* (Columbia, MS), 11 March 1954.

3. *Clarion-Ledger,* 14 March 1954.

4. *Columbian-Progress* (Columbia, MS), 18 March 1954.

5. *Columbian-Progress* (Columbia, MS), 14 July 1955; Rob Lee, Inmate Record Card #22539, Mississippi State Penitentiary, Mississippi Department of Corrections. Thanks to Tammy Wood for her assistance in locating a copy of this record.

6. *Clarion-Ledger,* 2 July 1955.

7. *Clarion-Ledger,* 27 September 1955.

8. Walter Watson, Inmate Record Card #21053, Mississippi State Penitentiary, Mississippi Department of Corrections. Thanks to Tammy Wood for her assistance in locating a copy of this record. Watson was discharged from parole on August 12, 1958.

9. *Columbian-Progress* (Columbia, MS), 24 September 1959. The relevant files for the administrations of Governors Hugh White and J. P. Coleman contain no letters or petitions from Lee or on Lee's behalf and no other indication of formal action on his case. Those files are contained in Records of the Office of the Governor (RG 27), Series 975, Paroles and Suspensions, Mississippi Department of Archives and History, Jackson. Dates of Lee's ninety-day and subsequent indefinite suspension are taken from Rob Lee, Inmate Record Card #22539, Mississippi State Penitentiary, Mississippi Department of Corrections.

10. *Enterprise-Journal,* 18 June 1964.

11. www.ancestry.com/family-tree/person/tree/162858958/person/222119709124/facts?_phsrc=OjJ28&_phstart=successSource.

12. *Columbian-Progress* (Columbia, MS), 13 March 1975.

13. *Hattiesburg American,* 29 July 1975; www.findagrave.com/memorial/24203893/rob-lee. His grave marker says simply "Rob Lee," with his birth and death dates.

14. *Columbian-Progress* (Columbia, MS), 30 May 1996.

15. www.findagrave.com/memorial/187590631/ruth-duggan; *Hattiesburg American,* 6 September 1997. For an obituary and a photograph, see *Columbian-Progress* (Columbia, MS), 18 September 1997.

16. *Enterprise-Journal,* 22 May 1989. For a photograph of Craft, see www.findagrave.com/memorial/84263779/edd-tunison-craft.

17. *Enterprise-Journal,* 16 April 1959.

18. *Enterprise-Journal,* 5 August, 21 August 1959.

19. *Enterprise-Journal,* 7 September, 21 September 1961; *Clarion-Ledger,* 21 September 1961; *Greenwood Commonwealth,* 21 September 1961; *Hattiesburg American,* 21 September 1961.

20. *Clarion-Ledger,* 28 October 1961; *Hattiesburg American,* 28 October 1961; *Greenwood Commonwealth,* 28 October 1961; *Enterprise-Journal,* 30 October 1961.

21. *Delta Democrat-Times,* 29 October 1961. A suit arising from that initial complaint is *United States v. Wood,* 295 F.2d 772 (5th Cir. 1961), 19237; available at https://law.justia.com/cases/federal/appellate-courts/F2/295/772/28673/.

22. www.mdah.ms.gov/arrec/digital_archives/sovcom/result.php?image=images/ png/cd05/036176.png&otherstuff=2|108|0|19|1|1|1|35601|.

23. *Clarion-Ledger,* 30 December 1961.

24. *Clarion-Ledger,* 14 March 1962.

25. *Enterprise-Journal,* 17 August 1962.

26. *Enterprise-Journal,* 16 May, 16 June, 10 August 1967.

27. *Enterprise-Journal,* 23 February 1962.

28. *Enterprise-Journal,* 24 August 1983.

29. *Clarion-Ledger,* 4 February 1973.

30. *Enterprise-Journal,* 3 October 1978.

31. In 1954, he said that "at last account," Barnes was "a tenant farmhand on a plantation of former Gov. Ben Laney of [Arkansas]" (*Enterprise-Journal,* 9 March 1954).

32. *Enterprise-Journal,* 2 August 1980.

10. THE REPORTER AND THE LAWYER

1. Details of Charles Gordon's habits are drawn from conversations with his children Mac and Nancy.

2. www.findagrave.com/memorial/62816131/charles-butler-gordon#view-photo=72816322.

3. *Clarion-Ledger,* 30 December 1982. As of 2020, the scholarship is still offered (https://jnm.olemiss.edu/category/scholarships/).

4. *Enterprise-Journal,* 5 December 1983. US Representative Wayne Dowdy of McComb also spoke at the event, as did Charles Overby, executive editor of the *Clarion-Ledger.* The event was sponsored by the Pike County Arts Council, chaired by Carroll and Suzanne Case (*Enterprise-Journal,* 1 December 1983).

5. *Enterprise-Journal,* 15 June 1992.

6. *Clarion-Ledger,* 16 November 1982.

7. *McComb Daily Journal,* 12 December 1941.

8. *McComb Daily Journal,* 12 December, 15 December 1941.

9. *McComb Daily Journal,* 16 July 1942.

10. *McComb Daily Journal,* 31 December 1941; *Enterprise-Journal,* 15 November 1982.

11. *McComb Daily Journal,* 1 June 1945; Mac Gordon, *Hometown: A Remembrance* (Magnolia, MS: Magnolia Gazette Publishing, 2011), 33; Mac Gordon to author, August 25, 2021.

12. Gordon, *Hometown,* 50; *Enterprise-Journal,* 4 January 1968.

13. *Polk's McComb (Pike County, MS) City Directory* (Richmond, Va.: R. L. Polk & Co., 1950).

14. *Columbian-Progress* (Columbia, MS), 2 December 1982.

15. *Enterprise-Journal,* 26 November 1982.

16. *Enterprise-Journal,* 26 November 1982.

17. Gordon, *Hometown,* 25.

18. Mac Gordon to author, 5 April 2020.

19. *Enterprise-Journal,* 17 November 1982.

20. Gordon, *Hometown,* 43.

21. *Enterprise-Journal,* 25 December 1983.

22. Nancy Gordon Lazenby to author, 28 May 2020.

23. Mac Gordon to author, 27 May 2020.

24. Charles Dunagin, telephone interview with author, 6 June 2020.

25. *Enterprise-Journal,* 29 April 1964.

26. Gordon, *Hometown,* 46.

27. *Enterprise-Journal,* 20 May 1968.

28. *Enterprise-Journal,* 21 November 1982.

29. *Enterprise-Journal,* 17 November 1982.

30. *Clarion-Ledger,* 17 November 1982.

31. *Enterprise-Journal,* 2 July 2017. For the Mississippi legislature's resolution honoring Pigott after his death, see http://billstatus.ls.state.ms.us/documents/2016/pdf/SC/SC0532SG.pdf.

32. *Enterprise-Journal,* 23 October 1957.

33. *McComb Daily Journal,* 3 August 1938; *Enterprise-Journal,* 6 July 1938; McComb (MS) *Semi-Weekly Journal,* 2 July 1935; *Enterprise-Journal,* 18 November, 1 December 1953; 28 October 1938; *Enterprise-Journal,* 15 July 1940.

34. *Enterprise-Journal,* 19 May 1942; www.findagrave.com/memorial/208246245/pattie-lou-pigott.

35. *Enterprise-Journal,* 11 June 1943.

36. *Clarion-Ledger,* 1 August 1943; *McComb Daily Journal,* 2 August 1943; *Enterprise-Journal,* 2 August, 5 November 1943.

37. *McComb Daily Journal,* 23 March, 25 July, 11 September 1944.

38. *McComb Daily Journal,* 16 November 1944.

39. See, for example, *Raleigh (NC) News and Observer,* 25 July 1945; *Shamokin (PA) News-Dispatch,* 28 July 1945; *Montgomery (AL) Advertiser,* 29 July 1945. For a brief history of the unit, written by one of their commanding officers, see Linnel Wallace, *Summary History of the 289th Engineer Combat Battalion—WWII* (Carlisle, PA: US Army Heritage and Education Center, 1990).

40. *Clarion-Ledger,* 30 August 1945.

41. *Enterprise-Journal,* 12 September 1945. Much later accounts describe Pigott as an "intelligence officer" or member of the OSS, forerunner of the CIA, during his European service. One account appears in a long feature article on Pigott's career, based upon an interview with him. "The chapters in Joe N. Pigott's life seem like fiction," observed the reporter, "but it's all too real

to Pigott" (*Enterprise-Journal,* 25 March 2005). Another telling of these events is Pigott's obituary (*Enterprise-Journal,* 8 November 2015). Pigott gave this information as well in an oral history at the National World War II Museum in New Orleans. Personnel files of the Office of Strategic Services are now publicly available through the National Archives (https://catalog.archives.gov/id/1593270). Like many other contemporary records, those of individual members of the 289th were destroyed in a 1973 fire at the National Personnel Records Center in Overland, Missouri.

42. *Enterprise-Journal,* 4 September 1946.

43. David G. Sansing, *The University of Mississippi: A Sesquicentennial History* (Jackson: University Press of Mississippi, 1999), 263.

44. *Clarion-Ledger,* 20 March, 23 March, 28 June 1947; *Enterprise-Journal,* 11 July 1947; 21 June 1948.

45. For a copy of the *Ole Miss,* the school's yearbook, see https://archive.org/details/olemiss53univ/page/n37/mode/2up/search/pigott. Among the members of Pigott's law school class that year was William Winter, future governor of Mississippi.

46. *Enterprise-Journal,* 7 September 1949.

47. *Enterprise-Journal,* 13 October 1953.

48. *Enterprise-Journal,* 17 February, 22 February, 3 July, 18 July 1950; 23 April 1951.

49. *Stone County Enterprise,* 22 October 1953; *Enterprise-Journal,* 13 October 1953.

50. *Enterprise-Journal,* 25 November 1953.

51. *Enterprise-Journal,* 20 January, 7 April 1954.

52. *Enterprise-Journal,* 23 October 1957.

53. *Enterprise-Journal,* 26 May 1954; 21 January, 11 February 1955.

54. *Enterprise-Journal,* 17 February 1955.

55. *Enterprise-Journal,* 6 May 1955.

56. *Enterprise-Journal,* 25 July, 1 August, 3 August, 26 October 1955.

57. *Enterprise-Journal,* 2 January 1963.

58. *Enterprise-Journal,* 16 August 1961; John Dittmer, *Local People: The Struggle for Civil Rights in Mississippi* (Urbana: University of Illinois Press, 1994), 101; *Enterprise-Journal,* 28 August, 5 October 1961; Joseph Crespino, *In Search of Another Country: Mississippi and the Conservative Counterrevolution* (Princeton, NJ: Princeton University Press, 2007), 119.

59. Crespino, *In Search of Another Country,* 120, 121. A contemporary journalist's account of the mood in McComb is Nicholas von Hoffman, *Mississippi Notebook* (New York: David White, 1964), 64–78.

60. Crespino, *In Search of Another Country,* 123–27; Dittmer, *Local People,* 303–13, Dunagin quote at 311.

61. https://da.mdah.ms.gov/sovcom/result.php?image=images/png/cd01/006613.png&oth er stuff=2|36|1|41|1|1|6447|.

62. https://da.mdah.ms.gov/sovcom/result.php?image=images/png/cd01/006903.png&oth er stuff=2|36|2|44|1|1|6729|.

63. https://da.mdah.ms.gov/sovcom/result.php?image=images/png/cd02/008789.png&oth er stuff=1|116|0|10|1|1|8575|.

64. *Enterprise-Journal,* 25 March 2005.

65. *Enterprise-Journal,* 6 May 1992.

66. *Enterprise-Journal,* 25 March 2005.

11. A RAPE, A STABBING, AND A MORALS CHARGE

1. *Enterprise-Journal,* 14 May 1956.

2. *Enterprise-Journal,* 14 May 1956.

3. Indictments and other matters related to the cases against the four men are found in Pike County Circuit Court, Case #10,664. *Clarion-Ledger,* 15 May 1956; *Hattiesburg American,* 15 May 1956; *Richmond (IN) Palladium-Item,* 15 May 1956; *Billings (MT) Gazette,* 15 May 1956; *Indianapolis Star,* 15 May 1956; *Monroe (LA) News-Star,* 15 May 1956; *Tampa Bay Times (FL),* 15 May 1956; *Newport News (VA) Daily Press,* 15 May 1956; *Anniston (AL) Star,* 15 May 1956; *Knoxville (TN) News-Sentinel,* 15 May 1956; *Oneota (NY) Star,* 15 May 1956; *Hagerstown (MD) Daily Mail,* 15 May 1956.

4. *Enterprise-Journal,* 16 May 1956.

5. *Enterprise-Journal,* 14 May 1956.

6. *Enterprise-Journal,* 4 September 1956.

7. *Enterprise-Journal,* 28 May 1956.

8. *Enterprise-Journal,* 28 May 1956.

9. *Enterprise-Journal,* 27 September, 5 October 1956; *Chicago Tribune,* 15 May 1956; *Jet,* 31 May 1956.

10. *Enterprise-Journal,* 3 October 1956.

11. *Enterprise-Journal,* 3 October, 27 September, 4 October, 8 October, 19 October 1956.

12. *Enterprise-Journal,* 20 March 1957.

13. *Enterprise-Journal,* 25 March 1957.

14. *Enterprise-Journal,* 26 March 1957; *Clarion-Ledger,* 27 March 1957.

15. *Anniston (AL) Star,* 30 October 1957.

16. *Enterprise-Journal,* 28 March, 29 March 1957.

17. *Pittsburgh Courier,* 9 November 1957; *Nashville Banner,* 30 October 1957.

18. *Enterprise-Journal,* 21 October, 28 October 1957.

19. *Clarion-Ledger,* 31 March 1957.

20. *Enterprise-Journal,* 24 December 1956.

21. *New York Times,* 6 April 1957; *Enterprise-Journal,* 5 April 1957.

22. *Enterprise-Journal,* 11 May 1962.

23. *Clarion-Ledger,* 1 January 1957.

24. *Enterprise-Journal,* 2 January 1957.

25. *Enterprise-Journal,* 4 January 1957.

26. *Enterprise-Journal,* 4 January 1957.

27. *Enterprise-Journal,* 25 March 1957.

28. *Enterprise-Journal,* 15 August 1957.

29. Mac Gordon, *Hometown: A Remembrance* (Magnolia, MS: Magnolia Gazette Publishing, 2011), 49.

30. *Enterprise-Journal,* 11 May 1962.

31. *Enterprise-Journal,* 13 May, 21 August 1957.

32. *Clarion-Ledger,* 3 March 1958; *Delta Democrat-Times,* 9 July 1958; *Enterprise-Journal,* 9 September 1958; *Clarion-Ledger,* 13 July 1959.

33. *Clarion-Ledger,* 6 November 1959.

34. *Clarion-Ledger,* 17 November 1964.

35. *Hattiesburg American,* 5 January 1965.

36. *Hattiesburg American,* 6 January 1965.

37. *Clarion-Ledger,* 7 January 1965.

38. *Hattiesburg American,* 15 January 1965. His appeal is: James W. Craft v. State of Mississippi, case #sc0000043640 [1965].

39. *Clarion-Ledger,* 18 December 1965.

40. https://cite.case.law/pdf/1852725/Craft%20v.%20State,%20254%20Miss.%20413, %20181%20So.%202d%20140%20(1965).pdf.

41. See, for example, www.law.mc.edu/judicial/briefs/2015-KA-01458-COART.PDF. For the case's citation in a law review article on police surveillance of public toilets, see https://scholarlycommons.law.wlu.edu/cgi/viewcontent.cgi?article=3629&context= wlulr.

42. *Clarion-Ledger,* 24 August 1966; 16 October 1969.

43. *Clarion-Ledger,* 6 February 1981.

44. *Enterprise-Journal,* 17 May 2019.

45. *Enterprise-Journal,* 7 May 1997.

46. *Enterprise-Journal,* 8 December 2009.

47. www.findagrave.com/memorial/106899838/james-wendell-craft; https://www.findagrave.com/memorial/76987796/emmett-lamar-kincaid.

12. FAME AND NOTORIETY AFTER THE BARNES CASE

1. *Hattiesburg American,* 7 April 1943; *Enterprise-Journal,* 19 November 1943; 11 October 1950. Another newspaper gives his affiliation as Pi Kappa Tau (*Clarion-Ledger,* 15 October 1950).

2. www.findagrave.com/memorial/84263810/richard-lamar-craft.

3. *Clarion-Ledger,* 27 March 1931.

4. *Enterprise-Journal,* 6 November 1935; 20 November 1936; 8 January 1937; *McComb Daily Journal,* 8 January 1937.

5. *Enterprise-Journal,* 19 January 1938.

6. *McComb Daily Journal,* 10 April 1942.

7. *Enterprise-Journal,* 29 March 1982.

8. *Monroe* (LA) *Morning World,* 18 April 1959.

9. *Enterprise-Journal,* 30 March 1982; 13 October 1960.

10. *Enterprise-Journal,* 21 September 1961.

11. *Clarion-Ledger,* 17 July 1975.

12. www.findagrave.com/memorial/81611313/breed-oliver-mounger.

13. *Enterprise-Journal,* 30 March, 29 March 1982.

14. *Enterprise-Journal,* 31 August 1951.

15. *Enterprise-Journal,* 3 December 1989. For a photograph of Lee, see www.findagrave.com/memorial/13849064/robert-eugene-lee.

16. www.mdah.ms.gov/arrec/digital_archives/sovcom/result.php?image=images/png/cd01/006118.png&otherstuff=2|31|0|11|1|1|1|5960|. A number of documents in the Commission's files indicate that Dale told them that he knew of no "racial unrest" in his district but that he would inform them should he learn of any. There is no indication that he ever did.

17. www.findagrave.com/memorial/40056785/thomas-pickens-brady.

18. https://digitalcollections.usm.edu/uncategorized/digitalFile_5836a78a-6ff7-4fde-8a0a-9d1ae935de16/.

19. https://mississippiencyclopedia.org/entries/thomas-p-brady/.

20. *Delta Democrat-Times,* 31 January 1973.

21. Baltimore *Evening Sun,* 1 February 1973.

22. *Clarion-Ledger,* 5 February 1973.

23. www.findagrave.com/memorial/47848397/thomas-j_-brady.

24. *Enterprise-Journal,* 10 March 1969.

25. *Enterprise-Journal,* 26 July 1976.

26. *Enterprise-Journal,* 29 November 1976.

27. *Enterprise-Journal,* 9 March 1983.

28. www.findagrave.com/memorial/145543170/richard-lamar-craft.

29. www.findagrave.com/memorial/93245620/marshall-ellzey-bullock.

30. *Enterprise-Journal,* 9 March 1954.

EPILOGUE

1. Ranney, *A Legal History of Mississippi,* 3.

2. *Enterprise-Journal,* 13 October 2018. For Dr. Clopton's full body of work, see https://blackhistoryplus.com/.

3. For a copy of the film, within the context of a one-hour "History Is Lunch" presentation at the Mississippi Department of Archives and History in Jackson on June 10, 2020, see www.youtube.com/watch?v=TOHvApOZKN4.

4. *Enterprise-Journal,* 18 October 2018.

5. *Mississippi Justice:* An NMHS Unlimited Film Productions Project, copy of undated press release in author's possession. On other publicity for the film, see, for example, http://themississippilink.com/2020/02/27/mississippi-justice-then-and-now/.

6. Other accounts of this speech before Judge Brady appear in *Enterprise-Journal,* 24 January 2010; a fuller version is given in *Enterprise-Journal,* 25 March 2005. "The judge was a stout segregationist," the 2005 story rightly points out. In 1951 Judge Tom Brady was certainly an outspoken supporter of segregation. He would develop an even broader reputation after the *Brown* decision and his book *Black Monday* (1955). Pigott's 2005 recollections of the case, at least as reported in the newspaper, contain an error, which is a caution about the work of memory in fifty-year-old cases: "The white boy who she killed was the son of the sheriff of Walthall County, and his brother

was the mayor of Tylertown." Edd Craft would not become sheriff for nearly a decade. Wendell Craft would not become mayor for nearly two decades. The text quoted here is from a document given to me early in 2020. It is word-processed, thus created many years after the trial. It bears the heading "State of Mississippi vs Hattie Lee Barnes" but carries no other provenance.

7. For outstanding examinations of Harper Lee's beloved attorney, see Joseph Crespino, "The Strange Career of Atticus Finch," *Southern Cultures* 6, no. 2 (2000): 9–29; and Joseph Crespino, *Atticus Finch, The Biography: Harper Lee, Her Father, and the Making of an American Icon* (New York: Basic, 2018).

8. A trial transcript was typically prepared when needed for an appeal, unnecessary here. Court reporter Miss Tommye Thomas no doubt left materials from which a transcript could have been prepared, but those notes, like others of the period, have not been retained by the Pike County Circuit Court.

9. The Citizens' Councils were founded in 1954, in the wake of the *Brown* decision. The definitive account is Stephanie R. Rolph, *Resisting Equality: The Citizens' Council, 1954–1989* (Baton Rouge: Louisiana State University Press, 2018). See also the pioneering work of Neil McMillen, *The Citizens' Council: Organized Resistance to the Second Reconstruction, 1954–1964* (Urbana: University of Illinois Press, 1971).

10. On a lynching in Mississippi that occurred well after the 1951 Barnes trial, see Howard Smead, *Blood Justice: The Lynching of Mack Charles Parker* (New York: Oxford University Press, 1984).

11. *Hattiesburg American*, 13 January 2019.

12. *Enterprise-Journal*, 5 March 2005. *Hattiesburg American*, 13 January 2019.

13. Trent Brown, *Murder in McComb: The Tina Andrews Case* (Baton Rouge: Louisiana State University Press, 2020).

14. Darlin' Neal, "The Black Side of the Aisle," *Mississippi Review* (Winter 2018): 79.

15. On these reenactments, see www.tribtown.com/2017/05/18/valuable_lesson/; https://www.al.com/opinion/2015/04/monroeville_board_no_more_to_k.html.

16. Neil R. McMillen, *Dark Journey: Black Mississippians in the Age of Jim Crow* (Urbana: University of Illinois Press, 1989), 206.

INDEX